"International organizations often boast of their experience and ability to deal and cope with sometimes very different national administrative cultures e.g. how to get civil servants from Sicily and Scandinavia to work together smoothly and effectively. Richard Lewis's books should be standard reading in the European Union's institutions, as they have been for years in the World Bank. Different cultural backgrounds enrich and enhance creativity in pooling intellectual resources but only if the members of the team understand and take into account the underlying cultural differences. I will gladly recommend this new book to my colleagues in Brussels. Richard's penetrative cultural insights combine with Kai Hammerich's in-depth understanding of corporate leadership to produce a valuable tool for executives in this era of globalization."

Eero Vuohula, former official of EFTA and Director at the European Commission's Directorate of External Affairs

"Organizational culture is too often an afterthought for businesses. Whilst many organizations believe they are global, they do not recognize how their heritage has defined their current culture. This book provides a well thought out methodology and pragmatic insights in organizational culture, to enable business outcomes. This is really important for leaders working in an international environment and Human Resources professionals who see culture as the glue for organizational effectiveness."

Hugo Bague, Group Executive Organisational Resources, Rio Tinto

"In essence the value of this book is in the successful linking of theory and reality: while insightful on several levels, it is factual, illustrative, and . . . . utterly practical for various audiences. Fish Can't See Water is not just an interesting read, but, most importantly, a useful guide for navigating the intricacies of the current, ever-changing (yet surprisingly the same), business world."

Dr Iouri Bairatchnyi, Former Director, Cross Cultural Programmes, World Bank, Washington DC

FISH CAN'T SEE WATER

HOW NATIONAL CULTURE CAN MAKE OR

BREAK YOUR CORPORATE STRATEGY

KAI HAMMERICH AND
RICHARD D. LEWIS

WILEY

This edition first published 2013
© 2013 John Wiley & Sons, Ltd

Registered office

John Wiley & Sons Ltd, The Atrium, Southern Gate, Chichester, West Sussex, PO19 8SQ, United Kingdom

For details of our global editorial offices, for customer services and for information about how to apply for permission to reuse the copyright material in this book please see our website at www.wiley.com.

Wiley publishes in a variety of print and electronic formats and by print-on-demand. Some material included with standard print versions of this book may not be included in e-books or in print-on-demand. If this book refers to media such as a CD or DVD that is not included in the version you purchased, you may download this material at http://booksupport.wiley.com. For more information about Wiley products, visit www.wiley.com.

Library of Congress Cataloging-in-Publication Data

Hammerich, Kai, 1960–
    Fish can't see water : how national culture can make or break your corporate strategy / Kai Hammerich and Richard D. Lewis.
        pages cm
    Includes bibliographical references and index.
    ISBN 978-1-118-60856-2 (cloth)
    1. Corporate culture—Cross-cultural studies.   2. Organizational behavior—Cross-cultural studies.   3. National characteristics.   4. Strategic planning.   I. Lewis, Richard D.   II. Title.
    HD58.7.H343 2013
    658.4'012–dc23   2013013592

A catalogue record for this book is available from the British Library.

ISBN 978-1-118-60856-2 (hardback) ISBN 978-1-118-60853-1 (ebk)
ISBN 978-1-118-60854-8 (ebk) ISBN 978-1-118-60855-5 (ebk)

Cover design: Dan Jubb. Front cover image: iStockPhoto/bora ucak.
Back cover image: iStockPhoto/Mirosław Kijewski.

Set in 11/14.5 pt Palatino Std by Toppan Best-set Premedia Limited, Hong Kong
Printed in Great Britain by CPI Group (UK) Ltd, Croydon, CR0 4YY

CONTENTS

PREFACE

It is no longer a secret that the biggest obstacle to successful globalization is the inability of most companies to understand the world view and aspirations of partners and competitors. Their culture is opaque, seems irrational. So does ours to them. But we are normal, surely? Looking at their behaviour, we perceive abnormalities. But the reverse seems true, too. Surely we can see ourselves? Clearly. Or can we? Can fish see water? Can we see our own cultural environment?

Where national traits are concerned, we are all experts and victims. Culture hides much more than it reveals and, strangely enough, what it hides, it hides most effectively from its own participants.

The two authors of this book come from very different backgrounds, consequently see things in a diverse manner. In writing this book, the authors learned a lot from each other. We have tried to share our flashes of enlightenment with you, our readers.

For more information, news and updates, blogs and articles and educational support materials including classroom presentations, cases, instructor notes etc please visit **www.fishcantseewater.com**.

RDL   KH

ACKNOWLEDGEMENTS

No work on cross-culture escapes the influence of Ed Schein and Geert Hofstede, and we would like to acknowledge their pioneering of central concepts which figure prominently in this book.

Numerous multicultural people have helped inspire us in the creation of the central ideas in our book, including: the Asian brand expert Martin Roll, Lars Terney of Nordic Capital, Mikkel B. Rasmussen of ReD Associates, Jørgen Vig Knudstorp of Lego, Tue Mantoni of B&O, Jim Hagemann Snabe of SAP, Juha Äkräs and Stephen Elop of Nokia, Vagn Sørensen of FLSmidth, Niels B. Christansen of Danfoss, Barbara Annis of Barbara Annis & Associates and Dean Stamoulis of Russell Reynolds Associates, Karsten Feilberg, Kim Berknov, Jens Schultzer, Christian Mariager, John Youngblood and Bill Hoover.

We would like to thank everyone at Wiley for their thoughtful editing, and in particular our publisher, Rosemary Nixon for her constructive comments and unwavering support. Rosemary also introduced us to our development editor, Katherine Armstrong, who had a profound influence on the final structure of the manuscript and helped crystalize many of the key messages, through many long and sometimes challenging, but always enjoyable conversations.

Finally, this book would not have been possible without the daily support of Frances Phillips and Ceri Erskine, who have read the manuscript many times and suggested multiple improvements.

Richard D. Lewis and Kai Hammerich
London, July 2013

INTRODUCTION

The idea we present in this book is simple: national culture, through its influence on corporate culture, has a powerful but often-invisible impact on the success of global companies. What's more, the very same national traits that accelerated growth in one stage of the corporate lifecycle may derail that growth at a different stage or when an inevitable crisis hits. When you, as a leader of a global organization, become able to recognize the impact of national culture, you will be in a stronger position to lead your company. We will present you with two concepts, Richard D. Lewis' renowned Lewis model and Kai Hammerich's new Cultural Dynamic Model®[1]. This framework will give you a precise language and a stronger conceptual understanding to discuss how national culture affects your organization and how it differs from other business culture influencers that you are more familiar with. It will outline what you, as a leader, need to watch out for and what actions you can take during a period of transformation. In a global world where most processes and products can and will be copied, culture matters more than ever and, as we will show, can be a source of sustainable competitive differentiation! As they say: "Culture eats Strategy for lunch!"

In this chapter and the following two, we will take you through the key concepts in the book. First, let's share four examples of what we mean.

Playing football in Brazil and Germany: Countries will go about getting things done in different ways, based on their national cultural traits. The Brazilian national football team plays a different style of football from the German. Their football skills and capabilities are different, as their players have developed differently due to their different national culture and socio-economic realities. In his book *When Cultures Collide*, Richard Lewis tells us that the

---

[1] © Kai Hammerich 2012.

Brazilians among other qualities are known to be relaxed, friendly, exuberant and emotional.[2] Many Brazilian star players started playing football barefoot, on uneven ground in a *favela* on the outskirts of a large city. These characteristics led to an individualistic style, with an entertaining game, to impress their friends with their ball-artistry. Through this, they would gain local hero status. In contrast, Germans are known to enjoy being organized, communal, disciplined, logical and task oriented. A young German boy will join a local club at an early age, use proper boots and learn to play the game in a well-organized youth team. The German players grow up to be technically competent, and with a more systematic approach to the game – yet equally effective in delivering results. Thus, the way the two teams play is fundamentally different, but both are world-class competitors and have won multiple world championships. From these national differences you cannot conclude that either way is more effective, just that they are different.

Samsung Electronics has in a few years become the world's most valuable and largest consumer electronics company. It has done this through an unrelenting focus on execution and being the "fastest follower". The Korean national traits of discipline, observance of protocol, competitive spirit, long-term orientation and suspicion of foreigners[3] have created a formidable and focused company. It is also somewhat insular, with virtually all senior executives and board members being Korean albeit many with extensive international experience. Samsung Electronics employees are highly disciplined and attempt to achieve their mission, however difficult it might be. Although the Korean culture's emphasis on hierarchy and rote memorization may facilitate swift, effective strategy execution and the rapid rise to global prominence, this same emphasis may also obstruct expression of creative or dissenting opinions.[4] If it doesn't proactively manage its Korean heritage, Samsung Electronics therefore could face significant challenges in maintaining its lead in the next business cycle and achieving its ambition of becoming the technological and creative leader and not just the fastest follower. Competing with American innovative and ambitious Google, Microsoft and Apple on their home turf of technological creativity and innovation is a tall order for anyone – and a challenge that will inspire Samsung's competitive spirits. The derailing effects of national traits can be overcome, but only with effort, time and dedicated leadership.

[2]Lewis R.D. (2006) *When Cultures Collide*, 3rd Edition. Nicholas Brealey, pp. 224–226 and 540–542.
[3]Lewis (1996), pp. 503–504.
[4]Chang S.-J. (2010) *Samsung vs Sony*. Wiley, pp. 99–100.

The Austin Motor Company initially developed a highly innovative and successful culture that demonstrated its native England's strong bias for innovation, action, get-things-done attitude and efficiency at fixing problems quickly. These national characteristics fed a "wing it" cultural business dynamic that helped the company navigate the uncertain times of an emerging cyclical industry, two war periods and ultimately propelled it to become the dominant local car manufacturer. However, when efficiency became the name of the game in the increasingly global and maturing industry, Austin's "wing it" culture paled in comparison with the quality and process focus of its German, French and Japanese rivals. By the 1970s, not even the efficiency-seeking mergers that created British Leyland could save Austin and its sister companies from this. Eventually, British taxpayers had to foot the bill for bailing them out.

GM: The American culture is at its best when displaying vibrant individualism, entrepreneurial spirit, risk-taking, innovation, ambition and results orientation combined with a focus on making money. "The business of America is business", as they say. These traits very much characterized General Motors in the first part of the 20th century, when it emerged as the dominant American car company. Initially, GM lost out to Ford's one-product, one-colour (black) and low-cost car strategy. GM, in contrast, focused on a strategy offering multiple car brands from the entry-level Chevy to the up-market Cadillac and in multiple colours. By the 1950s, GM had become the leading industrial company in the world with over 50% market share in the US car market. However, to avoid a break-up, GM felt forced by the US government to stop focusing on gaining share, and instead focused on increasing profits by reducing cost. Over time it developed a more introverted, bureaucratic and customer-distant culture with increasingly uncompetitive products. A new cultural dynamic emerged, where the internally recruited executives sheltered themselves from the real world in a clubby white male culture on the top executive floors of the GM building. In this case, GM exemplifies a potentially derailing side of the American corporate culture, which can also be hierarchical, bureaucratic and command-and-control oriented, if not managed in the mature phase of a company's lifecycle or in a crisis. The term "red tape" was, after all, invented in the USA. Ultimately, the US government in 2009 bailed out GM.

In the next chapter, we will discuss how the lifecycle of a company interacts with the national culture of various countries in more detail. Some cultures are better suited to the early and more innovative phase, such as in England and Denmark; others are intrinsically better suited to the more process-focused mature phase such as in Germany, Japan and Korea. The USA is unique in that it has strengths throughout all stages, which may help to explain the country's success after WWII. Pragmatic business China may prove to be similar to the USA in this respect, though it is too early to tell with certainty. The key point here is that a company needs to be aware when a national characteristic potentially can derail its strategy – or accelerate it. A company can learn to master a new work practice that may not seem natural to it, through effort, practice, training and consistent leadership – but first it has to recognize the need, which can be challenging as we shall see in many of the cases in this book. This is where the "Fish can't see water" effect raises its head. Management and the board are often culturally blind to the effects of their own company's culture, and thus may not realise when deep change is required.

An equally important point here is that one can't conclude that how a company is organized based on its national heritage is inherently better compared to how another company from a different country is organized. It is just different. After all, companies from all over the world dominate the many sectors of the global economy.

However, let's not get ahead of ourselves. Let's begin the journey by asking the simple question: What is culture?

What is "culture"?

Ever since humans gained consciousness, social norms, beliefs, rituals and group behaviour became the heart and soul of human activity. *Culture is the social programming of the mind that distinguishes the members of one category of people from another,*[5] as the famous Dutch cultural expert Hofstede says. We know from our own personal life that any group of people together for a longer period of time will develop its own culture whether explicitly or implicitly stated, based on the mix of people in the group and the task at hand.

Humans do not cooperate mindlessly. We are unlike other living creatures. In most groups of mammals, birds and fish, each member of the group will play exactly the same role and behave similarly to the others. Ants and termites establish elaborate societies, where the role of the individual is subordi-

---

[5]Hofstede G., Hofstede J., Minkov M. (2010) *Cultures and Organizations*, 3rd Edition. McGraw-Hill, p. 6.

nated to the greater good of the nest or hive. In contrast, humans are wired for culture and capable of expressing great individuality within a society, while at the same time contributing to the greater good of the group. Humans will specialize within the group, depending on their particular skills and personality and contribute using their specific talent, whether as a craftsman, carer or as an artist. We are usually seen as different from other animals because of our inherent traits of consciousness, language and intelligence. However, in his book *Wired for Culture*[6] Mark Pagel argues that we've had it the wrong way round. Many of these traits would not exist without our propensity for culture – our ability to cooperate in small tribal societies, enabling us to pass on knowledge, beliefs and practices so that we prospered while others declined.

Culture has a purpose, and the purpose is to help the group survive and succeed in their physical, political and spiritual environment, as measured by their own success criteria. A culture can be strong or weak, and effective or not, in achieving the objectives of the group. Only time will tell how long a culture can maintain its vitality before eventually leading to the demise of the group that created it. In business, strong corporate cultures emerge over time as repeated behaviour, results and success reinforce the existing behaviours, values and principles of thinking. A single individual, the founder or a very small group of individuals, most often shapes these core cultural values in the early phases of the group's existence, based on their own personal experiences, beliefs and values.

Culture is behaviour and behaviour is culture. Ed Schein, the American cultural expert, notes that "it is the consistency that is important and not the intensity of the attention". Consistency builds strong cultures. Whether they are effective in achieving their goals is another matter. This is why "walking the talk", as they say in America, is such a powerful way of influencing the culture of a company.[7] Hands-on leaders have a stronger impact when they, through their own example, show people what they value and therefore want them to copy. Toyota embraces the very Japanese concept that "every mistake is an opportunity to learn" and expects every manager to teach his organization this philosophy. It is a deeply rooted principle, which is ingrained in the work principles on

---

[6]Pagel M. (2012) *Wired for Culture*. Allan Lane.
[7]Schein E.H. (2004) *Organizational Culture and Leadership*. Jossey Bass Publishers, p. 247.

the shop floor at every Toyota assembly line. Every employee understands it and everybody does it. It takes Toyota years to teach these principles to the task- and results-oriented managers from Europe and the USA, who instinctively will criticize, pass blame or ignore it when a mistake happens. Anglo-Saxons are often more focused on short-term actions and results than investing in learning for the long term, as we shall see in the Toyota case. In Chapter 1 we will look deeper at how cultural influencers become imbedded in a corporate culture, through the actions of the leaders.

Fish can't see water. Our assumption in this book is that the vast majority of business organizations have a national culture at the heart of their corporate culture. An American company will be based on American values, think American and act American, just like a Japanese company will be Japanese at heart. However, this is also the blind spot of the organization. We can't easily see our own cultural programming in a mirror. In our own eyes we are normal, and that is what we see in the mirror. However, when we look at each other we see difference. That is what we mean by "Fish can't see water"! The proverb "You can take a Chinese person out of China, but you can't take China out of a Chinese person" could be said about most people. This book is about learning to identify the deep and often invisible national programming that affects the strategy execution of your organization.

The water that we couldn't see when analyzing culture

As we worked on this book, we wondered why so few authors on the two related subjects of corporate strategy and corporate culture had mentioned the importance of national culture and discussed its effect on corporate culture, and if they did, then often only in passing. We soon realized that there was a national cultural dynamic at play.[8]

Many influential business books on corporate strategy and corporate culture have originated in the USA.[9] These books often discuss the subject through the corporate strategy perspective with limited reference to national culture and mostly use American examples when presenting business cases.

---

[8]Schein makes a similar observation; Hofstede et al. (2010), p. 339.
[9]Collins J. (1995) *Built to Last: Successful Habits of Visionary Companies*. Harper Business Essentials; Peters T., Waterman R.H. (1982) *In Search of Excellence*. HarperCollins; Kotter J., Heskett J. (1992) *Corporate Culture and Performance*. Free Press.

They also use extensive data analysis to prove their points, usually based on more readily available American data. A small minority specifically discuss corporate culture, but again mostly use American examples. Both strains implicitly assume that since "the Business of America is Business" – and who can argue with the success of American business in the 20th century? – therefore the American way of doing business was superior. Consequently, it has been quite straightforward for them to implicitly conclude as evidenced through their recommendations and insights that global corporations would generally benefit from adopting an American-inspired performance-oriented and individualistically focused corporate culture. Trying to understand other national cultures and how those affected business performance was of less interest to them.

This implicit assumption is being seriously challenged. The world is changing. In 1980, the market capitalization of listed American corporations accounted for over 60% of the value of all major listed global companies, and by 2011 it had dropped to less than 30%.[10] This is not because the American companies are underperforming; it is because the emerging markets companies are overperforming. Today most of the largest countries embrace the capitalistic system one way or another and are quickly learning from their American masters. They are also increasingly finding their own way of organizing their companies, often rooted in their national heritage and not just adopting American or European work practices.

Generally, these books, whether from the USA or Europe, seek rational predictability. In the West, we like to deal with certainties and facts; if the input expressed in numbers is this, the output will be that. This perspective works well for strategy where the realm can be expressed in numbers: the price, cost, profits, market share, or a balanced scorecard. They recognize culture, but with less hard data to support the conclusions; they only mention it occasionally. Consequently, most of the influential books on strategy continue to analyze companies along the facts- and numbers-based business strategy and execution dimension, and look at the linear relationship between the strategy, the way a company organizes and executes and the results, as shown in Diagram I.1.

Unfortunately, culture is difficult to express numerically; it is by nature more anecdotal and in the realm of storytelling. We too would prefer culture

---

[10]http://seekingalpha.com/article/259736-china-surpasses-japan-in-percentage-of-world-market-cap/.

Diagram I.1: Relationship between strategy, work practices and results

to be part of a linear and measurable system; however, the subject is simply too complex and multi-faceted to allow for such a level of scientific predictability. There are simply too many variables interacting and they are difficult to measure with accuracy. This conclusion is indirectly supported by the largely vain effort to create a solid link between culture and performance in more recent American business literature on the subject, despite significant efforts. American academia largely abandoned its focus on corporate culture after an initial burst of interest in the 1980s and 1990s. "If you can't make money out of it, why bother?" would be an unsurprising American perspective.

In Europe there has been a stronger and somewhat more successful focus on using statistical analysis to identify the common five dimensions of national culture,[11] which best classify the people types in various countries. The risk with this approach, however, is that the uniqueness of each national culture ends up being confined to statistical noise. In this book we are particularly interested in this statistical noise – i.e. what makes nations and their companies unique and not just the commonalities. Richard's "Lewis model" is unique in that it captures both the commonalities as well as the uniqueness of the people from each country, as you will see in Chapter 2.

Lastly, national traits only change slowly over the years. Countries and their people simply don't change that fast. Hence, the importance of analyzing how the national culture impacts a corporation over business cycles spanning decades. This is rarely done in our short-term-oriented Western world, where the stock market analysts, and thus the companies, tend to focus on the next quarter and maybe next year. Management consultants and business theorists may take a longer view, though often using years rather than decades as their unit of time measurement.

Therefore, in our view, the area of corporate culture needs a different approach. In this book we will guide you through our diagnostic framework

---

[11] Hofstede et al. (2010).

that will help you identify and understand the root mechanisms, and the cultural dynamics at play in your or any other organization. Language is at the root of culture. Language is nature's tool for programming the mind. Therefore our aim is also to give you a more precise language to discuss these central aspects of culture.

While we use the abstraction of a single corporate culture throughout the book, we also recognize that the organizational culture in a company often is more homogeneous at the subsidiary level than at the corporate level and thus easier to analyze.[12]

The long-term view: corporate lifecycles and corporate culture

Corporations usually follow a similar path to greatness. Though, obviously, the time it takes will differ depending on the industry in which they operate. A Web 2.0 company like Facebook went global and big in five intense years, whereas companies relying on physical presence and physical goods will take longer. Until Web 2.0 came along, this normally was measured in multiple decades. However, there are sprinters too. Rapidly growing Chinese technology companies such as Huawei and Lenovo have managed to become dominant in China and a global top player in less than two or three decades, as has American Google, Apple and Microsoft, and German SAP. For each phase the particular national traits will have a different impact, sometimes benign, and sometimes derailing, as we shall see in the cases later in the book.

Below we have listed five lifecycle phases, which most companies will go through:

1. Innovation
2. Geographical expansion
3. Product-line expansion
4. Efficiency and scale
5. Consolidation

---

[12]Schein (2004). Schein also notes that one can argue that large global corporations may not have a single overarching global culture, but a set of significant regional and functional or divisional subcultures.

A large company will often encompass many product areas that are in different phases at the same time. Large companies normally have a mix of new ventures, smaller fast growing business units and emerging technologies that supplement the main business, where the majority of revenues and profits are derived from. As Samsung started to dominate the global TV set business in the early 2000s, they were working on establishing a new mobile smartphone line of business, which today is a main profit driver. We will define the lifecycle phase of a company, based on their main business, unless otherwise stated.

The innovation phase

This phase usually starts with an innovation or an innovative strategy. This is a volatile period for any company, where most struggle with getting commercial and technological traction, usually based on a single product or service. The founders are dominant in every aspect of company life and during this period will make the most profound impact on the corporate culture of the company. Sony rose to global prominence though a strong partnership between the founder and genius innovator Masaru Ibuka and his younger more commercial and internationally-oriented partner Akio Morita, who both influenced the core culture, as you will see in the Sony case. A particular critical moment is when the founders hand over the leadership to a more managerial regime, either during this phase or later. The perils of this early stage are well documented by the Macedonian, Dr Ichak Adizes, in his lifecycle model.

The geographic expansion

This phase is characterized by the rapid expansion of the company either regionally or globally, as the company sells its products and services in more markets. This is where the company meets the world for the first time. Some countries are more extrovert than others, which will impact their ability and ease of expanding. Maritime nations, for instance, tend to have a higher frequency of interaction with other countries and therefore are better used to dealing with cultural differences. Large nations will often find significant populations of immigrants from their country in the new markets, which may ease both the initial market acceptance and the ability to attract the first local employees with a good cultural fit. In this phase, the company should consider whether it will pursue a cultural dominant strategy with a single unified corporate culture or adopt a more locally-oriented model. In the intermediate hybrid model, it will adapt parts of the local cultures and work practices into its subsidiary work practice, which can dilute the core corporate culture. However, this choice is often not made consciously at this stage, as we will see later. This was a period where innovative Sony and Nokia both thrived, rapidly building a global business, using a largely hybrid model; both had explicit and strong corporate values to glue the decentralized organization together. Samsung and Toyota in contrast both used a dominant cultural strategy with little local interpretation allowed in the subsidiaries, and a strong central technical core. We will discuss the choice of subsidiary culture strategy in more detail in Chapter 7.

Product-line expansion

The company has a global presence and in this phase it will expand the number of product lines and broaden their product portfolio to cater to more customers and build stronger and deeper relationships with existing customers. Consumer goods companies expand their brand portfolio, while industrial companies add products to serve their customers in new areas, or use the same base technology to serve new segments. During this period the company needs to be innovative, agile and increasingly efficient at the same time. The national traits supporting innovation (individualism, agility) and efficiency (discipline and organization) may rub against each other and create significant conflicts and unintended cultural dynamics. The phase often marks the end of the organic growth period. This is a period where execution-oriented and ambitious Samsung thrived, expanding from DRAMs to television and consumer electronics to mobile phones.

Efficiency and scale focus

As the industry matures, there is a drive towards more efficiency often through sheer scale and a desire for a stronger market share position. This period is often characterized by the creation of global processes, discipline and tight execution focus using a global organizational structure. Companies from countries with strong individualism and an innovative creative bias, which thrived during the innovation phase, may well struggle in this period. Those countries, like Denmark, often have a high proportion of small and medium enterprise (SME) companies. Larger nations, in particular those with a history of organizing at scale at many levels of society, often thrive during this phase, though not always. As we shall see in the later cases, this is the phase where Austin stumbled and Toyota thrived, and execution-oriented Samsung Electronics rose to become the largest consumer electronics company from a revenues perspective.

Consolidation

This is the end game of an industry, with only a small handful of global or regional players dominating. This phase is characterized by less organic growth and a stronger focus on mergers and acquisitions (M&A), often of entities originating from different nations. The big challenge is making these acquisitions work. While they often make sense from an industrial and structural perspective, by reducing the number of players, the value creation for shareholders is frequently hampered by significant integration issues, often based in deeply rooted national and corporate cultural issues. In this phase, the two companies will both often come from a large nation, invariably with a strong culture, leading to the inevitable culture clash. This is the period where P&G and FLSmidth thrived, and GM stumbled.

While M&A is an important, fascinating and complex subject, we will not discuss this in detail here. It deserves a book on its own to be dealt with adequately, describing how tens of paired cultures, e.g. a French company merging with an American company, or a Chinese company buying a German company, are likely to play out across different industries at the different

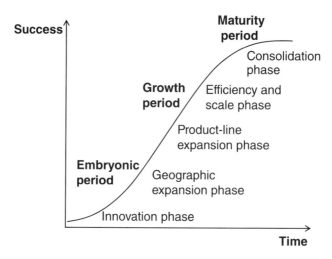

Diagram I.2: The normal corporate lifecycle

stages of their lifecycle. However, we will naturally touch the subject at times when relevant.

Diagram I.2 summarizes the normal corporate lifecycle.

You are probably able to identify the lifecycle stage of your company on the curve shown in the diagram. So that you can focus on the stage that is most relevant to you, we've presented case studies in chapters dedicated to each of these phases. Each chapter shares the story of how great companies thrived or dived in the phase because of a cultural dynamic influenced by its national culture.

We will at times refer to the simpler three-period version including the embryonic, the growth and the maturity period.

Interruptions of the lifecycle – when the crisis hit

Most companies will not continue to grow forever. At some stage they will invariably be hit by a life-threatening crisis, which they will either survive as Xerox did in the early 2000s or fail as Kodak experienced. Sometimes a company simply fades into economic irrelevance with the passing of time, as substitute products take over and habits change – like the coffee shops in 17th century London, now revived through Starbucks, the travelling theatre troupe or the craftsmen making knights' armour. As you read the cases, we will highlight what caused the crisis for each company and the role the national culture played in the events leading to the crisis. The typical causes of a corporate life-threatening crisis include:[13]

- Less competitive strategy[14]
- Poor execution – of a sound strategy
- Disruption[15]
- Technological innovation
- Process innovation
- Success – the success trap, which can lead to complacency
- Time – if you don't move forwards in business, you go backwards

[13]For an excellent discussion of the subject also read Collins J. (2009) *How the Mighty Fall*. Random House.
[14]Porter M. (1980) *Competitive Strategy*. Free Press.
[15]Christensen C. (1997) *The Innovator's Dilemma*. HBS Press.

- Change of leadership including the founder to managerial regime transition
- Navigating the transition from one lifecycle phase to the next.

As a company deals with the crisis it will ultimately either embark on a new and different growth curve, linger on or perish. Sometimes, it will have to reinvent itself as IBM did in the 1990s under Lou Gerstner's bold leadership, when it moved from hardware to services. Rarely will a company rediscover its original innovative spirits as Apple did with the return of Steve Jobs in 1997. Whatever it does, it often ends up in a new competitive environment, which will challenge its corporate culture and may rub against deeply rooted national traits, as we will see in many of our cases. During such a lifecycle transformation, the management needs to be acutely aware of what role the root national culture has and how they use the cultural accelerators to further the transformation and identify and deal with the potential cultural derailers. Diagram I.3 summarizes the full lifecycle model and the typical causes of the crisis.

In Chapter 9, we discuss the crisis in more detail, in particular how the national culture influences the company during a crisis. As a leader it is important for you to observe that *a company under crisis often will revert to its core national culture*, as the psychologist in post-traumatic experiences would predict. However global it may be, an American corporation under pressure will often become more American. It will become more hierarchical, more command–control oriented, more dogmatic and more rigid, showing another

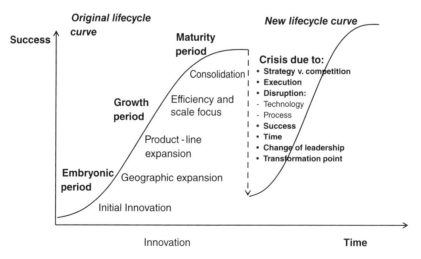

Diagram I.3: Typical causes of the crisis in the full lifecycle model
© Kai Hammerich, 2012

side of the American corporate psyche. The finance department will increase its strengths, and the employees will become more individualistically focused on myopic objectives and less team oriented. It is indeed rare that a crisis will make a company more global and inclusive in its perspective. The same obviously goes for German, Indian, French, Brazilian, Chinese, Japanese, Danish, Italian, Finnish and Korean companies. They will all react differently to a crisis, as they revert to their own national uniqueness. *No company and no leader can afford to ignore the effect of the national cultural heritage during a period of crisis!*

"Global" companies

So does the global corporation exist? Yes and no is the short answer! Many corporations rightfully claim they are global. They have a global footprint; they have global operations, global customers and global employees. They may even have some shared global values and therefore postulate having a global culture. However, this latter claim is often misleading. The perspective may be politically correct in a global world, but hides the fact that virtually all global corporations have a single national culture at heart. They may have a thick veneer of globalization that enables them to cooperate effectively with other nations and some broadly accepted values to go with it, but in their heart they belong only to one nation. P&G, GE, IBM and Coca-Cola are all proud American companies. Just as Huawei, Siemens, Renault, Toyota and Tata are proud Chinese, German, French, Japanese and Indian companies and culturally and operationally very different.

There are very few successful dual-country companies. One such example is Unilever, a consumer goods company that was created by the merger of British Lever and Dutch Margarine Unie. It is dual-listed in London and Rotterdam. However, on closer inspection using our national cultural lenses, the two countries are related from a cultural perspective.[16] They share a common mercantile, seafaring and colonial heritage and at Unilever this was combined with similar corporate values embedded by the founders of honesty, integrity and hard work, a belief in local autonomy (over centralization) and a belief in the value of human relationships.[17]

[16]Hofstede G. (1980) *Culture's Consequences*. Sage.
[17]Jones G. (2005) *Renewing Unilever: Transformation and Tradition*. Oxford University Press, Chapter 9.

The dual culture also created significant tensions. The consensus-oriented Dutch managers would enjoy a good open and honest debate about issues before making a decision. However, they would often feel outmanoeuvred by their British counterparts, who preferred to discuss and agree decisions among themselves in advance of a meeting. It may also have contributed to the development of a quite "clubby", networked and slow-reacting culture. The value placed on having "good" human relationships between managers from the different parts of the organization meant that dissent was often frowned upon and cross-national distrust masked behind apparent consensus.[18]

However, geographic proximity and a partly shared history do not guarantee cultural alignment. There are few, if any, successfully integrated Danish–Swedish corporations. A few national traits critical for the success of a business organization are fundamentally opposed. The Danish short-term pragmatism, agility and opportunism combined with jolly informality flies in the face of the Swedish desire for long-term planning, processes and consensus and a more formal social etiquette. These differences are caused by deeply rooted cultural differences that emerged in the two countries as they adapted to very different geopolitical environments after the Viking period, during the Mediaeval Age. Denmark – a small seafaring and fertile nation surrounded by bigger countries – needed to be agile, while Sweden benefited from developing its longer-term collectivist orientation to explore the rich, but hard to get to, natural resources.

International organizations like the UN and the Red Cross are global without having a unifying national culture at the core. Over time, such organizations may create a common culture based on the rules and procedures that have been adopted as their organizational etiquette, and will use bureaucracy and policies to reinforce the behaviour and habits. However, the resulting culture will rarely be as consistent and homogeneous as in an organization with a single national culture at heart or a unifying "raison d'être". International organizations where the main and most influential donor is from a single country will often reflect those national values while international organizations, which are largely administrative – versus being in the frontline – often adopt many work practices from the country in which the HQ is located.

It is possible to create a homogeneous organizational culture for an international organization, when it is based on a professional culture, a common

---

[18]Jones G. (2005), Chapter 9.

sense of purpose or having most of the employee base in the front line. An example of this would be Médecins Sans Frontières. The organization employs medical doctors, who share a common professional culture. They also share a strong sense of purpose of assisting people, without regard to race, political affiliation, gender, religion or nationality, who are in need in areas of armed conflict.

Summary

Kai recently met with a friend who is a director of a major management con-sultancy firm. He reflected on some of the change projects he was working on: "It is just so difficult to get a UK organization to adopt the Lean philosophy.[19] With the French and the Germans it is much easier – they get it." Essentially, the efforts to adapt Lean run against a number of deep national cultural traits in the English people – the independence, the anti-authoritarian perspective, the individualistic approach to life, their respect for the individual, the prag-matism, etc. Contrast this with the French and German cultures, where people are more at ease with designing, running and operating in organized systems and using what the English would consider quite rigid processes. Bureaucracy as an organizing principle was originally invented in Germany and success-fully adopted by the French.

There are compelling benefits in having a single nation-state culture at the heart of an organization. It gives the employees a clear, moral, ethical and behavioural compass to work from, as any organization benefits from knowing where true north lies! It enhances consistency, which when reinforced repeat-edly, will create a stronger culture. With a true north defined, everybody understands what is right and wrong, and can get on with the job. In the end, a consistent culture is superior to a vague one in terms of getting things done, as long as it doesn't derail itself and is focused on the task at hand.

One can't say if a particular nation is inherently more effective in getting things done than another. Most, if not all countries, have proven their ability to defend their own territory and establish a national culture. They have done this either through sheer might and scale in the case of China, Russia, Britain

---

[19]Japanese manufacturing philosophy originated by Toyota, particularly important in the efficiency and scale phase.

and the USA or through their ability over the centuries to resist the military powers of enemies, or potential cultural integration by occupiers in the case of Denmark, Switzerland and Vietnam. All countries have had leaders who at some point in their history made significant military, economic, technological or social progress by organizing their people to achieve whatever they set out to aspire to. Most nations have also faced a national disaster, e.g. a period where geopolitical trends weakened them or a war. National traits are often the by-product of such major events. They are neither good nor bad, they are simply different.

The Prussian General Von Moltke personally changed the culture of the Prussian Army over a 30-year period, as a response to a devastating defeat by the Napoleonic Army in 1806, to combine tactical disobedience with strategic discipline. He first used his new principles of leadership in battle, when the Austrian–Prussian Army defeated the Danish Army at Dannevirke in 1864. This led to the loss of one-third of Denmark's territory (Saxe-Lauenburg, Schleswig and Holstein) and started a period of introverted mourning. This, however, eventually also inspired the industrial revolution in Denmark, where young entrepreneurial companies with a global outlook, such as the cement engineering company FLSmidth, helped rebuild the Danish economy.

All companies are affected by their national heritage. Over the corporate lifecycle and during a period of crisis, the national traits will impact companies from different nations differently. Some countries have national traits that are better suited to the early innovative growth phase, while others thrive in the maturity phase. As a leader, it is important that you understand how this may impact your company.

As human beings, we are culturally programmed to view the world from our own national perspective. This makes us blind to our own culture. Just as fish don't see water, leadership teams from the same nation as the company, or who have worked at the company for a long period, may struggle to see when a potentially derailing cultural dynamic is at play.

Will the global company, without strong national roots, become more prevalent in the future? Maybe the digitalization and our own personal awareness and exposure to other countries will create more global companies. More companies today start out with a global outlook, not going through the local, then regional and then global expansion that characterized companies from the 19th and 20th centuries. Yet, digitalization also means that you don't need to have a physical presence in other countries to do business, which reduces the actual exposure and thus influence beyond the analytics of the data. The current dominant Web 2.0 companies, Google, Facebook, Amazon and eBay, with the exception of Skype, a Microsoft subsidiary, are all very American, having gone global almost instantly after quickly conquering America. Our own national culture is embedded at a young age and the organizational national culture, as we shall see in Chapter 1, is embedded through the founders, thus it may take some time before we see a rapid increase in the number of truly successful global companies without a distinct national culture at heart.

A brief chapter overview

In Chapter 1 we discuss how values, beliefs and assumptions are embedded in the organization, through the founders and leaders. We introduce the concept of business influencers and national influencers, and how they impact a company in different ways. We present the simple version of the Cultural Dynamic Model®, and use most of the chapter to discuss the effects of business influencers.

Chapter 2 will introduce the Lewis model, which triangulates national cultures between linear-active, multi-active and reactive national types. We use it to describe national traits and national types across the globe, and how the national influencers impact a company's corporate culture through its history, the national types and the founders and leaders.

In Chapter 3, we discuss the key national traits of a few countries in more detail: the USA, Sweden, France, Japan, Italy, Germany and Great Britain. From America's frontier spirit that laid the foundation for its entrepreneurial focus and short-term results orientation, and the idea that "The Business of America is Business", to the more long-term oriented, elitist and intellectual business culture in France. We also look at the complex social values and rules in Japan that profoundly affect both corporate behaviour and how other cultures should interact with the Japanese. The main point is that no culture is perfect. All national cultures have different strengths and traits that may derail their success at each stage of their lifecycle.

Chapter 4 presents the full Cultural Dynamics Model® and introduces the key concept of a cultural dynamic. We will use the Austin Motor case to demonstrate the idea. A cultural dynamic describes the dynamic effect when the national and business influencers, through the company's work practices, start interacting with each other and often unintentionally change the corporate culture. The case also demonstrates how a highly innovative company stumbled in the efficiency and scale phase.

In Chapter 5 we will continue the detailed discussion of the lifecycle periods. We start with the embryonic period, which includes the early innovation phase and continues with the geographical expansion phase. We will present three cases, first Finnish Nokia and how it, in less than 20 years, became the global leader in mobile and then was hit by a crisis. We continue with two short cases describing the global expansion of Finnish KONE, and American Walmart's international expansion. These cases, in addition to the previous case on Austin Motors, illustrate the dynamics of this period and the influence of national culture.

In Chapter 6 we discuss the growth period when companies continue their geographical expansion, expand their product offerings and start focusing on efficiency and scale. We use the comparative case of Samsung and Sony to compare and contrast the fortunes of these two consumer electronics giants and crystallize key learning. During this period, the company will expand its number of product lines and the number of customer segments it addresses. It will establish itself as a more mature global corporation with global processes. The company needs different skills and capabilities to be successful, and thus different national traits will impact the success compared to the earlier embryonic period.

In Chapter 7, we describe the maturity period with the efficiency and scale phase and the ultimate consolidation phase through the cases of Japanese Toyota, Danish FLSmidth and American P&G. As the industry matures, there is a drive towards more efficiency often through sheer scale and a desire for a stronger market share position. Consolidation is the end game of an industry, with only a small handful of global or regional players in the segment. Again, this period requires different capabilities from the growth period and again different national traits will impact success. We will summarize the key learnings from the eight cases at the end of this chapter.

In Chapter 8, called "Whither the West", we discuss how this new balanced global world will affect countries in the West and outline a few golden rules for dealing with people from reactive and multi-active cultures.

In Chapter 9, we will discuss how an existential crisis ultimately will hit most companies and what effect the national culture will play in both identifying it and handling its effects.

In the final Chapter 10, we will summarize our findings and present eight recommendations that the boards, management and investors should consider. We also list common traits that may switch from being an enabler to a derailer and vice versa in different countries, and in the Appendix we list common national enablers and derailers in over 25 countries. Finally, we briefly discuss what countries may learn from these findings and what implications they could have for them if they want to strengthen innovation and entrepreneurship and deal more effectively with national enablers and derailers that affect their ability to compete in a rapidly globalizing world.

Part I
DEVELOPING THE CULTURAL DYNAMIC MODEL®

1

In this chapter we discuss the mechanisms by which values, beliefs and assumptions are embedded in organizations through the behaviour of their leaders and their work practices. Drawing on the work of Ed Schein and Geert Hofstede, we go on to use the Cultural Dynamic Model® developed by Kai Hammerich, to guide our discussion of how business influencers and national influencers impact the corporate culture in fundamentally different ways: the staid *national traits* that are slow to change compared with more fluid *business traits* that can be influenced by management over a shorter time scale. In this chapter our discussion focuses on the business influencers, and in Chapter 2 on the national influencers, using the Lewis model – a triangular representation of national types. In Chapter 4 we bring it all together in the complete Cultural Dynamic Model®.

When Kai Hammerich was a newly minted and hopeful MBA from Kellogg Business School in 1984, he got his first job in marketing at Hewlett Packard in Denmark. To spur sales he came up with a promotional concept to expand the use of administrative computers , as servers with ERP (enterprise resource planning) applications on them were called at the time. The simple idea was to target secretaries rather than the heads of finance, and offer a 90% discount on word processing, email and graphics software, hoping that with use, the customers would need to upgrade to the then much more expensive computers. The campaign was a runaway success. HP Denmark more than tripled software revenues and profits.

Initially, the European software division was delighted, but they soon complained that the CFO was less than pleased with the deep discount. As the more pricey hardware upgrades started to roll in the software division had the sensible idea of asking the hardware division for a cross-subsidy. They argued that it was their discount solution that had enabled the hardware division to significantly increase sales and therefore profits. The response from the German head of the European computer division was disappointingly clear: "Over my dead body" – sophisticated business talk for a NO! Kai was disheartened. He felt this was not rational, and escalated the issue. Eventually, a senior CFO tersely told Kai that while he understood his frustration, the principle of the independent product division was sacrosanct at HP. Kai was right by MBA standards, but here was a fundamental belief at stake and that was more important than short-term MBA logic, and the campaign was called off. This belief in the independent product division was central to HP and had been inculcated in the organization by the two founders Bill Hewlett and Dave Packard. This was a principle that was not up for debate! It had become an embedded value – based on a business influencer.

The next sections explore the ways in which such beliefs become embedded in an organization.

First, let's look at the nature of organizational culture, or corporate culture as it is also called when describing a business organization.

What is corporate culture?

The three levels of culture

There are several definitions of corporate and group culture. The American guru of culture and leadership, Edgar A. Schein, defines culture in a particularly useful way for our purposes. Schein defines organizational culture as[1]:

> "A pattern of shared basic assumptions that was learned by a group as it solved its problems of external adaptation and internal integration, that has worked well enough to be considered valid and, therefore, to be taught to new members as the correct way to perceive, think, and feel in relation to those problems."

From this definition it follows that:

1. Culture is learned and reinforced and handed on as learning to the next generation and new members of the group

[1]Schein E.H. (2004) *Organizational Culture and Leadership*. San Francisco: Jossey Bass Publishers, p. 246.

Three Levels of Culture (Schein)

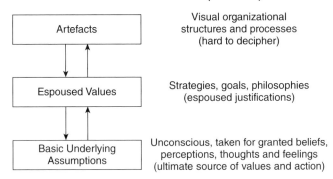

Diagram 1.1: Schein's three levels of culture
Source: Organizational Culture and Leadership, E.H. Schein. Reproduced by permission of Jossey-Bass, San Francisco.

2. Culture has a purpose in terms of achieving common objectives. Perceived success will reinforce the culture and make it stronger
3. A group will develop its own distinct patterns of behaviours and beliefs to support the culture, and the internal socialization process.

Schein notes that the early stages of a company's life are critical in defining the culture at three levels (Diagram 1.1).

At the top level is what one can physically observe about the culture: the buildings, the physical workspaces, the visible behaviour, the rituals, the advertising, the organizational charts, and documented work processes, or artefacts, in Schein's words. These elements are easy to observe, but difficult to decipher. We can admire the pyramids, but have little idea of why they were built!

At the middle level you find the articulated shared goals, strategies, philosophies, and explicit values and beliefs, which Schein calls the espoused values. The P&G Way, outlining the guiding principles of Procter & Gamble, would be an example of an espoused value, used to justify decision making principles.

At the lowest level one finds the often invisible or difficult to detect values and beliefs or assumptions in his terminology, which guide the culture and the actions in the organization. These are the concepts or behaviours that are taken for granted; they are non-debatable and difficult to change. Assumptions based on the national heritage will be prevalent at this level. An American's right to individualism is such a fundamental national assumption, as is HP's belief in the independent business division. The American national value, though, is deeper-rooted and more staid than the more contextual HP value, which management would be able to influence and alter.

The popular mission, vision and value statements that most companies promote are often a mixed bag of how the culture actually is and how the company would like it to be or not to be. Most American companies have included a statement about collaboration and teamwork in their corporate values. This may be an appropriate *corrective value* in a company with an invisible assumption of everyone's right to individualism, but may not necessarily reflect how people actually behave. In Chapter 4, we will explore how a company's value statement often includes different types of messages with different purposes. They will tell you quite a bit about the culture and values of the company, once you have deciphered them, which may not always be what the company intended to communicate.

How leaders embed their values, beliefs and assumptions early on

Schein also observed that leaders embed their beliefs, values and assumptions in an organization.[2] The primary embedding mechanisms take place early in the lifecycle of a company creating its cultural foundation, while the secondary mechanisms take place as the company matures and moves from a personal to a managerially oriented culture.

The *primary embedding mechanism* includes:

- What leaders pay attention to, measure and control on a regular basis
- How leaders react to critical incidents and organizational crises
- How leaders allocate resources
- Deliberate role modelling, teaching and coaching
- How leaders allocate rewards and status
- How leaders recruit, select and promote
- Stories about important events and people
- Formal statements of organizational philosophy, creeds and charters.

Reinforced by the daily work practices in the mature organization

These embedded values, beliefs and assumptions are reinforced in the mature organization, through the daily work practices, in what Schein calls the *secondary articulation and reinforcement mechanisms*, which include:

[2]Schein (2004), p. 246.

- Organizational design and structure
- Organizational systems and procedures
- Rites and rituals of the organization
- Design of physical space, facades and buildings.

For simplicity and variety, we will use the words corporate or organizational values or just values to represent the values, beliefs and assumptions in the remainder of the book.

The six dimensions of corporate culture

P&G is a company that seeks the truth. This is a deeply-rooted belief that was inculcated by its purist and religious founders. When P&G launched Ivory Soap in 1881 its slogan said that the soap was 99.44% pure. Not 100%, not 99% – no, 99.44%, and scientifically proven to be purer than other Castile soaps. With that fact in hand, P&G, also keen on making a good profit, advertised it intensively and soon became the undisputed market leader. Anyone who has worked at P&G has toiled with frustration over the infamous one-page-memo. That single page that will summarize any major business decision. It is used to recommend an action, whether it is a billion dollar investment or a more mundane new advertising campaign. Every word is evaluated until it is perfect – and the "truth" is found. It can take weeks and tens of iterations between the writer and managers above to get it approved. Over the years, the P&G culture became centred on artefacts like that and at times developed cult-like traits. Either you enjoyed it and stayed for long, or you left early, as there was little room for cultural dissent. However, virtually all people who have worked in P&G are impressed by the principled and uncompromising nature of its culture.

In his classical IBM questionnaire-based study, Hofstede established six dimensions of what he terms Organizational (read corporate) Culture through statistical analysis.[3]

1. Process oriented versus results oriented (means v. goals)
2. Employee versus job orientated (people concern v. getting the job done)
3. Parochial versus professional (a person's identity derived from company or profession)

[3]Hofstede G., Hofstede J., Minkov M. (2010) *Cultures and Organizations*, 3rd Edition. McGraw-Hill, p. 354.

4. Open systems versus closed systems (inclusive culture v. exclusive-secretive-clubby)
5. Loose versus tight control (of people and what they do)
6. Normative versus pragmatic (following procedures v. market/customer driven).

These are very useful when describing a corporate culture in a consistent manner. However, as indicated repeatedly by Hofstede, Schein and others, this is a complex field and not easily captured in simple models. There are simply too many variables. You may be able to use a simple model to describe a business culture, but will probably not achieve much in terms of predictability of the performance of the organization. When it comes to culture, the devil is in the proverbial detail and the detail is multi-faceted.[4]

It is obvious that national values will have a significant influence on these six dimensions. For Danish companies, the culture is generally described as open and inclusive, whereas Japanese companies are generally considered more closed. Does this make either of them more or less effective in reaching their objectives? The answer is more complex, will depend on the particular circumstances and is not a simple yes or no, as we shall soon see!

Companies from every country can be grouped along these six dimensions; however, there can still be significant variances between companies from the same country. Google and Procter & Gamble are both American, but obviously very different, companies, that originated in different eras with somewhat different expressions of the basic American values – yet both are successful; and there are Danish companies that are closed and successful and Japanese companies that are open and successful.

Corporate culture and strategy: the cultural dynamic model®

At its simplest level, the relationship between strategy and culture can be looked upon as two intrinsically linked objects. They can't be separated; they are as yin and yang (Diagram 1.2).

[4]Hofstede et al. (2010), p. 358.

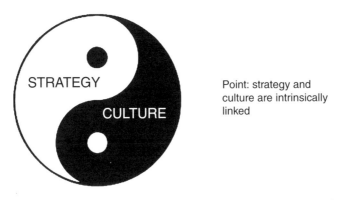

Diagram 1.2: The yin and yang relationship between strategy and culture

Results come from work that gets done: "the work practices"

In the Toyota case we describe how work practices deeply rooted in the Japanese culture enabled Toyota to gain a sustainable competitive advantage during a 30-year period. The international subsidiaries would adopt the Japanese work practices and philosophy with limited opportunity for local interpretation. We will use the term *work practices* throughout the book. By this we mean all the tangible processes, structures and systems that go into delivering the products and services the company offers. *Work practices are a central concept for us. This is where culture meets strategy.* In the case of Toyota, they include the Toyota Production System, the Just-in-Time Philosophy, the Lean manufacturing processes, as well as the skills and capabilities of the people employed, the physical plant, the decision-making processes and reward philosophy. Work practices are artefacts that can be observed by an outsider; the organizational values behind the work practices are more difficult to decipher.

Work practices influenced by . . .

The business strategy and execution perspective

When we focus on the culture side, we present you with a model that Kai developed, called the Cultural Dynamic Model®. It combines the strategy and execution dimension with the culture perspective, and their yin and yang relationship. You have probably already read one or more of the many influential business books that have been written on strategy by leading American

Diagram 1.3: Business strategy and execution dimension

business theorists, from Porter's *Competitive Strategy*, to Clayton Christensen's *The Innovator's Dilemma* and Collins' *Built to Last*, just to mention a few. We won't repeat them here, though we may refer to their conclusions. These books focus on the link between the *strategy*, and how a company will competitively organize to serve its customers, through the *work practices*. The outcome of this effort or the *results* is normally expressed as the revenues, profits, market share and more recently the balanced score card. Analysis along this dimension is factual, rational and numbers oriented. This is the stuff that is taught at most business schools and refined by management consultancies. We call this the business strategy and execution dimension (Diagram 1.3).

When Henry Ford decided to go for a strategy of providing affordable transportation to the masses, it ultimately resulted in the creation of the largest industrial complex in the world: the River Rouge Plant. In the 1930s, it employed over 100,000 workers in a single vertically integrated process. Steel virtually came in at one end and cars came out at the other. This is an example of how a strategy will dictate a new set of work practices. The aim for Ford was to be the most efficient producer of cheap reliable cars, a strategy that helped Ford dominate the automotive market in the first part of the 20th century in the USA. This strategy required new work practices and thus a new corporate culture emerged that was different from the small workshop that assembled a few Ford Ts per day in 1909, when it was originally launched.[5] The impersonality of the industrial revolution with its large assembly lines was powerfully portrayed in Charlie Chaplin's *Modern Times* movie from 1936. While clearly having a social and political mission, it also articulates a common resistance to change and the reverence of the bygone!

---

[5]History of Ford (Sept 2012) (http://en.wikipedia.org/wiki/History_of_Ford_Motor_Company).

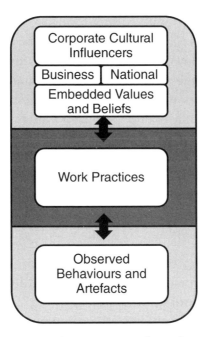

Diagram 1.4: The corporate culture dimension

The corporate culture perspective

The cultural perspective, our focus, can be expressed in Diagram 1.4.

Starting from the top, the two main factors shaping a company's values, beliefs and assumptions and thereby the corporate culture are the *business influencers* and the *national influencers*. The origin and nature of the two influencers are fundamentally different, as we shall see in this and the next chapter. Hofstede touched on this when he wrote:

> "The difference between national and organizational cultures is based on their different mix of values and practices. National cultures are part of the mental software we acquired during the first ten years of our lives, in the family, in the living environment, and in the school, and they contain most of our basic values. Organizational cultures are acquired when we enter the work organization as young or not-so-young adults."[6]

[6]Hofstede et al. (2010), p. 346.

Together, these two corporate culture influencers will have a fundamental impact on work practices. They are embedded in the organization through the values of the leaders. They are reinforced through the repeated behaviour of the employees and managers in the daily work practices. Finally, the influencers, through the work practices, will express themselves in what we can observe: the cultural artefacts and espoused values of the organization and the observed behaviour! This is the top of the iceberg that is visible to the outsider; however, what is under the water is the fascinating part.

It is important to observe that the employees and the leaders are the glue that bonds the business and national influencers together – affecting both, but in different ways.

Let's dive into the water and first take a look at the business influencers. These include:

1. The industry in which a company operates and its professional culture
2. The competitive dynamics of the industry
3. The market and brand position of the company
4. The innovation rate
5. External forces and trends.

The industry in which a company operates and the influence of the professional culture

What a company makes for a living and the types of people it employs will influence the corporate culture. The sophisticated culture of a fashion retailer will differ from that of the mainstream supermarket chain. However, a French and an American supermarket chain may share many values and work practices, as companies in the same industry often share traits and values transcending borders, through a common professional culture. Car companies share values through having a high concentration of mechanical engineers in critical positions and pharmaceutical companies sometimes get their ethos from medical schools.

People with the same educational background often share common personality characteristics which are useful for success in their profession, or simply a by-product of their particular talents and education. Lawyers share many personal characteristics; they are often detail oriented and have a good memory for facts. They are factual in their orientation and often seen as being emotionally balanced and not easily upset; all traits that are useful for a lawyer and judge. The same could be said, with different characteristics of course, for many other professions. Expect airline pilots to be predictable and unemotional in their reactions. You really don't want to be in trouble in an aircraft with an emotional and creative pilot at the steering column, except, of course, if it happens to be Tom Cruise in *Top Gun*. This also creates potentially opposing subcultures within a company – "R&D can't speak to sales" – and importantly a source for cultural distinction between industries.

The educational system in most countries will seek to get the most out of the talent available. It therefore filters young people with appropriate competencies and skills into the most relevant degree programmes for them. Engineers will be selected based on being rational, analytical, mathematically oriented and facts oriented – all useful talents for an engineer. Engineers are also often viewed as having the common personality traits of being practical rather than visionary, introvert with a relatively low self-awareness and often not at ease in complex social situations. These traits are not necessarily essential for being a good engineer, but rather a by-product of their talents and background. However, they will impact the ethos of the company in which they work. Obviously, we do recognize the need to be very careful in not taking this stereotypical perspective of a profession too far. Human beings are diverse, and we have met many creative and entertaining engineers and introverted sales people.

The competitive dynamics and lifecycle of an industry

The competitive dynamics of an industry will influence the requirements for the work practices and organizational capabilities and through this influence the corporate culture. Are you in a regulated industry or in a fragmented industry or do you play a scale game in a mature industry with few competitors? Depending on the industry, different qualities are needed to succeed. Those qualities are often expressed as a combination of behaviours and cultural capabilities, similar to the six dimensions of organizational culture outlined above. Typical dimensions may include: urgency/bias-for-action, customer orientation, quality/detail focus and process orientation. If your company is operating in a rapidly changing industry then short-term agility, innovation and creativity, customer focus and empowerment may be the key cultural traits that need to be honed in the work practices to be competitive. However, if you work in a regulated, more mature industry, a focus on process and planning, disciplined execution and the long term may be more appropriate.

Across industries, the industry's stage in the lifecycle evolution will impact what qualities define the competitive battleground. For each main lifecycle period, we have listed some of the typical enabling competencies and traits:

- **Embryonic period**: Innovation and initial international expansion.
  - Creative innovation
  - Growth orientation, focus on revenues
  - Strong customer orientation
  - Risk taking, empowerment and trust
  - Agility, short-term orientation and pragmatism
  - Building relationships across cultures
- **Growth period**: Continued, international expansion with a broader product offering, and initial focus on scale and efficiency.
  - Disciplined innovation – to broaden the product portfolio
  - Process and discipline; mastering planning, budgeting and execution
  - Commercial orientation; balancing risk, revenues, costs and margins
  - Relationship building; partnering and collaboration
  - Balancing agility with a control and quality orientation
  - Longer-term and more strategic orientation, while still being agile
- **Maturity period**: Consolidation and M&A
  - Strategic orientation; managing complexity in a global scale business
  - Commercial orientation; mastering continuous restructuring and reinvention
  - Mastering change; integration of acquired entities and new organizational structures
  - Process orientation; focusing on systemic efficiency and cost control
  - Quality focus; mastering all key disciplines; sales, marketing, R&D, supply chain, etc.

The transition from one phase to the next is the critical point where companies can stumble. This is where the national influencers will be seen most vividly. Austin stumbled in the transition between the innovation phase and the growth phase partly because it didn't manage the transition from the founder leadership to a new managerial regime and partly because its cultural heritage derailed its efforts to establish effective manufacturing processes and achieving scale by expanding internationally. Nokia was challenged when Apple and Google redefined the competitive landscape for mobile smartphones with the iPhone and Android technology. The new strategic imperatives facing Nokia demanded Web 2.0 software development and managerial skills and capabilities, which were in short supply at Nokia – and in Finland. Ultimately, Nokia decided to partner with Microsoft, using the Windows Mobile platform to speed up the acquisition of those skills. As we shall see in the Nokia case, Nokia's Finnish heritage played a significant role in it not recognizing and responding to the threat from Apple and Google in time. In several cases, a trait that was an enabler in one phase may become a derailer in the following.

However, sometimes smaller issues get in the way during a transition phase. When the mature and 60-year-old, process-oriented Hewlett-Packard and the 20-year-old brasher Texan Compaq merged their global PC and Enterprise operations in 2002, to gain scale, the two cultures and work practices clashed on the sales side. Compaq, as you would expect of a younger company, had a more aggressive, agile sales culture, and handed more decision-making authority to the local subsidiary, with weekly up-to-date financial information provided. HP, as you would expect of a more mature company beyond the initial expansion phase, had stronger central control mechanisms in place to balance the business, and gave less empowerment to the local subsidiary, only sharing financial information once a month. The Compaq Enterprise team successfully fought to adopt their model of local empowerment in the merger with the newfound empowerment embraced by the HP Enterprise team; however, the HP financial systems would prevail. So, when after the merger a Compaq-inspired subsidiary was given a new aggressive quarterly sales revenue target, but no weekly financials, the sales skyrocketed, but at the end of the month, the gross margin had dropped dramatically from being in the 30s to less than 10%. This led to a timely review of what IT systems and management practices were needed to support local empowerment to avoid a repetition of the incident. Work practices and systems will reflect where a company is on its lifecycle curve and its underlying values. During a merger of organizations in different phases, these systems may derail the integration.

Position and brand

The position and brand of your company will influence the corporate culture. Are you the leader or the challenger in your industry? The challenger profile often includes being short-term, execution, results and action oriented. A challenger is more agile and pragmatic, and will respond quickly to changes in the market and to new customer requirements. If you are the market leader, being process oriented and strategic may be key competencies that should be embedded in the culture, obviously without being complacent. Different industries and national differences will impact on how the market position translates into an appropriate set of capabilities and thus the corporate culture.

The type of products you sell will also influence the corporate culture. If you walk into Tiffany's in New York you expect professional, smart and intimate customer service in line with the company's brand position and prices. You expect the personnel to be sophisticated and knowledgeable, well groomed and possibly well educated, espousing aspirational middle-class values. If you walk into a hypermarket like Walmart you expect and get a different experience. The people employed impact the ethos of the company and its corporate culture, espoused values and work practices. A low-margin, low-salary retail type business will typically hire people from a working-class background. Thus, it is not uncommon for mass retailers to have a quite practical, no-nonsense and results-oriented culture; however, as a consequence, senior managers promoted from within may lack abilities in strategic and long-term thinking.

A word on cultural fit

In the past couple of decades, companies have increased the use of psychometric analysis when hiring people. Psychometrics is concerned with the measurement of knowledge, abilities, attitudes and personality traits. A popular methodology is the Myers-Briggs Type Indicator (MBTI) assessment. This is a psychometric questionnaire designed to measure psychological preferences as to how people perceive the world and make decisions.[7]

Companies will use these tests to guide the hiring decision. They will tend to hire people who share behaviours, values and beliefs with the company and, thus, who are considered a good cultural fit. Hiring against a well-defined psychometric profile therefore will reinforce the existing values, traits and possibly the assumptions. The consequence of this is that it can create a lack of behavioural and value diversity and thereby leave the door wide open for insular and myopic thinking and potentially "group think".

You would expect that the diversity that comes from hiring nationals from different countries will enhance the company's diversity of thinking and ability to see the water. However, an executive from a country other than the

[7]Wikipedia on Psychometrics and Myers-Briggs (http://en.wikipedia.org/wiki/Myers-Briggs_Type_Indicator).

company's heritage who has stayed at the company their entire career, usually has been successful because they have a strong cultural fit. Therefore, they probably share and accept many of the invisible values, beliefs and assumptions. Consequently they too may be culturally less clear-sighted and provide less diversity of thinking than you would expect.

The innovation rate in an industry

The innovation rate of an industry will also influence the corporate culture. Many excellent books have been written on "disruptive innovation" in recent years. However, the majority of innovation is evolutionary in nature rather than disruptive. Creating a company culture that supports evolutionary innovation is essential for many of today's global companies.

American and mid-western, 3M has perfected the art of commercializing even mundane product improvements. Who else would have put glue on the back of a square piece of yellow paper, thereby creating a multi-billion dollar business with its Post-It notes? Another example of its innovative culture was when, in the 1960s, it found a new process for precision cutting crystals to concentrate light, and the overhead projector was born. Forty years later, an offshoot of the same crystal cutting technology laid the foundation for a significant new global business in self-adhesive, light-reflecting materials, used on all types of sports, leisure and security clothing, enabling us to safely exercise in the dark.

3M has a strong belief in basic research and a longer-term perspective than competitors, in particular US-based competitors. It will nurture an idea for longer, when other companies would have dismantled the project. On average, the company is probably wrong, but once in a while, it will hit on a Post-It note product and create a new billion dollar business and recoup all its investments in the projects that failed.

Companies will strive to establish a corporate culture and work practices that support this type of day-to-day innovation, though this may fly in the face of their national instincts. The Open Innovation paradigm was coined in the USA in 2009 at Berkeley University – a university with a distinct communal culture and radical reputation. With Open Innovation, the simple idea is that employees from different companies are encouraged to share IP (intellectual property) with potential collaborators, rather than guarding it. The point is to overcome the complex web of IP rights controlled by different companies that hinder progress. If successful, this new model of co-invention and co-creation between individuals and companies will challenge the traditional innovation model of the individual inventor, who found an IP gold nugget, became rich and won the Nobel Prize. It may also give the corporate IP lawyers, CEOs and shareholders many sleepless nights!

A good example of how such a fresh way of thinking can revolutionize innovation comes from the (American) Bill & Melinda Gates Foundation. In order to spur innovation in the fight against diseases such as malaria, it funds product development partnerships made up of consortia which share IP. Obviously, having access to far more of the newest knowledge accelerates innovation for everyone, without a Nobel Prize syndrome hampering progress. It took an outsider, who could see the water, to break the sector's gridlock!

In the future, it will be interesting to observe how quite independently minded American companies will evolve this new concept. Maybe it will prove to be more popular and effective in countries with more communal and collaborative national cultures, or maybe the short-term financial benefits are so significant that it will be embraced widely in America first!

External forces and trends

How do you make an oil company green? This is the multi-billion dollar question that executives at BP, Exxon, Shell and French Total are struggling with every day. Sometimes a change in public opinion of what is right will force a company to review its value and belief system. Today, being green is important, as is corporate social responsibility (CSR) and sustainability. The American focus on diversity and inclusivity is gaining ground worldwide. These new trends often fly in the face of practices deeply steeped in national traits or business traits and to embrace them takes courage and leadership. This is not about advertising or PowerPoint presentations; this is about changing people's behaviour on the ground, and establishing a leadership culture to support it. Ultimately, leadership of business organizations comes from the top. Many companies will publically subscribe to these aspirational goals; the key test is if they are just words or valued and embraced in the day-to-day operations. After all, Enron's tombstone corporate values also included excellence, respect and integrity![8]

---

[8]http://www.prweb.com/releases/2006/02/prweb342169.htm.

The business influencer: summary

Leaders embed their values in the organization. Some will be more transient in nature and some more deeply rooted in national beliefs and therefore more resilient to change. If we compare the HP and Toyota cases, we can see the difference. The sacrosanct belief at HP in the independence of the business division versus the sales organization is a value that can best be described as having been embedded through the business influencers. At Toyota, the belief in simplicity and elimination of waste more firmly originates in Japanese national beliefs, embedded in the work practices by the founder.

An embedded national trait such as Toyota's simplicity and elimination of waste will be an embedded business influencer for non-Japanese staff and naturally a national belief for the Japanese employees. Thus, employees from many nations may accept a certain value that has strong national roots, but it is not as firmly embedded with them. Nokia's international employees may take pride in the fact that Nokia is a Finnish company, and part of working for Nokia is working for the success and pride of Finland; however, for them it is an adopted value rather than a firmly embedded national belief!

The water people don't see: the national influencers

Here is how Toyota itself describes its dedication to the elimination of waste and the concept of continuous improvement that created the Toyota Production System (TPS).

> "TPS is steeped in the philosophy of 'the complete elimination of all waste' and imbues (permeates) all aspects of production in pursuit of the most efficient methods. Its roots go straight back to Sakichi Toyoda's automatic loom developed in 1896. The TPS has evolved through many years of trial and error to improve efficiency based on the Just-in-Time concept developed by Kiichiro Toyoda, the founder (and second president) of Toyota Motor Corporation. Waste can manifest as excess inventory in some cases, extraneous processing steps in other cases, and defective products in yet other cases. All these 'waste' elements intertwine with each other to create more waste, eventually impacting the management of the corporation itself . . . By practicing the philosophies

of 'Daily Improvements' and 'Good Thinking, Good Products,' the TPS has evolved into a world-renowned production system. Furthermore, all Toyota production divisions are making improvements to the TPS day and night to ensure its continued evolution."[9]

This belief is central to Toyota's ethos and work practices, and implicit in all they do. It came from the founder Kiichiro Toyoda, who in one of his five precepts said: "Avoid Frivolity. Be sincere and strong." In modern language it would probably read: "You should eliminate waste, and concentrate your energy on what is truly effective and build a lean and fit company."[10] This is a belief deeply rooted in the Japanese national values of modesty and prudence.

The *national influencers* which we will discuss in detail in the next chapter can be divided into three groups:

1. The history of the country (geopolitical history, geography/climate, spiritual orientation, the era in which the company was founded, etc.)
2. The national types (the Lewis model) of the country
3. The values, beliefs and assumptions of the founders and the key leaders.

The key difference between national and business influencers is their time perspective. National cultures are imbedded into people at a young age, and thus staid. Business influencers are acquired later, and can be impacted by management on a shorter timeframe. This is the reason why it is critical to understand whether you as a leader, facing a period of transformation, are dealing with national influencers or business influencers. If national influencers have the potential to derail a new strategy, you may be in trouble, unless significant corrective action is taken!

We will not go into a detailed analysis of the national influencers here, but note that the values, beliefs and assumptions of an organization, as Schein indicated, often are invisible and therefore require deeper analysis to identify. This is best done through observation, though this is not always possible, for

---

[9] http://www.toyota-global.com/company/vision_philosophy/toyota_production_system/origin_of_the_toyota_production_system.html.
[10] Hino S. (2006) *Inside the Mind of Toyota*. Productivity Press, p. 51.

instance when describing historical events. In the cases in this book, we have used a mix of observations based on our personal experiences with the companies, and extensive analysis of secondary materials. The acid test of having identified the right values and assumptions is: can they explain the actual observed behaviour and artefacts with a high degree of certainty? The analysis based on the Cultural Dynamic Model® uses a mix of factual and anecdotal material, and is prone to be impacted by the cultural bias of the analyst. However, when done prudently, it is a factual analysis, where independent observers will arrive at similar conclusions.

For a corporate organization, it is often possible to identify a few fundamental values or assumptions that can explain most of the core organization's unique character and the observed work practice behaviour. We call this the organization's "cultural universe". To fully verify this requires extensive hands-on observation. In our cases we will limit our analysis to discussing one or two assumptions that are pertinent to the key learning in each.

In Diagram 1.5 we have summarized how the business and national influencers define the core values of a corporation.

We will discuss this further in Chapter 4, when we complete the Cultural Dynamic Model® with the concept of a cultural dynamic, describing how the strategy and cultural dimensions dynamically interact over time as behaviours and values are reinforced through the work practices.

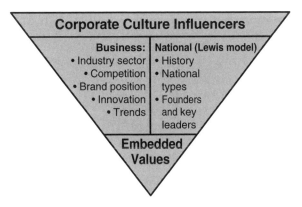

Diagram 1.5: How the business and national influencers define the core values of a corporation

The three levels of culture

Changing the behaviours, work practices and habits of people takes time, dedication and most importantly leadership from the top. *Culture exists at three levels* at the same time: the executive level, the middle management level and at the front-line level. Transformational change only happens if it is embraced effectively through new behaviours at all three levels simultaneously. Inconsistency in behaviour may lead to organizational cynicism, like when the management asks employees to constrain their salary demands in tough times, and then pay themselves high bonuses! In some cultures, this may be acceptable, but not in others.

Diagram 1.6 shows the three levels of culture.

Which?, a UK consumer magazine, published an article about pricing policies at mass retailers in the UK. They pointed out that often multi-pack offers were more expensive per pack than the products sold individually. A customer experienced this at his local Tesco store, prominently displaying the "Peel" tomatoes multi-packs. He complained to the store manager twice, insisting something be done about it. When he returned the following week, the multi-pack offer was still in place but they had increased the price of the individual packs by 50%! At Tesco, the corporate guiding value and the advertising slogan is "Every Little Helps"! In this case it didn't quite guide the behaviour in the front line as well as the leadership may have hoped for, assuming of course that the slogan is directed towards their customers and not the shareholders. Maybe the store manager didn't want to lose his investment in the large displays for the multi-packs, or maybe he had specific KPIs that would focus him on promoting these multi-pack products over individual products.

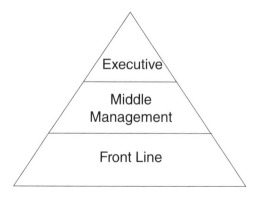

Diagram 1.6: The three levels of culture

Or maybe there was an oversight in the complex IT system that manages pricing of tens of thousands of products in thousands of stores.[11] The same could happen in most companies, every day, anywhere the world. Which brings us to a key observation:

> *At its very best, corporate culture guides judgement and enables people to overrule man-made systems driving inconsistent decisions or behaviour.*

It is this reinforcement thousands of times every day, when the systems don't provide final guidance to decisions where you need the cultural values to assist you. If done consistently, repeatedly and over long periods, a stronger and more consistent culture will emerge.

During a transformation period it is not unusual to observe that the top management is well ahead of the organization in embracing the new behaviours. They become visibly frustrated with the apparent reluctance of the wider organization to enthusiastically embrace the new principles. The reason is both the time lag of culture, as we will discuss next, and because the new values haven't been translated into actual behaviour. If you want to empower your organization to take more commercially prudent, customer-oriented decisions in the front line, you will have to explain in detail what that means for the individual middle manager and employees, and what the new rules are. You can't just say "Just use your common sense!" – because the sense that was common before may not be the same as is common now.

The organization will always be somewhat sceptical about a new regime, as nobody likes change. Any hint of reversal to the old management behaviour, i.e. punishing someone who misinterpreted a new value in good faith, to do what he or she thought was the right for a customer, will be monitored intensively by the organization. If found, it will be used as proof that nothing has changed, and therefore that change is not needed!

The time lag of culture and cultural agility as a competitive advantage

During a transformation, the change in corporate culture will lag behind the strategy implementation. It can easily take three or five years for a strategy

---

[11] *Which?*, October 2010, p. 56.

change to work its way through the work practices and become inculcated into the corporate culture. A change in culture only happens when the actual behaviour is changed and repeatedly reinforced in the work practices. This takes effect through the actions of the leadership and the substitute leadership elements including: the rewards systems, performance management indicators (KPIs), the organizational structure, the decision-making processes, and training in both the formal and informal organization. It also creates a dilemma for corporations. With the increased cycle speed of change in our hectic globalized world, there is a real risk that the static nature of culture change will clash with the more frequent need to change strategy, and therefore could lead to the culture being perpetually out of sync with the strategy.

Consequently, it is important for your organization to consider how you can speed up the cultural change to align with your new strategy. This may well be the most critical challenge to international management teams in the years to come. We believe that *cultural agility is a sustainable competitive advantage for the 21st century.* To accomplish this, your organization will have to more effectively identify and deal with the derailing effects of national traits and embrace the accelerators. Diagram 1.7 conceptualizes this point. The graph on the left side shows how the culture can be permanently out of sync with the strategy except for brief moments, when the line crosses, in perfect harmony. Areas in grey are the cost of the misalignment to the organization. The alignment of culture and strategy is much closer on the right side. It would, however, be foolish to suggest that any organization will ever find 100% alignment, except for the brief moment when lines cross.

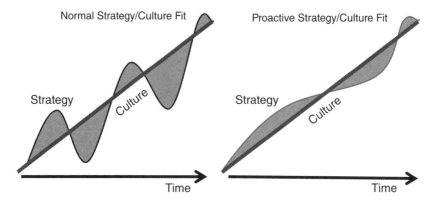

Diagram 1.7: How culture and strategy interact

As we will see in the Sony, Nokia and FLSmidth cases, corporate cultures can be annoyingly rigid when you need to respond firmly to changes in the strategic imperatives or when you are being hit by a life-threatening crisis.

Chapter summary

Every company has a corporate culture, whether implicitly or explicitly stated. The organizational culture is the result of all the decisions made and actions taken in an organization over time. *Behaviour shapes culture and culture is behaviour*, and success is the engine that feeds it! Culture is not created using PowerPoint slides or with impressive tombstones with lofty aspirations carved on them. No, culture is slowly formed by people interacting and by repeating behaviours that lead to success as defined by the organization. Leadership comes from the top, and as we will see throughout the cases in this book, continuous and consistent leadership is a very good starting point for building strong cultures. Walk the talk, as they say in America, is a very effective way to create deep culture.

Culture is embedded in the organization through the national and business influencers. The nature of the two differs; national influencers are deeply embedded through the values, beliefs and assumptions of founders and leaders. The business influencers are embedded through people and how they respond to the business realities facing them; the industry they operate in, their professional culture, the lifecycle stage of the company, their brand and positioning, the innovation rate of the industry and wider societal trends such as diversity and sustainability.

Culture operates at three levels at the same time; the leadership, middle management and the front line. Consistent behaviours across the three levels will help create a stronger culture. However, culture often lags behind strategy by three to five years, as change has to be consistently repeated in the work practices to become firmly embedded.

You can change behaviours in an organizational culture that are based on deeply rooted national cultural traits, but be aware that it takes significant effort and time. In the case of General Von Moltke we discuss how he fundamentally changed the values and behaviour of the generals in the Prussian army in the 19th century, to be strategically obedient, yet tactically disobedient when in the mist of battle. This was a value that went against a strong Prussian upper class trait of hierarchical thinking and obedience in accepting orders, which had helped create a strong army culture with a deep command–control orientation. Such a change takes time, in this case over 30 years and only through hands-on personal leadership in selecting and educating every single new commanding officer.

In the next chapter we will explore the three key aspects of national culture that influence corporate culture.

2

The best-selling cross-cultural analysis *When Cultures Collide, Leading across Cultures* (Richard D. Lewis, Nicholas Brealey, London 1996, 2003, 2009, 2011) examined the cultural characteristics of 85 nation-states on six continents. Although the study was geared to some degree to the business community, it dealt in principle with general national traits as they pertained to society as a whole, looking at the role they played in what has been sometimes termed "the clash of civilizations".

It indicated that cultures developed on a grand scale, engendered by such mighty issues as history, geography, climate, religion and language, and evolved not just over centuries, but during historical millennia and indeed inheriting some characteristics from the pre-historic era. In human terms, cultures are ancient, powerful and incredibly complex phenomena, changing reluctantly, at glacial pace, possessed of great momentum and endurance.

When Cultures Collide also recognized the numerous layers within most national cultures: regional, professional, generational, educational, and those deriving from differences of religion, gender or class. Such variants *spice*, but do not basically change, the thrust of the national culture. People live and work inside countries and their behaviours, customs, habits, tastes, preferences and priorities conform with remarkable consistency to the national norm. It has been assumed that the Internet and other technological advances in the area of international communication will, in the long run, standardize people's behaviour, aspirations and activities. One talks of the "global village" and how disparate national cultures will be diluted and eventually dissipated in the face of the interconnectedness of countries, especially where youth is concerned. This has, however, not yet happened. One must remember that national agendas are not set or implemented by the young, but largely by older people, in governments, academia, political strongholds and other august bodies. Older people tend to resist change and cling to established procedures and ancestral traditions. Thus, while the diverse societies of the world are modernizing (at different rates), they are not necessarily drawing closer together and are certainly not homogenizing.

There is another type of culture which, to some extent, stands apart from the bulldozing national ethic and which may enjoy a certain independence by virtue of its own creativity and solvency. This phenomenon is *corporate culture*. Many of the people living and working inside a nation are also living and working inside a company or corporation. It is often said that a national culture is a blueprint for survival of the nation. Obviously corporations and other commercial organizations are interested in, and strive for, survival – even prosperity. They may achieve this by aligning the corporate culture with that of their country – this certainly tends to attract customers in the domestic market. But there may occur situations or circumstances where conducting business strictly according to the nation-state rules does not lead to prosperity, but to something less satisfactory. Examples are communist regimes controlling commerce in Cuba and North Korea (and formerly in Vietnam, Russia and several East European countries) or overly go-getting US corporate cultures that alienate clients in countries like Japan, France and Sweden, where a more sophisticated approach is mandatory.

There are no universal rules uniformly beneficial to the establishment of a corporate culture. They vary enormously even inside one country and one branch of commerce – the chasm between the business styles of IBM and Apple is a good example.

What goes to make a corporate culture? Which ingredients combine to create its shape and character?

Nation-state traits are usually influential at the beginning. It is hard to imagine laying the cornerstone of a German company without a semblance of hierarchical structure, a Swedish one without adequate employee welfare or a Japanese firm without any group or network connection.

Historical factors bear upon the creation of corporate cultures just as they do at the national level. In which historical period did the company first see daylight? Was it born during a depression, boom time or war? Three revolutions – agricultural, industrial and technological – have parented commercial enterprises with very different agendas, aims, aspirations and avenues of ambition.

Who were the *founders and early managers of the company*? Did the emerging corporate culture reflect their image? If Henry Ford stamped his character on the Ford Motor Company, how influential have been leaders such as Carnegie, Rockefeller, Krupp, Konosuke Matsushita, Akio Morita (Sony), Jorma Ollila (Nokia), Bill Gates, Steve Jobs, Jack Welch, Axel Wennergren, Axel Johnson, Pekka Herlin (Kone), Carstedt, Agnelli, Siemens, Richard Branson and Howard Hughes?

The character of a company may also reflect the *region* it inhabits. Californian firms are culturally very different from those on the eastern seaboard or in the Midwest. Executives from Pittsburgh and West Virginia live in a different world from those in Washington, Arizona and Texas. In Italy, companies in the northern industrial areas around Milan, Turin, Genoa and the Veneto show little enthusiasm for the lifestyles and corporate cultures of Sicilians, Neapolitans and Calabrians, whom they see as living in a previous century. Bavarian firms act differently from those in the northern half of Germany. Parisians contrast in sophistication with Marseillais; the corporate styles of northern English firms – children of the industrial revolution – bear little resemblance to the "Establishment" boards of the City of London.

The tripartite categorization of the Lewis model – distinguishing between linear-active, multi-active and reactive cultures – will, in the main, engender corporate cultures which follow this pattern. Thus we might expect board members in linear-active Holland to install procedures based on facts, planning, action and implementation, while their multi-active French counterparts would place more emphasis on elegant discourse, theoretical models and the company's reputation in the larger society. Japanese companies and conglomerates (reactive) are seen as semi-sacred entities where self-sacrifice, paternalism and internal cooperation combine to reinforce a strict, albeit benign, hierarchy (Diagram 2.1).

The tendency for corporate cultures to pay homage to national traits is clearly persuasive, but other factors introduce variety. As we have said above, a company might be the offspring of a particular era (war, peace, revolution, crisis, scarcity or surfeit of commodities, new discoveries, etc.) which would define its nature or character. Regional traits would weigh in, as would the personality of the founder and leaders. In hot and cold wars, corporations such as Boeing, BAE, Krupp and Siemens would work closely with the military authorities. *Hot and cold climates* are also powerful factors: multi-active behaviour thrives in hot places such as Africa, the Middle East, Mediterranean countries and South America. All linear-active cultures are located in cool or cold nations (the only exceptions being Australia and certain regions in the United States).

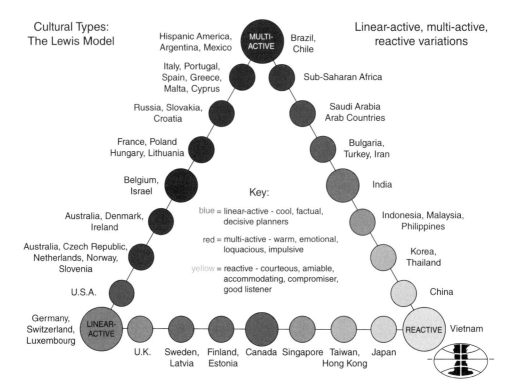

Cultural Types: The Lewis Model

Linear-active, multi-active, reactive variations

Hispanic America, Argentina, Mexico / MULTI-ACTIVE / Brazil, Chile

Italy, Portugal, Spain, Greece, Malta, Cyprus

Sub-Saharan Africa

Russia, Slovakia, Croatia

Saudi Arabia Arab Countries

France, Poland Hungary, Lithuania

Bulgaria, Turkey, Iran

Belgium, Israel

India

Australia, Denmark, Ireland

Indonesia, Malaysia, Philippines

Australia, Czech Republic, Netherlands, Norway, Slovenia

Korea, Thailand

U.S.A.

China

Germany, Switzerland, Luxembourg / LINEAR-ACTIVE

REACTIVE / Vietnam

U.K. / Sweden, Latvia / Finland, Estonia / Canada / Singapore / Taiwan, Hong Kong / Japan

Key:

blue = linear-active - cool, factual, decisive planners

red = multi-active - warm, emotional, loquacious, impulsive

yellow = reactive - courteous, amiable, accommodating, compromiser, good listener

Diagram 2.1: The Lewis model
(this figure appears in colour at the end of the book after the index)

Religion also plays its part. Indian companies observe Hindu tenets; a good Arab manager is a good Muslim; Lutheran corporate cultures prioritize hard work, profits, clean offices and equality for women. In the USA, a number of large corporations acknowledge and publicize their Christian affinities and values. The Roman Catholic Church influences corporate behaviour world-wide. Modern Turkish companies are currently torn between adhering to Kemal Ataturk's secular legacies and cultivating an increasingly Islamic image favoured by the government. African corporate cultures in most countries are shaped by tribalism. Apart from largely secular Europe, only Japan and China conduct business with little or no reference to religious considerations, since Confucianism and Buddhism are codes of behaviour that impose their own ethical standards, separate from theological doctrine.

Nation-state cultures – like human beings – have *masculine and feminine* characteristics. In 1980 Gert Hofstede analyzed data collected in detailed questionnaire format from hundreds of individuals in 40 countries. When we correlate his results with equally exhaustive data in the Lewis model concerning linear-active, multi-active and reactive cultures, some interesting points come to light. One would expect the linear-active cultures, with their emphasis on job orientation, products, action and results, to be located firmly in the masculine category. In fact, as Diagram 2.2 shows, half of them are among the world's most feminine cultures (Netherlands, Norway, Sweden, Denmark and Finland). The cluster could be called "Lutheran". Another cluster (Anglo-Saxon) is moderately masculine, though Canada and New Zealand are borderline. A "Catholic" multi-active cluster is (expectedly) feminine, while a multi-active/reactive Asian cluster is somewhat surprisingly masculine. Italy seems out of place in this cluster and one would perhaps question Hofstede's data in this instance, though it is strengthened by his finding that Italy rates seventh in his individualism index, hard on the heels of English-speaking USA, Australia, Britain, Canada and New Zealand. Were the Italians who were interviewed perhaps from the north?

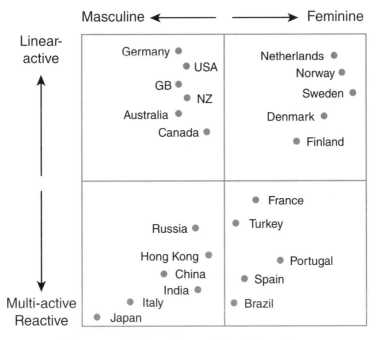

Diagram 2.2: Masculine and feminine cultures

Corporate cultures in each country will inevitably be shaped to some extent by the masculine/feminine dichotomy. In the Lutheran cluster the well-established welfare states of the Nordic countries and the Netherlands engage the companies' executives with the rights and benefits of the employees as top priority. This contrasts markedly with Japan's masculine paternalism where employee welfare, though imperative and well taken care of, is seen as generosity from above (a boon) rather than an inexorable right.

If we correlate Hofstede's *individualism* index with the Lewis model's linear/multi/reactive categories, we find that *no* linear-active cultures are collectivist. The top left-hand square (linear and individualist) is exclusively Anglo-Saxon and Germanic. Collectivism is most evident in multi-active and reactive cultures – principally Asia and *Latin* America. Western European Latins (France, Italy, Spain and Wallonia) have their own moderately individualist cluster (Diagram 2.3).

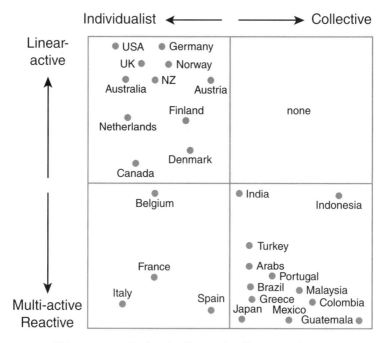

Diagram 2.3: Individualist and collective cultures

A company creating and establishing its corporate culture has a wide variety of choice and simultaneously faces many challenges. We have seen how national values, the era of inception, the personality of the founders, the regional location, climate, religion, considerations of masculinity and femininity and individualism and collectivism are all factors in shaping it. Taking everything into account, what are we looking for? Reputation? Efficiency? Survival? Profits? Which economies are the most successful? First, let's look at the *linear-active cultures*. The 15 most linear-active countries in the world are the United States, Canada, Britain, Australia, New Zealand, Germany, Switzerland, Austria, Sweden, Norway, Denmark, Finland, the Netherlands, Luxembourg and Flemish Belgium. Their citizens are well aware that their linear, disciplined, largely Protestant-influenced way of life differs sharply from that of multi-active and reactive populations. They are also very aware that their 15 economies account for 50% of world production and that in the GDP-per-capita league, all of them except New Zealand are in the top 20 countries. (Two of the others – Singapore and Hong Kong – have strong linear-active influences.)

But other indices may erode Western complacency. In the last decade of the second millennium, China was by far the fastest-growing economy (over 11% per annum) and only *one* Western nation, Ireland, appeared in the top 20. Ireland has a basically linear-active lifestyle diluted by marked multi-active tendencies (also supported heartily during the decade by generous EU subsidies).

The writing is on the wall, and it is largely pictographic. In two, three or four decades at the most, China's economy will surpass that of the United States. At the beginning of this century, the world's 10 biggest economies were, in order of size, the United States, Japan, Germany, France, Britain, Italy, China, Brazil, Canada and Spain. By mid-century the ranking is more likely to be, again by size, China, the United States, Japan, India, Brazil, Mexico, Germany, France, Korea (North and South) and Canada. Linear-active champions in the top 10 will have been cut down to the United States and Germany, with multicultural Canada squeezing in. Britain may not make it.

We are, of course, only talking economics. If we look at population size, the only linear-active country in the top 10 is the United States (third). By mid-century the US population may have been overtaken by those of Indonesia, Brazil, Pakistan, Bangladesh, Nigeria and possibly Mexico. The total linear-active population will probably be approximately 3–4% of the world's total. Even now, it is no higher than 8% and is decreasing daily.

We cannot consider these statistics (of economic growth and burgeoning populations) without drawing certain breathtaking conclusions. Since the fall of Arab civilization in Andalucía in 1492, Europeans and their North American descendants have dominated world affairs politically, commercially, militarily and culturally for five centuries – half a millennium. This was largely thanks to mammoth China looking inward and letting the rest of us get on with it. Even now, it is unlikely that China will try to dominate the rest of the world in this century. They have a very good record of non-interference.

However, we are approaching a watershed. Whatever Chinese intentions may or may not be, the 21st century will be the one in which the balance tilts. During the century, the economic growth of Asian and Latin American countries will enable them to call the tune in international commerce and politics. Not only will most of the mightiest engines of industrial production be located in China, India, Japan and Korea (as well, of course, as the United States), but the world's hungriest markets cannot fail to be the burgeoning populations of India, China, Indonesia, Pakistan, Bangladesh, Brazil, Mexico and Nigeria. Their needs, requirements, tastes and appetites will transform not only the world economy but also the way the world works and lives.

At the time of writing there is not a lot of evidence to suggest that linear-active societies are drastically altering their ways of doing business. In spite of the ominous rapid advance of nonlinear societies (economic, political and demographic), linear-active business communities continue to feel comfortable within their systems. It is a proven category, so why change it? Why should one not concentrate on selling to the 600 million linear-active customers in the world? They think like we do, and they have the money to buy. But what about multi-active and reactive customers? The fact is, there are a lot of them: about 6 billion at the last count. Don't hard-headed Americans, British, Germans and Nordics want their custom? Of course they do. The teeming populations of the future – China, Japan, Korea (reactive), Brazil, Mexico, Nigeria (multi-active) and Indonesia and the Indian subcontinent (hybrid multi-active/reactive) constitute an unimaginably huge mass of consumers. But how to capture these markets? How to compete with savvy China, India and others?

The current reply would be that we have systems and these systems assure efficiency. What are these systems? Why don't other business cultures adopt or imitate them? What is so special about linear-active business methods?

Linear-active cultures

To begin with, linear-active people tend to be task-oriented, highly organized planners who complete action chains by doing one thing at a time, preferably in accordance with a linear agenda. They prefer straightforward and direct discussion, depending on facts and figures they obtain from reliable, often printed or computer-based sources. Speech is for information exchange, and conversationalists take turns talking and listening. Truthful rather than diplomatic, linear-actives do not fear confrontation, adhering to logic rather than emotions. They partly conceal feelings and value a certain amount of privacy. Results are key, as are moving forward quickly and compromising when necessary to achieve a deal.

Linear-actives believe that good products make their own way and sometimes fail to see that sales are based on relationships in many parts of the world. They normally use official channels to pursue their aims and are usually not inclined to use connections, take shortcuts or influence opinions through presents or undercover payments. Normally law-abiding, linear-actives have faith in rules and regulations to guide their conduct.

They honour written contracts and do not unduly delay payment for goods or services received. When doing business, they are keen on punctual performance, quality and reliable delivery dates. Mañana behaviour and over-loquacity are frowned upon. They are process oriented, brief on the telephone and respond quickly to written communication. Status is gained through achievement, bosses are often low key and money is important. Rationalism and science dominate thinking more than religion does.

The term *linear-active* refers to cultures which emphasise "linear" qualities such as punctuality, step-by-step planning in a straightforward manner, single-mindedness, observation of deadlines, quick responses to written communication and completion of action chains, and which are very "active" in supporting and buttressing these goals with an elaborate system of medium- and long-term strategies embedded in a complex mesh of processes and doctrines. These are so copious and jargonistic as to take one's breath away. Different linear-active corporate cultures pay lip service to concepts such as "business process re-engineering", "de-layering" and "balanced scorecards". Others include: rightsizing, downsizing, change management, Team Flow Model, Cultural Dominance Model, managing transition, matrix management, quality circles, "best practice", performance appraisals, organizational change, rolling quarterly forecasts, JIT production, Total Quality Management, global realization process, macro-engineering, MBO (management by objectives), KPI (key performance indicator), benchmarking, leveraged buy-outs, power as change model, de-levelling, what-if analyses, career-pathing, feedback loops, distributed cross-organizational teams, collaborative software, affinity networks, concurrent re-engineering, Corporate Purpose Breakdown, negative performance indicators (complaints!), information obesity, M-form society, CTA (critical thinking appraisals), CORE principles, SWOT analyses, OPERA approach, virtual facilitations, MIO (major improvement opportunities), CALS (Computer-assisted Acquisition and Logistics Support), mushroom management and Shamrock, Trapezium and Honeycomb patterns of organization.

Many of these terms and concepts are American in origin; they are used extensively (albeit selectively) in Western linear corporate cultures. Managers are expected to be familiar with and practise those that are appropriate to the activities of the company. The terms, though used mainly in English, can be translated into other languages (e.g. German and Dutch) though Nordics tend to use the English versions. They are not very popular, and sparingly used, in multi-active and reactive cultures. French, Italian and Japanese business-people tend to see *business formulae* as insignificant alongside *business relationships*. Wary of rigid rules, processes and constrictive systems, they take psychological shortcuts to efficiency by deepening relationships, getting close to customers and markets, sharing of emotions, mutual help in difficulty, free interpretation of the rule book, gift-giving and acknowledging tacitly that it is flexibility that makes the world go round. This is the basic problem for Western linear-active companies pursuing business in Latin countries, Africa and the Middle and Far East. In these countries linear-actives see a lack of regulation, elastic ethics and perceived inefficiency. On the other hand, they also witness overabundant production and rampant growth. What must they do to compete in these markets?

Let us now look at the multi-active world.

Multi-active cultures

Multi-actives are emotional, loquacious and impulsive people; they attach great importance to family, feelings, relationships and people in general. They set great store by compassion and human warmth. They like to do many things at the same time and are poor followers of agendas. Conversation is roundabout and animated as everyone tries to speak and listen at the same time. Not surprisingly, interruptions are frequent, pauses in conversation few. Multi-actives are uncomfortable with silence and can seldom tolerate it.

In business, relationship and connections are seen as more important than products. The former pave the way for the sale of the latter. Relationships are best when they are face to face; they cannot be maintained over a protracted period simply by written correspondence or phone calls, although the former has less effect with multi-actives than the latter. They much prefer to obtain their information directly from people and trade in rumour and gossip. Multi-actives show less respect than linear-actives do for official announcements, rules or regulations. Although they have limited respect for authority in general, they nevertheless accept their place in their own social or company hierarchy. Strong bosses are admired and are also expected to protect their employees.

Multi-actives are often late with delivery dates and paying for services or goods received. Less interested in schedules or deadlines than linear-actives are, multi-actives often move only when they are ready. Therefore, procrastination is common, punctuality infrequent. Multi-actives' concepts of time and discourse are decidedly nonlinear, and they fail to understand the importance that timetables have for linear-active people.

Multi-actives are flexible and frequently change their plans, which in themselves are not as detailed as those of linear-actives. Improvisation and handling chaos are strong points.

Multi-actives borrow and lend property rather freely. They are gregarious and inquisitive, valuing privacy less than company. Often epicurean, they adhere less to strict Protestant values than linear-actives do. In business, they use charisma, rhetoric, manipulation and negotiated truth. They are diplomatic and tactful and often circumvent laws and officialdom to take "shortcuts". They entertain lavishly and give presents or undercover payments to secure deals and contracts.

Multi-actives live in a different world from linear-actives and unless the latter tailor their business methods and objectives to enter this world, they will continue over the next few decades to surrender business to China, India, Korea and the next wave of Tigers (Vietnam, Indonesia, Brazil?). Western companies have a head start and a decent technological platform to sustain growth in certain fields, but what is sure is that a major re-engineering of processes and change of business strategies are going to be required – and soon.

Let us first define the term *multi-active* more closely. The majority of the world's inhabitants fall into this category, therefore it is important for people belonging to other categories to fully understand the term. Hall's counterpart is *polychronic*, Tomalin and Nicks use *flexible*, Duke's ICE uses *expressive*. None of these descriptions penetrate adequately the psychology of the people in this category. Hall's term is again limited to time: polychronic = people who are capable of doing several things at the same time; Tomalin's "flexible" is reasonably descriptive, though fails to "get inside" the flexibility. ICE's "expressive" refers principally to speech and possibly body language, which is basically surface behaviour. Lewis's term *multi-active* connects closely with not only the ability to do several things at once but implies and spotlights the often equivocal *activities* and *action-mode* of the persons in the category. These activities include the use of flexible or situational truth, frequent manipulation of the situation or environment, seeking favours with key people and pulling strings, often disregarding regulations and even laws, gaining status through connections, ignoring principles of punctuality, maximizing power distance, replying tardily to written correspondence, resorting to improvisation after inadequate planning, often changing plans, allowing religion to influence business decisions and "renegotiating" contracts (which they regard as ideal documents in an ideal world).

This analysis of multi-active behaviour sounds initially negative, but has to be seen in the context of attitudes of people who do not necessarily enjoy the commercial, social and legislative benefits of the established linear societies. The multi-active world is a human one (over 3 billion humans belong to it!) and sets the standards for human comportment. They live that way because they like it and are unlikely to conform to linear-active standards anytime soon. It is probable that adaptation will be required of the minority (linear-actives), rather than the other way around.

Reactive cultures

The *reactive* segment of society also poses a problem for would-be Western traders. Another psychological attitude – different from the multi-active – becomes apparent.

Richard Lewis's extensive exposure to Asians (he spent five years in Japan) inclined him to think that European and American cross-culturalists had failed to categorize Asians succinctly. Japanese are not polychronic (like Italians), but neither are they monochronic (like Germans). Asians generally do not fall into Western categories; they have one of their own which Lewis called *reactive*.

Hall ignored this mindset; Hofstede and Trompenaars did not mention it. Tomalin and Nicks, as well as Duke's ICE, both followed Lewis's example and included a third category. Tomalin and Nicks called it the *listening* category, while Duke's ICE called it *reserved*.

Both "reserved" and "listening" only touch on superficial aspects of the category. Reactive describes a psychological stance which penetrates the Asian mindset and intention. The genius of reactive listeners is that they exercise their ability to adapt towards linear-activity or multi-activity within the framework of their reaction to their interlocutors, e.g.: Japanese stress their undoubted qualities of punctuality, factuality, planning and calm when dealing with the Germans, but adopt a more flexible, people-oriented approach when confronted with multi-active Spaniards, Italians or Latin Americans. Like them, they excel in the cultivation of relationships.

When negotiating, reactive cultures invariably ask the other side to speak first. This custom, shared conspicuously by Japanese, Chinese and Koreans, denotes the Asian predilection to hear the other side's position before declaring one's own. By speaking second, they are enabled to modify the degree of variance between their opinion and that of the other side (a preliminary alignment of views might be available); at the very least a head-on collision can be averted. In this way, Asians are fundamentally reactive, not in the sense of being passive (the opposite of proactive), but with the aim of avoiding possible pseudo-conflicts due to different degrees of self-assertion or pontification. Another advantage gained by this tactic is that it leaves one's options open for a little longer. Reactivity is the key to Asian negotiating (Diagram 2.4).

Reactive cultures listen before they leap. Reactive cultures are the world's best listeners inasmuch as they concentrate on what the speaker is saying, do not let their minds wander (difficult for Latins) and rarely, if ever, interrupt a speaker while the discourse or presentation is ongoing. When it is finished, they do not reply immediately. A decent period of silence after the speaker has stopped shows respect for the weight of the remarks, which must be considered unhurriedly and with due deference.

Even when representatives of a reactive culture begin their reply, they are unlikely to voice any strong opinion immediately. A more probable tactic is to ask further questions on what has been said in order to clarify the speaker's intent and aspirations. Japanese, particularly, go over each point many times in detail to make sure there are no misunderstandings. The Chinese take their time to assemble a variety of strategies that will avoid discord with the initial proposal.

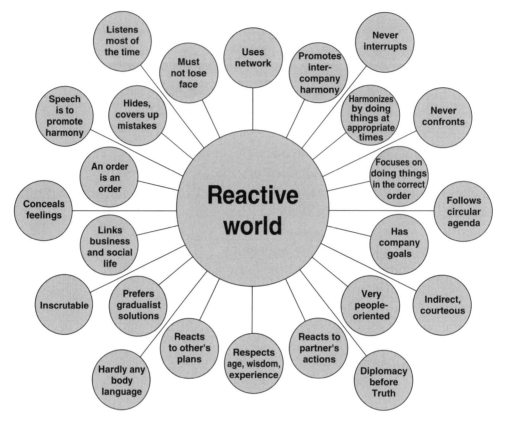

Diagram 2.4: Reactive communication style

Reactives are introverted; they distrust a surfeit of words and consequently are adept at nonverbal communication. This is achieved by subtle body language, worlds apart from the excitable gestures of Latins and Africans. Linear-active people find reactive tactics hard to fathom because they do not slot into the linear system (question/reply, cause/effect). Multi-active people, used to extroverted behaviour, find them inscrutable – giving little or no feedback. The Finns are the best example of this behaviour, reacting even less than the Japanese, who at least pretend to be pleased.

In reactive cultures the preferred mode of communication is *monologue* – pause – reflection – monologue. If possible, one lets the other side deliver its monologue first. In linear-active and multi-active cultures, the communication mode is a *dialogue*. One interrupts the other's monologue with frequent comments, even questions, which signify polite interest in what is being said. As soon as one person stops speaking, the other takes up his or her turn immediately, since the Westerner has an extremely weak tolerance for silence.

Reactives not only tolerate silence well but regard it as a very meaningful, almost refined, part of discourse. The opinions of the other party are not to be taken lightly, or dismissed with a snappy or flippant retort. Clever, well-formulated arguments require – deserve – lengthy silent consideration. The American, having delivered a sales pitch, leans forward and says, "Well, what do you think?" If a reactive is asked for an opinion, he or she begins to think – in silence.

The reactive "reply-monologue" is context-centred and will presume a considerable amount of knowledge on the part of the listener (who, after all, probably spoke first). Because the listener is presumed to be knowledgeable, Japanese, Chinese, or Finnish interlocutors will often be satisfied with expressing their thoughts in half-utterances, indicating that the listener can fill in the rest. It is a kind of compliment.

Reactives not only rely on utterances and partial statements to further the conversation, but they also indulge in other habits that confuse the linear-active or multi-active. They use, for instance, a "roundabout" style, with impersonal verbs ("one is leaving") or the passive voice ("one of the machines seems to have been tampered with"), either to deflect blame or with the general aim of politeness.

As reactive cultures tend to use names less frequently than multi-active or linear-active ones do, the impersonal, vague nature of the discussion is further accentuated. Lack of eye contact, so typical of the reactive, does not help the situation. A Finn or a Japanese, embarrassed by another's stare, seeks eye contact only at the beginning of the discussion or when he wishes to signal the interlocutor to take up her turn in the conversation.

Small talk does not come easily to reactives. While Japanese and Chinese trot out well-tried formalisms to indicate courtesy, they tend to regard questions such as "Well, how goes it?" as a literal request for information and may take the opportunity to voice a complaint. On other occasions their overlong pauses or slow visible reactions cause nonreactives to think they are slow-witted or have nothing to say.

It is always important to bear in mind that the actual content of the response delivered by a reactive represents only a small part of the significance surrounding the event. Context-centred utterances inevitably attach less importance to *what* is being said than to *how* something is said, *who* said it, and what is *behind* what is said. What is *not* said may be the main thrust of the reply.

Self-disparagement is another tactic of reactives; it eliminates the possibility of offending others. Such humility may draw the other person into praising one's conduct or decisions. Linear-actives and multi-actives must be aware of presuming that self-disparagement is connected with a weak position.

Getting things done

Linear-active, multi-active and reactive people live in their different worlds. In order for globalization to be harmonious and effective (the "global village"), a certain amount of congruity would seem to be required. Can commercial methods, aims and strategies – business cultures – be standardized? Linear-actives are ready and willing to introduce (impose?) an impressive array of well-tried systems, doctrines, formulae and scientific theories which have proved efficient in their own experience. Getting others to adopt these business theories is what the West understands by the term "globalization". Most of these systems originated in the United States and are explicit in a large number of business manuals that have been used in western and northern Europe for several decades. The problem is that multi-active and reactive cultures (French, Italian, Arab, Japanese, Chinese, Indian, etc.) do business in other ways. They see many of the Western precepts as examples of over-organization – too rigid, often assertive and lacking humanity. Operating inside these systems, people who do not think in linear fashion feel themselves restricted, constrained – in a kind of corporate strait-jacket. They miss their comforting ambiguities and feel their options have been decimated.

Looking first at multi-actives, how do they attain efficiency when they show little adherence to linear virtues such as punctuality, planning, appraisals, analysis and contracts? An Italian might reply that we save time by bypassing officialdom and using shortcuts to key people and connections. We have a practical approach to rules, regulations, laws and rigid formulae, and though you may not approve, we think that we are closer to reality than you are. You worry about lack of control undermining trust and you have problems with ethics (or lack of them) but we take such things in our stride. We understand humanity and we enjoy physical and mental closeness not only to colleagues, but often to our customers and even opponents. We appreciate your preoccupation with company re-engineering, but we do not need complicated processes for this, as it is likely to be effected in one sweep by our boss. Vertical structures often simplify such matters. Often changes reflect the image or opinions of the boss, but we are usually happy with this, as we rarely use committees to make important decisions. We dislike too many doctrines and though our decisions are less scientific than yours, they are more instinctive. Instinct is one of our strong points. You say our planning is inadequate and while we might agree, we can improvise and handle chaos better than you can. Moreover improvisation is fun. It allows us to express our originality.

You can imagine Americans and Germans shuddering at these attitudes. And what about reactive Japanese and Chinese and hybrid India? Few would question Japanese efficiency, but they have a different route to success from that of Westerners. It is an open secret that a Japanese company is a semi-sacred organization whose goal is to create harmony among its staff members. This is achieved by a particular brand of Japanese paternalism – a from-cradle-to-grave system where employees on moderate salaries can benefit from medical care, cheap company loans to buy their house, sizeable bonuses twice yearly, generous entertainment expense accounts and funeral expenses. They cannot be fired, neither do the companies wish to fire them, as they work long hours and take short holidays. The subsequent harmony results in collective behaviour, general conformity with company rules and mutual trust between staff and management.

The impressive collective efforts and the all-pull-one-way nature of Japanese workers are enhanced by the almost uncanny telepathic features of employee cooperation. Japanese company and intercompany networks are second to none. Conflict with opponents is avoided whenever possible. The big Japanese conglomerates have almost identical corporate cultures to the foreign eye. Change management is effected usually in a smooth manner due to the hierarchical nature of the firms and "telepathic" agreement. Japanese companies, however, do not make changes for change's sake. They tend to go for change only when they consider it necessary and even then they prefer to look at best past precedents rather than bold innovation. They are not impressed by Western business doctrines; they have *their own formulae* (after all, JIT (just-in-time) and Quality Circles were Japanese inventions). American black-and-white doctrines are unpopular in Japan and in Asia in general, where things are rarely judged to be black or white, right or wrong, good or bad, true or false.

Differences of opinion are seen as a circular pattern of scattered points, which can hopefully converge to reach agreement. This may take some time and Japanese, particularly, are often criticized by others on account of their slow decision-making. They do not regard negotiation as a process to be hurried; they also hate deadlines (failure to meet one would mean loss of face). Japanese are aware of the American ability to make quick decisions, but they point out that many of them are about minor issues. They say that Japanese too can make quick decisions about small matters, but that complex issues cannot and should not be settled quickly. It has been said that Japanese do not make decisions, but that decisions *are made*. This often occurs when all choices have been examined exhaustively and all but one eliminated. Americans used to dealing with Japanese put it another way: if the Japanese company does nothing over a period of weeks or months, then a solution will appear!

The multi-active-reactive Indians have another solution. Lack of scheduling and blatant procrastination frequently lead to a serious crisis, whereupon the well-known Indian quality of *jugaad* is called upon.

Jugaad is a Hindu word or concept which means "to get the job done, somehow or other". Vikas Swarup, the Indian diplomat who wrote the novel that the film *Slumdog Millionaire* is based on, said in a recent interview that jugaad is "really the spirit of India".

In a physical sense a jugaad is also a type of cheap makeshift vehicle found in Indian villages. Basically a wooden cart made by a carpenter, with a diesel engine bolted to it. The brakes may not work, but – no problem – someone can jump off and throw a wooden block under the wheels.

More jugaad . . .

As with many concepts which get to the heart and soul of a nation, it is complex to define all the elements of jugaad. The very fact that such concepts *are* so peculiar to a culture is what makes them so hard to get across to other cultures. Wittgenstein believed that the most important things could not be put into words, and jugaad is a prime example.

It is ultra-resourcefulness; it is being able to come up with solutions with the bare minimum of, or with unlikely, materials; it is generally a *collective* effort; it tends to be done under time pressure; it may involve getting around established procedures through personal connections; it could have some slight legal ambiguity; the results may leave you scratching your head wondering "how does this work?"

With your eyes and ears open to it, you start to see it all over India – the individual lunchboxes prepared by women for their husbands and personally delivered to their desks every day; the phone dealer who fixes a mobile when his Western counterpart would have shaken his head and told you to buy a new one; the team who come up with an out-of-the-box solution to a business challenge.

This spirit of "whatever it takes" is something Westerners could learn from. It is a great skill to have in times of change and crisis – a skill involving taking risks (which *karma*-believing Indians excel at), the willingness to go beyond one's job description, networking ability, collaborative skills, an open mind and boundless flexibility. Rather good competitive skills to gain ground over product-based, slower, more linear and regulated Western corporations.

3

Different cultures have diverse concepts of leadership. Leaders can be born, elected, or trained and groomed. Others seize power or have leadership thrust upon them. Leadership can be autocratic or democratic, collective or individual, meritocratic or unearned, desired or imposed.

It is not surprising that business leaders (managers) often wield their power in conformity with the national set-up – for instance, a confirmed democracy like Sweden produces low-key democratic managers; Arab managers are good Muslims; Chinese managers usually have government or Party affiliations.

Leaders cannot readily be transferred from culture to culture. Japanese prime ministers would be largely ineffective in the United States; American politicians would fare badly in most Arab countries; mullahs would not be tolerated in Norway. Similarly, business managers find the transition from one culture to another fraught with difficulties. Such transfers become more and more common with the globalization of business, but the composition of international teams and particularly the choice of their leaders requires careful thought. Autocratic French managers have to tread warily in consensus-minded Japan or Sweden. Courteous Asian leaders would have to adopt a more vigorous style in argumentative Holland or theatrical Spain if they wished to hold the stage. German managers sent to Australia are somewhat alarmed at the irreverence of their staff and their apparent lack of respect for authority.

All the above indicates that company managers, from day-to-day executives to board directors, are going to be more comfortable in their activities if the corporate culture which serves as a guideline aligns itself to a major degree with the traditional characteristics of the country's inhabitants.

This alignment may exist from the company's birth – it would be less than natural if it did not – but subsequent changes in business strategies, new partnerships in the home country, or (more importantly) a partnership, joint venture or merger with an entity belonging to another culture, might jolt or dislocate the initial alignment. The question arises, how serious is this dislocation going to be? Can the corporation maintain its wholeness after such a tectonic shift? Could there be benefits in differently benign nation-state combinations (e.g. American risk-taking and German caution) compensating for each other in a corporate culture?

More general, philosophical questions also arise. Do certain nation-state traits possess negative aspects? What about when certain traits viewed as positive by, for example, Americans (individualism, speed, directness, etc.) are seen as negative by other cultures (Japan, Sweden, Thailand)? What policy should we adopt when two companies with (powerful) wildly different cultures merge? What can we learn from cases where small states, adapting to the cultures of bigger ones, have produced superior performances, e.g. Nokia? How important is the role of international teams in propagating certain cultures or blending diverse ones?

Before we attempt to answer these questions, let us examine the extent to which a nation-state culture, big or small, will influence corporate behaviour within its borders.

The United States

Key nation-state traits

- Confidence (the American Dream)
- Bias for action (speed)
- Bottom-line focus
- Masculinity

Historical background

It is often said that there is no American culture; it is better defined as a collection of subcultures, even as a *lack* of culture. These opinions are short-sighted: there *is* an American *mainstream* culture. It is largely a business-oriented culture (the business of America is business). In this culture you turn up for your job and observe certain rules: you must be punctual, well dressed, clean, energetic, focused, aware of the objectives of the company, diligent in your pursuit of them, work hard, not time-wasting or slacking, take short holidays, be sensible in avoidance of red tape, stay on at the office in a crisis, learn English, show stamina and listen to the boss – if you fall down on more than two or three of these issues, you will be fired.

That is the job culture and it produces a clearly definable American worker or executive. Looking deeper, however, an underlying national historical culture has been evolving since independence in 1776, with its earlier roots visible in the struggles of the *Mayflower* pioneers, the Indian and Mexican wars, the Louisiana Purchase, the astounding expedition to the Pacific by Lewis and Clark and the eventual conquest of a vast continent in an incredibly short space of time.

Expression of nation-state traits within corporate culture

If we today take stock of the culture of the US nation-state, the bottom line is succinct: at base, it is young, successful, rich and powerful. This solid foundation gives the American people – and their businessfolk – a dominant and enduring trait: that of confidence. Intertwined with the concept of the American Dream, this characteristic makes the American corporate executive act boldly, show a willingness to invest, get the biggest piece of the pie and subsequently, through his control, expand the American Dream by using American methods that will ensure emulation of the nation's success.

If we look at a more detailed analysis of modern American corporate behaviour, we find it emanates largely from "the frontier spirit". This term has often been used to describe the psychology of the original settlers in the American continent, starting with the *Mayflower* landing in 1620 and leading to the establishment of 13 colonies on the eastern seaboard. The settlers were initially almost entirely persecuted groups from the British Isles, who emigrated principally to seek freedom of activity and belief and start a new life in a new country.

It is not hard to imagine that these settlers were a hardy lot who, in the ensuing decades, became rapidly aware of the historical opportunity that beckoned. They had a precarious foothold at the edge of a huge continent rich in virtually every imaginable asset. It was not empty – there were up to 10 million Native Americans living there – but this made America one of the most thinly-populated areas in the world; moreover, the "Indians" were politically divided into hundreds of tribes and – significantly – poorly armed according to European standards.

One could say the tough, strong-willed settlers were the right people in the right place at the right time. The vast land was there for the taking. This study is less concerned with the ethical aspect of the conquest than with the effect it had on the character of the immigrants who later became known as the Americans. The "frontier spirit" – the urge to expand westwards and ultimately to rush to California – demanded sterling qualities from the individuals who undertook and accomplished this epic task. The journey was long and hazardous, the Indians were often hostile, and the equipment of the settlers was mainly primitive. We all know that they succeeded, after much travail and great hardships, in winding up with the land, the rivers, the mountains, the oil and the gold. Out of the pursuit of these targets evolved the American character.

The journey was long, the land mostly untamed. Stamina was of the essence – developed over years of hardship, setbacks and determined continuance. The 21st century American executive retains this stamina. If we tick off the characteristics of the American businessman, we cannot help but see his origins in the frontier spirit. He does things quickly and with a sense of urgency (let's get to California before the gold runs out); he is pragmatic and simplifies issues (I have my wagon, horses and a gun – those are my cards); he is a hard negotiator (I have to know how to barter and live off the land); he is egalitarian (I left the dukes and earls back in England); he is individualist (I can only rely on myself and my horses); he is informal and uses first names (sit down at my camp fire, Jack, and have a cup of coffee); he takes risks (I've staked out a thousand acres and am ready to defend them); he shows little sentiment in business (my priority is survival); he is essentially mobile (we gotta move on); he is future-oriented (I didn't have much of a past); he is tough (young America was a dog-eat-dog society); he is optimistic (so much land, so few people to share it); he is mercenary, obsessed with the bottom line (otherwise I can go no further); nothing is impossible in the United States (from Virginia to California we have lived the American Dream).

This American spirit – a national credo – continues largely unabated in spite of political, military and economic setbacks (Vietnam, Iraq, Afghanistan, corrupt corporate governance, recession) experienced in the second half of the 20th century and the early years of the 21st. One should never underestimate the resilience of the United States and its continued adherence to the nation-state traits which made it great. Politics are politics and there has been much agonizing at this level since the turn of the century, but American confidence ebbs slowly (if at all) and corporate America has changed little in its approach to business methods which remain largely in alignment with national beliefs and principles.

This steadfastness is not necessarily advantageous in the area of international business and aspiring globalization. While US companies are more ubiquitous around the globe than those of any other country, they are less successful than they might be if they were to learn some lessons from other cultures.

Potential advantages/disadvantages of US nation-state traits

▪ Confidence (the American Dream)

Most Americans believe that nothing is impossible in the United States, particularly in regard to personal advancement. This belief can be termed as a CBH (cultural black hole) – that is to say, it is adhered to so completely and intensely that it overrides any opposing argument, however logical it may be. While confidence, boldness and firm decision-making are great assets to have in business, they are not always unarguable in complex situations that demand more than one perspective. In post-1945 Europe with the healing effect of Marshall Aid, clear-eyed American affirmative action was just what the stricken continent needed and welcomed. Who would question American power, dominance and commercial know-how? Yet in the following decades, and particularly after 1970, the German and Japanese economic "miracles" raised the curtain on the emergence of business models strikingly different from and arguably superior in some ways to the American. Germans and Japanese had learnt from, and possibly ameliorated, strengths associated with the Anglo-Saxon cultures. Here we see the American cultural trait of supreme confidence – no doubt originally an enabler – acquiring the category of a derailer.

As the world grew smaller and trade and commerce globalized, the Americans, ubiquitous in their penetration of world markets, had every chance to learn and absorb strengths and skills demonstrated by energetic cultures. The Japanese, Chinese, Koreans, Finns, Danes and Germans all had distinct success stories in the closing years of the last century. Unfortunately the USA – still immersed in her Dream – has been slow to afford recognition of others' cultural advantages. The major trading nations, including Japan, got to know the basic American cultural traits – and how to handle many of them. The reverse was rarely the case. American self-confidence, born of success, often morphed into arrogance, even disdain of others' cultural behaviours. Visiting delegations of US executives seeking to establish joint ventures in Japan were invariably warned by the ACCJ (American Chamber of Commerce in Japan) that first meetings with Japanese were for making the acquaintance of the potential partners only. In spite of this seasoned advice, more than half of US teams started negotiating (even discussing profit split) during the initial get-to-know-you lunches! American unwillingness to study local cultures in some depth, and to adapt to them, still remains a major weakness in the furtherance of American initiatives in Asia, South America and elsewhere.

- **Bias for action (speed)**

The frontier spirit, inculcating a sense of urgency, bequeathed to Americans a desire and subsequent ability to pursue their objectives and goals more speedily than nationals of more settled nations. The completion of the settlement of the United States has not been accompanied by the discontinuance of this characteristic in the US business world. Unfinished tasks must be addressed and completed *tomorrow*, if not yesterday! American executives are restless. They are products of a newborn nation that knows no other culture.

The enabling virtues of speedy action are apparent for all. But haste can be a derailer too. Japanese, who may take three months over a decision which Americans would make in one day, are less than impressed by American quickness. Japanese, as well as Chinese, point out that they, too, are capable of making a series of rapid decisions like anyone else. But that concerns *small* decisions. Big decisions necessarily take longer, and in these, Asians (and others) will not be hustled. Patience is certainly an Asian virtue, particularly in the Confucian cultures (Japan, China and Vietnam) though less so in risk-taking India and Korea. Other cultures regarded as slow-moving by the USA are Mexico and most Hispanic countries, as well as Sweden, France, Germany (caution) and even Britain. This bias for action is evident not only in American business but also rears its head in the political sphere (wars in Korea, Vietnam, Afghanistan and Iraq, when allies were slow to follow).

- **Bottom-line focus**

"The business of America is business" and for Americans that means profits in the not-too-distant future. Few executives would argue with accurate calculations of early revenue, good budgeting and solid financials. This type of focus is surely an enabler. But today's competition is fierce. Contracts are often brought home by long-term strategies. In Europe, the United Kingdom and Germany are particularly adept at securing business though patient structuring of projects that often require long-term loans or investments on the part of the supplier. France, in theory at least, safeguards reputation at the expense of profits. Both France and Sweden were quick on decisions to support and bail out industries that they considered household names or flag-bearers (Renault, Volvo, Saab, Aerospatiale). Norway foregoes quick revenue from its North Sea oil with an eye to preserving a key national asset (to the extent that her own citizens have urged a quicker freeing up of some income). Chinese stand out for their willingness to invest long and middle term in various countries around the world, not only buying in advance years of Angolan oil or Brazilian soya bean crops, but placing vast sums in the US economy. Japan has traditionally been active in long-term investment strategies. Koreans, on the other hand, often sought quick profits, but Hyundai, LG and Samsung have in the last decade reversed this tendency.

▪ Masculinity

Major enablers in US business have been the masculine characteristics of key objectives: persistent growth, steady profits, accumulation of wealth enabling ubiquitous acquisitions, a plethora of worldwide products sold through aggressive marketing and advertising. The combination of these factors and methods for many years gave American business seemingly unstoppable momentum and success. But, as has been mentioned earlier, world business has been "Asianizing", which means to some degree "feminizing". Social progress was a buzz-word in the last decade of the 20th century. Millions have been lifted out of poverty. The concept of nurture – so long advocated by cultures in Sweden, the Netherlands, Canada, Finland, Norway and Denmark – is making inroads with corporate sponsors and governments in Brazil, China, India, Indonesia, Botswana, Namibia and Colombia. The Arab Spring, with luck, may help in the acceleration of this process. The USA may have to review its masculine image. Growth cannot be limitless and may take second place to prudent development. Profits are harder to come by, as competitors' low wages and low pricing narrow US margins. American wealth is offset by serious deficits and acquisitions are reduced, also snatched by China and India. US products worldwide are rivalled by those of China ("the factory of the world"). Aggressive marketing – American-style – is no longer the name of the game in markets becoming more collective in nature. Other cultures are starting to "gang up" against American commercial dominance (read BRICS, which unites half the world's population and GDP).

Summary

The USA is a resilient nation and can be expected to set up a rigorous defence of her pre-dominant positions in the world's political and economic scenarios. She cannot, however, afford to be tardy in adopting enabling policies vis-à-vis other extremely important cultures – Asian, South American, even European and Russian – in areas where her essentially masculine and driving traits are quickly morphing into derailers in a more collectivist planet.

The phenomenon of diminishing Americanization of corporations in favour of increasing Asianization since the 1980s has been discussed at length in *The Cultural Imperative* by R.D. Lewis (Nicholas Brealey, 2007). Nevertheless US firms continue to conduct business in accordance with inherently masculine values that evolved from the frontier spirit. These are in stark contrast with increasingly popular and viable feminine values which are deferred to in most European countries and many in Asia and Africa, and to some extent in South America.

Masculine and feminine values may be listed as follows:

Masculine	Feminine
wealth, power assets	non-material benefits
material progress	social progress
growth	development
products	relations
profits	reputation
results	solutions
boldness	subtlety
facts	feelings
logic	intuition
duties	rights
quick decisions	right decisions
speed	timeliness
competition	co-operation
individual career	collective comfort
personal honour	sense of proportion
success	quality of life
leading others	nurturing others
commanding	rendering service

If you run your eye down the left-hand column above, you have a virtual check-list of the targets of the American executive. The right-hand column gives us a similar behavioural checklist for countries with more feminine values such as the Netherlands, Denmark and particularly Sweden. On the North American continent, Canada subscribes to many of the values in the right-hand column.

In summary, the overwhelmingly masculine character of the modern US executive, in faithful alignment with American nation-state traits, does little to facilitate interaction with representatives of the majority of the world's cultures – particularly the multi-active and reactive categories. He is comfortable functioning in an American environment, and strives to project his own rules and principles in US subsidiaries abroad, but makes little progress in familiarizing himself with the characteristics of other cultures, even though he aspires to have them as customers. There are 5 billion of them, and counting . . .

In the pages that follow, let us see to what extent other nation-states and cultures affect corporate behaviour within their own borders and as they venture abroad.

Sweden

Key nation-state traits

- Ideal welfare state
- Obsession with human rights
- Feminine characteristics

Historical background

Sweden, albeit a Western democracy like the United States, has national traits and a business culture very different from America's. Sweden is many things that America is not, and shuns many qualities that the Americans hold dear. If one looks at the masculine/feminine checklists above, one has a fairly comprehensive description of how Sweden and the USA differ. Basically, Sweden is the world's number one welfare state, whose citizens are coddled from cradle to grave with an interminable array of rights, privileges and benefits which no American government is able (or willing) to guarantee and which few countries of the world can aspire to (only the other Nordic countries would have a chance).

Expression of nation-state traits within corporate culture

The Swedish business culture reflects national beliefs and credos perhaps more than in any other country, apart from Japan's corporate flexibility (or lack of it) and is curtailed strictly by governmental laws, practices and restrictions. It is virtually impossible for an employer to fire anyone, even though employees may be indolent, disloyal and without talent. Such is the state's obsession with human rights, the corporation is encumbered with laws regulating treatment of employees that would make Americans and Britons shudder. Most Swedish staff are honest and conscientious, but a minority are not, and they ride the system with impunity. Swedish managers strive to look powerless in order to retain some influence. Foreign managers working in Sweden frequently throw up their arms in frustration or despair. Americans suffer particularly, but British managers, French, German and even Norwegians, Danes and Finns find the rules too stringently anti-management.

Another problem with the concept of a welfare state interfering with business culture is its obsession with the necessity for consensus. Swedish managers (and their unfortunate foreign counterparts) are not allowed to make "important" decisions without seeking the consensual agreement of staff. In some companies, "staff" is interpreted as middle and lower management, secretaries, tea-ladies and even cleaners. Ask foreign managers who have had to conduct business in Sweden for any length of time to describe the experience and they will say "meetings, meetings, meetings". This is a serious problem for Swedish companies employing foreign staff or interacting internationally with customers or partners. Swedes are seen as being among the world's slowest decision-makers. When a Swede works individually as a member of an international team, he often shines as being modern, innovative and energetic. Within the confines of Swedish corporations, he loses momentum. Many Swedish managers are acutely aware of this phenomenon – some like Gyllenhammer, Carstedt and Barnevik have "broken the rules" and succeeded – but foreign partners would welcome the time when Swedish lawmakers might consider reducing the constraints imposed by a system they one day may not be able to afford. The criticism levelled at Swedish companies, with the constant consultation going on at all levels, the endless meetings, habitual deferment of decisions, obsession with people orientation, ultra-cautiousness, woolly personnel policies and unclear guidelines for managers, spotlights weaknesses that arise out of the business culture unquestionably aligning itself with national exigencies at a time when 21st century conditions require something else.

Taxes are so high that they hurt, and the country is aging fast. Every year, there are fewer breadwinners for more dependants. In a non-competitive world, Swedes might go on selling quality products at high prices to support their living standards, but competition in the 21st century will be ferocious. Asians and Americans do not take six-week holidays plus all kinds of long weekends and rush out of their office at four o'clock in summer. One suspects there is more wrong with the Swedish system than the Swedes themselves. They are kind, intelligent, steadfast people who want to do well, but it will not be easy for them to eradicate their work-to-rule mentality when things get tougher.

Potential advantages/disadvantages of Swedish national traits

- **Ideal welfare state**

It is clearly beneficial for a company to feel that its staff is motivated, well paid, well housed and protected against injustice, ill-health and misfortune. The legislation enshrined in the Swedish welfare state has, during the second half of the 20th century, provided these advantages for Swedish citizens. Swedish business has been, since the end of WWII, largely successful, apart from one or two short lapses, both domestically and in the field of exports. Comfortably-off Swedes have impressed other nationals by their honesty, modernity, transparency and focus on quality. It appears that the influence of a well-organized welfare state has a good effect on corporate culture. Swedish firms are profitable and happy. But, of late, they are not happy. As discussed above, well-fed citizens have a tendency to focus more on rights than on duties. Foreigners working in Sweden, and since the turn of the century many Swedes themselves, question the ultimate destination and fate of a welfare state, where an ageing population, a diminishing workforce, coddled pensioners and more desire for leisure combine to lessen the challenge that a nation can present to competitors.

- **Obsession with human rights**

While human rights are obviously salutary, Sweden's obsession with the concept goes much farther than those of most countries. It is clear that Chinese notions are going to differ greatly from Swedish, but even British, Americans and Finns find Swedes finicky on this issue. Small and middle-sized Swedish firms can be considerably embarrassed when half a dozen year-long maternity and paternity leaves crop up simultaneously. US firms in Sweden fail to comprehend continual employee absences in times of crisis. Can one never fire anyone in Sweden? The world financial crisis beginning in 2008 (we don't know when it will end) could put a different complexion on Swedish human rights.

- **Feminine characteristics**

According to the well-known survey carried out by Geert Hofstede, Swedish culture is the most feminine among major countries. This feature is clearly interwoven with the human rights issue and the structure of the welfare state. The list of masculine and feminine values on page (76) starkly contrasts the chief features of American and Swedish behaviours. If we evaluate the feminine traits, it would seem that many of them have served Swedish companies well in the post-war era: development, reputation, subtlety, right decisions, timeliness, cooperation, quality of life, nurture would be among them. Yet what is wrong with (American) masculine traits, including growth, profits, results, duties, quick decisions, speed, competition, material success? It would be normal to consider both lists as beneficial. But how will these qualities play out in the modern era?

Summary

The world is changing fast and corporate cultures will have to adapt to changes taking place in Asia, Africa, the Middle East and South America. There is some evidence that US firms have begun to incorporate some feminine values (cooperation, sense of proportion, nurturing others). Swedes may have to pay more attention to some masculine traits (e.g. duties, quicker decisions, individualism).

France

Key nation-state traits

- France-centred self-esteem
- Strong on theories, ideas, process
- Sense of intellectual superiority

Historical background

French business leaders rival those of Sweden in the way they conduct their affairs in conformity with national credos. Like the Swedes, they are hampered in attaining best practice, as a number of their national traits do not align easily with international attitudes.

What are French values and core beliefs? To begin with, they are France-centred. Convinced of their intellectual superiority vis-à-vis other nations, they consider it their mission to civilize the rest of us. André Malraux, when appointed Minister of Culture by Charles de Gaulle in 1974, declared in his first broadcast *"La mission de la France, c'est civiliser l'Europe."* Resentful of Anglo-American political and military dominance, they regard it as a duty to safeguard European (and particularly French) culture. To this end they spend more money on the offices of the Alliance Française around the world than the British and Germans spend combined on the British Council and the Goethe Institut. The French education system is highly centralized and attaches great importance to language, literature, oratory and philosophy, incorporating elements of these subjects into the curricula of their elite business schools, HEC and Ecole Normale Supérieure.

Expression of nation-state traits within corporate culture

French corporate leaders, especially company presidents, emanate largely from these or similar establishments, bringing with them the appropriate cultural baggage – a sense of history, deep respect for culture and language, elegant theories of business and administration, and an in-built suspicion of and distaste for Anglo-American commercialism.

The elite training and education of high-ranking French business leaders does not necessarily equip them for likely success. Their preference for theories in the face of facts causes them to err with some frequency. When they do make mistakes, they are not likely to be fired, as French boards consider they appointed the best-qualified person in the first place. Profits may not accrue, but in French business, reputation is more important than profits. The government has shown its willingness on more than one occasion to bail out household names such as Renault and Citroën when times are hard.

In France there is no doubt that the importance of general well-being is seen as a preferable alternative to the mania for economic growth. Swedes (and their corporations) agree; Americans do not. Most British, Canadians and Swiss are somewhere in the middle.

Potential advantages/disadvantages of French national traits

■ **France-centred self-esteem**

French self-esteem parallels and equals that of Americans, though with a slight difference in perspective. Americans see themselves as champions of action and effective business; French as the flag-bearers of European civilization, with the duty of having to civilize Britons, Germans, Scandinavians and all other inhabitants of the continent. This is in itself a worthy aim, though whether the French will ever get up to civilize the Norwegians and the Finns is questionable, as they are still having problems with the English. This self-confident attitude of the French has served the furtherance of their ideals in the same way as it did for the Americans. It helped them to establish and administer with no little success their colonies in North and Central Africa and a couple of islands in the Caribbean, not to mention a lengthy though troublesome entanglement in Vietnam, Cambodia and Laos. Their conviction of French civic superiority has left an indelible stamp on former French African colonies, in particular Senegal and Morocco, where French administrative techniques and moral values enjoy continued adherence to this day. The trait has produced far less enthusiasm in Algeria and other African nations and has few current devotees in Southeast Asia. The French civilizing urge and its adoption had to be discarded in the post-colonial era and must be considered as a derailer in the 21st century. Neither do fellow Europeans show much enthusiasm for French tutoring. Acceptance of joint moral and political equality with her EU partners (e.g. Germany and Britain) is a more appropriate stance for the coming decades.

■ **Strong on theories, ideas, process**

French business leaders are fond of (often obsessed by) commercial theories and sometimes pursue them in the face of incompatible pragmatism. Elegant theories, though attractive in themselves, have been known to blind French leaders to fairly obvious truths. A workable theory is indeed an enabler and can unite groups with different perspectives by its elegance. If it does not work, however, pragmatic Germans, Dutch and Finns will soon disown it. French often have displayed reluctance to abandon a theory or philosophy which, according to their logic, should succeed. Often they are the last signatories to international agreements such as GATT rounds. When (French) logic does not work it becomes a derailer (obstinacy).

- **Sense of intellectual superiority**

This attribute characterizes a significant number of French both in the political and business arenas. French people relish assuming leadership, convinced of their intellectual credentials for doing so. It was an enabler for hundreds of years inasmuch as it lent their leaders poise as they moulded European institutions according to their tenets and aspirations. If the 20th century was American and the 19th British, the 18th, 17th and 16th centuries certainly belonged to the French. Their achievements and experience in this period extended to primary roles in the fields of science, medicine, the arts, architecture, infrastructure and political and civil administration, not to mention military organization and supremacy. Their presence and activities in many parts of Africa, Asia, Oceania, round the Mediterranean and North America gave them justification of their mental prowess based if not on intelligence alone but on worldwide political and commercial experience. What could a desert-bound Hottentot or a backwoods Finn tell a seasoned world citizen, a Frenchman?

In view of scientific advancement in anthropology and what we know about human intelligence, such self-imagery becomes a derailer in modern times. Our widened knowledge of ancient history certainly would encourage Chinese and Indians with their 5000-year-old civilizations (and significant list of inventions) to dispute any European claim to intellectual superiority. It is worth noting that both the Chinese and Japanese are not unlike the French in their (quieter) sense of uniqueness, a quality not unrelated to superiority.

Summary

With the emergence of new giant powers and markets (China, Brazil, India, Russia), France is now a relatively small country. It is unlikely that she will attain her once-lofty aims; more likely she will have to settle for third or fourth place in Europe. Her reluctance to learn and use English may well lose her markets on all continents. Those in French-speaking Africa are a consolation but relatively unimportant.

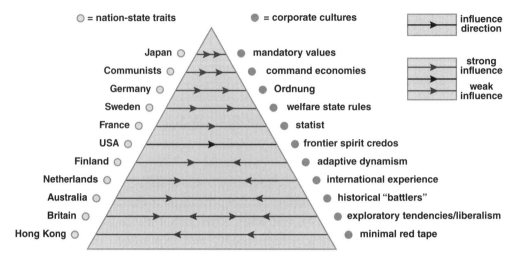

Diagram 3.1: The convergence/divergence of nation-state traits and corporate cultures

If we were to divide nations into two camps – on the one side those whose corporations adhere faithfully to nation-state characteristics and on the other side those who have freer corporate cultures – then the former would include the United States, Sweden, France, Italy, Germany, Japan, China and Singapore; the latter would consist of Britain, Australia, the Netherlands, Finland and Hong Kong (Diagram 3.1).

Japan

Key nation-state traits

- Poor linguists
- Face protection, honour
- Ultra-courtesy
- Age-based hierarchy
- The company (*kaisha*) is sacred
- Long termism

Historical background

The country whose corporate behaviour is most closely tied to nation-state traits is unquestionably Japan. Japanese people are culturally very different from all others – in fact, they are unique. This uniqueness derives from excep-tional historical and geographical circumstances as well as their special thought processes in a language very different from any other. Why are Japa-nese so different, not only from Europeans but also from other Asians? A major factor was the 250-year period of near-complete (self-imposed) isola-tion up to 1853, an accentuation of her general geographical remoteness over two millennia. In isolation, Japan developed a distinct society that has no equal in terms of group cooperation, national spirit and high-context, almost telepathic understanding. These traits make Japanese people instinctively proud of their nationality and culture, which they consider has attained unri-valled standards of honesty, loyalty, self-effacement, stoicism, bravery, self-sacrifice, unselfishness and unfailing courtesy. Only a native of Japan can aspire to speak pure Japanese; no other individual can therefore gain access to the superior thinking and culture of which the language is the vehicle. No Japanese corporation or enterprise can ignore or disregard this dogma. From my 30 years' experience dealing with Japanese companies, I have concluded that digression from these norms on the part of executives is not only unthink-able, but almost impossible. Apart from one striking exception which I shall describe below, officers and employees of Japanese firms give the impression of generally behaving in an identical manner. Westerners usually see them-selves as individuals; the Japanese sees himself representing a company which is part of a group which in turn represents Japan. The oft-quoted term "Japan Inc." conveys to what extent Japanese corporations identify with their nation-state.

Expression of nation-state traits within corporate culture

This solidarity is not necessarily an advantage for Japanese enterprises. Tra-ditionally, the Japanese *salaryman* regards the company as sacred. Once he is accepted he shows complete loyalty to the company and there is no clear dividing line between life and job. His loyalty is rewarded by lifetime employ-ment and regular promotion. He steadily climbs the ladder in a vertical society and is completely satisfied with his status on every rung. His fidelity and long hours will guarantee him promotion to important positions, whether he is intelligent or effective or not. This often leads to problems in companies which are anxious to make good profits. How does a firm promote brilliant young men to influential positions?

The late Akio Morita, the charming and perspicacious former president of the Sony Corporation, once told me the following: in a company as dynamic as Sony he could not allow executive action to be solely in the hands of mediocrities. Yet older men had to be promoted according to seniority schedules and given corresponding wages. Even Morita could not defy the Japanese system. He was able to introduce dynamism at the top by placing power in the hands of younger, more efficient men who had titles such as third assistant in the planning department or accounts clerk or vice-section leader in packaging. These men had low salaries, but they had Morita's ear and access to his office when they needed it. They were trained in languages and other skills and sent round the world on frequent study tours. They built Sony up to what it is today both in Japan and abroad, while their senior vice presidents played golf and entertained visiting American vice presidents.

Since the recession in the last decade of the 20th century, many younger Japanese employees have opted to resign for various reasons, not necessarily for remuneration, but more so for personal advancement, gratification and challenge. This may be caused by the restructuring of huge corporations. Since cross-century some companies have begun to promote staff on the basis of skills, ability and contribution to profits. Even today, however, most executives gain promotion according to age seniority.

Potential advantages/disadvantages of Japanese national traits

- **Poor linguists**

A serious disadvantage emanating from Japan's national traditions is the poor performance of most Japanese in the area of foreign languages. This is unquestionably a derailer, as Japanese never really aspired to become a world lingua franca, even though it was fairly current in Korea and other parts of Asia from 1845 to 1945. Japan exists behind a language curtain and is unfortunately unaware of her intellectual isolatedness. While millions of Japanese attempt to learn English, results are generally poor and consequently Japan's voice in the world is not heard to the extent which her economic might justifies. Few Japanese politicians have understood this problem, though business leaders are beginning to realize more and more the disadvantage they are at. One great barrier is the Chinese script unfortunately adopted by the Japanese early in their history. This makes it extremely difficult for foreigners to learn

Japanese and Japanese schoolchildren lose valuable time mastering two or three thousand complex characters, when they could be learning English. Why don't the Japanese simply switch to the Roman alphabet? First, they would cut themselves off from their literature and calligraphic art. More important still, Japanese people are bound up emotionally with the visual aspect of the written characters. They have a kind of magic quality. A European text written in Roman characters can only be linear or factual. A complex Chinese character, with perhaps 10 or 15 strokes, conveys not only the meaning but has an aesthetic value. Visual aspects are important for the Japanese, as can be seen in their pretty ways of arranging food. Where Westerners often imagine things in words, Japanese can imagine them visually. This is difficult to explain to anyone who has not studied written Japanese.

Japanese managers in Europe and the USA often impress with their ability to speak English. However, they have often spent a sufficiently long period abroad to improve their language skills. If we look at Japanese executives as a whole, these travelling managers represent a small minority. Most corporate employees, including seniors, back in Japan are pathetically inadequate in language skills or simply too shy or inhibited to practise them. In this respect the Japanese nation-state's reluctance to involve people more in linguistics hampers their ability to compete with Asian countries such as India, Malaysia, Singapore and Hong Kong (all virtually bilingual). Even China and Korea – once lagging in foreign languages – are bypassing Japan in the acquisition of English.

■ **Face protection, honour**

Concern with loss of face and efforts taken to protect an individual's reputation in this respect is the most significant of Japanese characteristics. When one considers that virtually every decision taken on a daily basis and every word spoken by a Japanese salaryman is against a background of face protection, one realizes how much influence it has on his interaction with interlocutors. It also imposes a well-defined code of behaviour on whoever is dealing with him (for instance, you). While face protection is comforting for all concerned and is a reliable enabler in smoothing business relationships, it can be a derailer when Japanese are dealing with nationalities that do not trade in white lies or subtle cover-ups. Germans, Finns and Dutchmen are known for their frankness and adherence to truth, even though it might be somewhat unpleasant. Also Americans like to spell it out and tell it as it is. In such cases, face protection hampers both clarity of meaning and the prompt correction of errors during a business project. While Japanese and other Asians may have to learn to be more frank and truthful when dealing with Northern Europeans and North Americans, it would help matters if the non-Asians would also restrain to some extent their habitual bluntness.

- **Ultra-courtesy**

No nationals are more ultra-polite or innately courteous than the Japanese. This is another trait (sometimes linked to face protection) that starts as an enabler in the process of creating an amiable business or social relationship, but ends up as a derailer when overdone with non-Japanese. Foreigners often leave a meeting with Japanese only vaguely aware of what has been said and agreed, whatever language was used. Even all-Asian meetings (and, believe it or not, some all-Japanese ones) suffer the same fate. In their respect for courtesy and their subtle use of language, forms, concepts, proposals and items agreed on can be lost in a fog of impenetrable courtesy.

- **Age-based hierarchy**

As indicated above, all big and middle-sized Japanese companies are structured along hierarchical lines in conformity with Confucian precepts. Few managers (Morita was an exception) dared challenge these rules. The outstanding success of "Japan Inc." from 1965 to 2000 confirms the merits of the system – one in which discipline, obedience and tranquillity prevailed. This tried and trusted mechanism enabled Japanese firms to become household names – Sony, Mitsubishi, Hitachi, Toshiba, Toyota, Honda, Nissan, etc., not only in the Japanese islands but throughout the consumer world. Who would contemplate changing it?

Changes are taking place, slowly. Morita's promotion problems were all the more acute if foreign managers working in Japan spotted talent in the lower ranks which they wanted to utilize and reward outside the limits of the system. Moreover, young Japanese salarymen, more world-savvy through Internet or stints abroad, have begun to lose patience with the brake on their personal promotion or lack of take-up on their youthful ideas. Since 2000 the virtues of Japanese hierarchy have begun to be outnumbered by the disadvantages of a system that now seems out of touch with fast-moving enterprises in Korea, the USA, the Netherlands and even India (IT, automobiles). We have seen now more than a decade of Japanese industrial stagnation and witnessed China bypassing her for the No. 2 spot in world GDP. Underutilization of young talent, as well as of women, has been increasingly obvious in a patently static system where collusion between government, banks and industrial concerns has stifled new initiatives that were so typical of Morita and Matsushita and Toyoda in the 1960s, 1970s and 1980s. The extent of this collusion between the politicians and big business, apparently determined to keep the status quo, was starkly revealed and reached scandalous proportions in the investigations of the Fukushima nuclear disaster and the attempted cover-up that followed. Confucius rules (still), but for how long?

■ **The company (*kaisha*) is sacred**

The hierarchical Confucian system defines the structure of Japanese companies which, in the eyes of its employees, are almost sacred entities. The salarymen devote more time, thought and effort to the *kaisha* than to their own families. Tokyo males typically travel one or two hours to the office in the morning and remain at work till normally 6pm or longer if the section chief stays on. After that, it is not unusual for them to spend the time until 10pm discussing business projects in the numerous bars of the Ginza with opposite numbers in other companies. Sundays are devoted to the family, often spent shopping in the incredibly overcrowded supermarkets of the capital. The *kaisha* is in itself a kind of family (and a very important one) for all its employees, both junior and senior. It commands respect, awe and unwavering allegiance. It is even spoken of in a hushed voice, not dissimilar to that used by North Koreans when referring to The Beloved Leader.

Devotion to the *kaisha*, long hours, short holidays and overtime without pay ensured economical running of businesses throughout the second half of the 20th century. Though its days are numbered, the traditional Japanese *kaisha*, with its cowed middle-aged salarymen and boilerplate programmed managers, has not yet disappeared from view. The belated recognition that it is now a definite derailer is a precursor to a tectonic shake-up which has to take place soon in the Japanese business world, not to mention her archaic political parties and glacially-geared pressure groups. If the nation is to hold her ranking in the world's economies, this reorganization cannot be delayed long, as Japan continues to be stuck in the mud and heading nowhere. Japanese corporate culture, eminently successful in terms of results over decades, is one of the best examples of enabling philosophies becoming derailing ones as the world around them changes and progresses in an accelerated phase of globalized trade.

- **Long termism**

Japanese companies are not terribly interested in immediate profits. They are very interested in long-term ones, as their chief goal is market share. This has enabled them to secure many long-term contracts not only when trading around the world but also in business-to-business transactions with each other. One of the reasons for the success of Japanese exports has been the strength of her domestic market, which has given a firm platform for the country's *keiretsu* (conglomerates). Fast moving initiatives, new technologies, fresh players in the markets (India, Russia, Brazil, Indonesia) are in the process of rendering long-term agreements obsolete. Wise, long-term planning by Japan's *keiretsu* will soon be a derailer and will ultimately be discarded along with the other archaic features of Japanese business.

Summary

Her present economic plight and stagnation (2012) indicates that Japan has a more urgent need than other major countries to revise her corporate cultures to meet the demands of globalized trade. In her case, it is largely a matter of discarding very traditional structures, philosophies and habits that have previously benefited the nation greatly but have now outlived their usefulness and appropriacy.

Italy

Key nation-state traits

- Humanitarianism
- Flexibility
- Idealism

Historical background

A scrutiny of Italian corporate culture leads us initially and most significantly to Fiat. A well-known Italian proverb says "As Fiat goes, so goes Italy". Fiat has long been Italy's major industrial enterprise; many families have seen it employ their grandfathers, fathers, uncles, nephews and sisters, and, hopefully, it will provide work for their growing sons. Job switching, endemic in the United States and Britain, is not a problem in Italy, especially not in the south. To what extent is Fiat's corporate culture linked to Italian nation-state traits? What *are* the salient characteristics of Italian governmental rule?

Subsequent to two decades of Fascist domination and the overthrow and execution of Benito Mussolini, a new Italian government was set up in conformity with the democratic traditions of the Allies. The first post-war Italian premier, Alcide de Gasperi, oversaw a parliament and cabinet whose composition left no doubt as to its political direction. It was an essentially democratic institution which reflected, to all appearances, the aspirations of the voters. In the post-war climate, in a country struggling economically, such representational voting led to the emergence of a powerful Communist party, headed by Palmiro Togliatti, which came within a hair's breadth of winning the parliamentary elections of 1948 and forming a government. If this had transpired, Italy would have been the first European nation to produce a Communist government in free elections. It did not happen, but the extreme left wing element has continued to remain influential in Italian politics.

If left of centre traits have proved durable in the Italian governmental scene, other characteristics emanating from Italian people's psychology have persisted at the national level. Northern Europeans often describe Italian governments as volatile; certainly they changed tack with bewildering rapidity. In the period after the war, 1946–1956, 12 Italian governments succeeded each other, to the astonishment of other recently-elected European governments in countries such as Germany, Denmark, Holland and even changeable France. This volatility was also reflected in the variegated form of Italian rule and influence. While democratic principles remained unquestioned, they certainly did not go unchallenged, since certain politicians and power brokers of various kinds created their own empires and pressure groups, particularly in the south, where the Sicilian Mafia, the Neapolitan Camorra and the Calabrian N'drangheta exercised virtual control over the economies of their regions.

Expression of nation-state traits within corporate culture

Such "ruling bodies" introduce another major characteristic in Italian life – that of not just corruption, but the tacit *acceptance* of corrupt practices in the running of the country. While Berlusconi was unquestionably elected by democratic processes, his monopoly of the media, his controversial decisions, his scandalous appointments of beauty queens to ministerial posts and his increasing image of buffoonery have emphasized the willingness of the Italian electorate to tolerate practices which few, if any, other Western populaces would permit.

The volatility, recognition and partial acceptance of corruption and toleration of buffoonery in a premier indicate another Italian trait – that of flexibility. Italy has laws like everyone else, but to what extent are laws applied when a prime minister can break them with impunity, when key connections prevent officialdom from being able to bring transgressors to court and when three "mafias" control a black market reputedly accounting for 10% of Italian GDP?

Italian flexibility is linked to three other national traits – humanitarianism, idealism and a tendency (especially in certain areas) towards laziness. If we take the first of these qualities, few would take issue with the Italian reputation for compassion and humanity. Italian life is based on close family ties where feelings and emotion trump cold facts or logic, and these human outreachings tend to extend to other social and even business relations, where Italian warmth is regarded as a trump card in furthering one's aims. This national sense of humanity, so visible in Italian literature, music and fine arts, also permeates commercial life and corporate activities. Such human feelings are naturally linked to a penchant towards idealism, which in turn lessens the Italian's propensity for realism. It was noted during Italy's term for the EU presidency in 2005 that sweeping idealistic aims of their presidency had little chance of being completed in the six months allotted. Even at ministerial levels, Italians are vulnerable to bouts of euphoria which blind them to the likelihood of underachievement. Little was accomplished during the Italian presidency in contrast to solid but more modest achievements of Finnish and Dutch presidencies.

Italians are capable of working hard and long, but years of underachievement in the economic sphere, resulting in their earning the unenviable title of "the sick man of Europe", have led to the development of a lifestyle (especially in the often-sweltering southern half of the country) that values flexibility and less exigence for workers. This has made it difficult for governments to close the divide between Italian productivity and that of her northern neighbours. It is common in southern Italy to skip work with a fake doctor's note, even to call in sick while doing another part-time job to earn more money. The nature of Italian welfare legislation tends to protect workers who adopt these practices.

Can a company as large and powerful as Fiat break such traditions of indolence and install policies which will embrace the kind of change needed for Italy to skirt financial ruin and become more competitive with the countries of Northern Europe and the rest of the world?

In 2010, the chief executive of Fiat, Sergio Marchionne, fresh from rescuing Chrysler in the United States, began pushing workers to be more devoted to their jobs, echoing a larger effort by the government to improve Italian competitiveness. At both levels, departure from Italian traditions proved difficult. Berlusconi introduced an austerity package that included tying public salaries to productivity gains, raising the retirement age and reducing government spending. One million workers went on strike to protest against these measures. In the case of Fiat, Marchionne called on employees to radically alter their work ethic to compete in the global marketplace. While this type of encouragement makes sense to workers in Germany, Britain or the Czech Republic, Italians saw such proposed changes as Fiat drawing the curtain on a humane working life. "He wants to impose American-style standards" declared a senior union official, on hearing Marchionne's requirements to work longer hours and cut back on absences, "but too much work is going to kill our workers".

From the perspective of another union Marchionne was accused of "marching Italy on a path towards China". "There they work super shifts that lead to increased suicide rates, and workers are no longer humans, but machines." Fiat in some instances is by no means unwilling to show a human face: in Pomigliano, near Naples, they have kept open a car plant operating at 32% capacity for the past two years, since demand collapsed during the global economic crisis. Keeping the plant open was a corporate decision which made little economic sense, but the decision was taken in the face of intense political pressure to safeguard the livelihood of 15,000 families in a poor area gripped by organized crime. Marchionne's plan to invest a billion dollars in the factory, which would operate 24 hours a day, six days a week, adding a third daily shift to double output to 280,000 cars annually, was a corporate proposal that would be music to American ears, but water off a duck's back to quality-of-life-minded Italians.

Fiat is a big and essentially Italian enterprise which has been hugely successful in the European industrial marketplace, in cars and other vehicles. Other Italian companies have captured markets in domestic appliances (white goods). These successes, however, have derived principally from traditional

Italian traits – high standards of design, flexibility in pricing and nimble customer relations. Adoption of US-style thrust or Chinese work ethic, signalling a departure from alignment with Italian priorities, is an unlikely route for increased prosperity.

Potential advantages/disadvantages of Italian national traits

- **Humanitarianism**

As a constant characteristic of Italian mentality humanitarianism facilitates easy customer relations, general warmth and closeness among employees and colleagues, and ready compassion for those faced with hardship. On the downside it could lead to overprotection of "underdogs", failure to control miscreants, turning a blind eye to laziness, even conspiring with absentees with weak excuses.

- **Flexibility**

Italian flexibility – so useful in skilful negotiating and in their ability to quickly adapt to changing conditions – appears, when overdone, often as volatility, even licentiousness. Acceptance of endemic corruption at all levels, and particularly throughout large areas in the south, where powerful regional mafias get away (literally) with murder, has been and remains a lingering problem for Italian business.

- **Idealism**

The Italian propensity towards idealism, though linked positively to worthy corporate aims and goals, as well as their ability to use charm and charisma in their business activities, has its downside in frequent lapses of realism. This has manifested itself in poor state and corporate finances, unbalanced budgets, abandoned construction and reformist projects, and also a periodic decline in work ethic.

Summary

Faced with ferocious Asian competition in the coming decades, Italians need to revamp and manage their corporate cultures to match Asian pragmatism and productivity, honing their own skills of adaptability, creativity and speed of thought.

Germany

Key nation-state traits

- Factual planning and process
- *Ordnung*
- Work ethic
- Focus on exports
- Hierarchical bureaucracy

Historical background

After Japan, Germany is the country where nation-state traits impose themselves most thoroughly on corporate behaviour. Germans are clear-eyed about their national qualities. In their eyes, they are the most honest, straightforward and reliable people on earth. They believe in scientific rather than contextual truth and conduct their private and professional lives on this basis. They have great respect for facts and figures, the law, property and rank. Their standards of cleanliness, neatness and punctuality are beyond reproach; their work ethic and efficiency are surpassed by none. They stand by their commitments and keep their word. Concepts such as fidelity, loyalty and honour are very much alive in modern Germany.

Expression of nation-state traits within corporate culture

The values listed above are mandatory for German corporations. The most important word in the German language is *Ordnung*. Roughly translated into English it means "order" or "orderliness". German *Ordnung*, however, is far more orderly than its British or American equivalent. It demands orderliness in the home, the office, one's general environment, one's car and other possessions, neatness of dress and accessories, orderliness of one's social manners, working habits – above all orderliness of mind.

When these conditions have been fulfilled, one can say *Alles in Ordnung*. Working in a German company, one hears this phrase a dozen times a day. It is an expression of satisfaction, a compliment, a felicitous summary, a convivial conclusion. German corporations strive for *Ordnung*; they achieve it by following rules and processes that have been successful in the past. In German companies there is no substitute for experience. Firms are strictly hierarchical, with the most knowledgeable individual occupying the highest rung of the ladder. The structure is vertical: orders are passed downwards to the person immediately below you. Instructions are rarely horizontal; cross-departmental communication is rare and may be frowned upon.

This corporate discipline works well and smoothly among Germans, but can be seen as restrictive and perhaps disadvantageous by more free-wheeling cultures. It is to be expected that companies in democracies feel they have more freedom or at least flexibility in conducting their business. It is true that Germany and Japan are modern democracies, but they were undemocratic for long periods in their histories. Executives in Britain, Australia, Canada, Finland and the Netherlands feel less constrained by national norms (or they feel that the very norms give them flexibility and behavioural choice).

Potential advantages/disadvantages of German national traits

- **Factual planning and process**

It is rare for a German company to have to improvise or make rapid changes in their activities, as they rank among the world's best planners, creating processes that are based on facts, figures, intelligent analysis and experience. This trait has served them very well over a century and a half in the industrial era. Such meticulous planning has generally led to accurate budgeting; most German enterprises have sound finances. This corporate behaviour facilitates steady growth (few surprises) and only rarely are German firms deemed sluggish or unprepared. However, their serenity was disturbed by unforeseen developments in the period immediately after German reunification, when several large construction projects were badly miscalculated. Failure to allow for huge costs in sanitizing contaminated ground at large eastern factory sites and problems concerning the exchange of deutschmarks and east-marks gave indications that overplanning and strict processes can also lend difficulties. Quick-moving strategies emanating from Asia may catch out stolid German planners in the future.

- *Ordnung*

This very German concept, involving self-discipline, has clearly benefited companies in the past. Linked to processes, clear thinking and unerring completion abilities, it will continue to facilitate German commercial success. It may in the future require some modification of principles when faced with others' strategies (Korean shortcuts, Turkish workers, swelling numbers of *Gastarbeiter*).

- **Work ethic**

This trait has been durable, unflagging and of enormous benefit to German corporate culture. It applies not only to the number of hours worked, but also to the quality of the work. However, Germans now take longer holidays than most nationals (up to six weeks) and like to travel. It is therefore hard to discount the possibility that increasing German proclivity towards leisure will lead to a lack of competitiveness vis-à-vis productive (low wage) Chinese, Koreans, Turks and others.

- **Focus on exports**

This admirable and well-planned aspect of German business has been one of the chief reasons for the country's prosperity. It is all the more remarkable considering the fierce competition supplied by export-minded China, Japan and Korea. So far (2012) German export levels have been maintained, in spite of wages being higher than those of their Asian rivals. Though Chinese wages are rising steadily, German exporters will have to maintain agility with price levels, especially when other countries with cheap labour (Indonesia, Thailand, Vietnam) try to export more. Fortunately, it is likely that German quality (part of their strategy) will win the day, especially in the luxury goods area.

- **Hierarchical bureaucracy**

The strictly hierarchical nature of German leadership lends strong support to the traits of *Ordnung*, planning and work ethic. Discipline and clarity of command are maintained in German corporate culture, both vertically and horizontally across different departments. Traditional processes (successful for decades) are cemented and profitable. Hierarchy, however, is usually accompanied by bureaucratic rules and procedures, which can be slow moving. It is not easy to change the structure of a German company, or aspects of its basic corporate culture, very quickly. Many vertical and lateral clearances are required. When a crisis demands a change of strategy, German firms of the future may prove less agile than, say, Korean or Indian rivals, or even American.

Summary

If solidity is a German strength, a national weakness may be reluctance to abandon well-tried, proven processes that have served the nation well in the past. Many German firms are encumbered with lengthy manuals prescribing exactly how tasks should be carried out. These may have to be shortened or discarded, when and if competitors are prepared to "wing it". Also, in the Internet age, when information and ideas are available to young and junior employees, step-by-step hierarchical promotion may prove too slow for whizz-kids – only too welcome in corporate cultures such as the USA, Finland, Canada and Australia.

Great Britain

Key nation-state traits

- Individualism and inventiveness
- Engineering strengths
- Class system
- Insularity

Historical background

The British, in the days of the Empire, set up huge bureaucracies (especially in India) and the financial institutions in the City of London are pillars of British conservatism. In general, however, the country's democratic record, her exploratory instincts, her industrial and administrative creativity, her bouts of invention, her sense of humour and willingness to "muddle through" inevitably led to nation-state traits characterized by liberalism, individualism and freedom of choice. British companies are extremely variegated in nature both in structure and size. In no other countries, apart from possibly Denmark and Hong Kong, do SMEs occupy such a large share of the economy. Companies can be registered and set up in a few days, conditions for registration are undemanding. There may be state interference in the areas of taxation and social welfare, but in the UK businesspeople are not told how to run companies or given a set of norms or standards to conform to. It would be hard to define "a typical British corporation". Richard Branson and his enterprises have attained their popularity through their diversity and originality.

Expression of nation-state traits within corporate culture

As we have stated above, British companies are not dominated by a set of national values. As Britain was the first country to undergo her industrial revolution, a host of local companies sprang up, which, under the circumstances, were structurally quite different from anything that had existed before. Firms that were hastily established to meet the needs of the new technologies understandably had little in common with the rural, agricultural and feudal enterprises of previous centuries. There were no strict precedents as to how industrial firms should be run. A certain hierarchical discipline was imposed but as the nature of the labour was new, different owners in different industries (cotton, mining, steel, shipbuilding, armaments) devised diverse models of management structure, rules, procedures and ethics. Heavy industry factories were novel environments. In general, the working classes of the 19th century inherited the worst of the new conditions, in Britain at least. Other nations going through their industrial revolutions at a later stage were able to benefit from observed precedents, and modern facilities made factories in countries such as Denmark and Sweden more pleasant workplaces than those of Dickensian England.

British companies, well after the industrial revolution, developed a variety of corporate structures which reflected the nature of the industry, the character of their founders, the traits of their region (London, Lancashire, Yorkshire, Tyneside, Scotland, North and South Wales, the Black Country and Ireland) as well as the effects of collective bargaining and ultimately vigorous trade union activity. As said earlier, there is no national blueprint or boilerplate pattern for British commercial enterprises. In this respect, they are quite different from their Japanese, German or French counterparts. This does not mean that they do not possess enabling traits that ultimately will morph into derailers – in fact, they do. But they are not likely to be the same in each company, since early British enterprises emerged from diverse, exploratory crucibles.

Common traits visible in British corporate structure are rarely mandatory, but include self-deprecation, humour, wit, eloquence and coded speech. Managers portray themselves as diplomatic, tactful, laid back, casual, helpful, willing to compromise and seeking to be fair. Subordinates, workers, are proud of their inventiveness and lateral thinking.

Potential advantages/disadvantages of British national traits

▪ Individualism and inventiveness

Renowned as early inventors at the dawn of the Industrial Age, Britons can rightfully claim originality and individualist achievement as a national characteristic. This trait was a powerful advantage in the 19th century and enabled the islanders to establish an empire covering 15 million square miles on five continents. As we state earlier in this work, the same trait led British car manufacturers to continue making boutique cars on small-scale production while American, German and Japanese car-makers swamped the planet with less exciting, but more economical, automobiles produced by large-scale modern processes. Today more cars are made in Britain per capita than anywhere else, but they are produced by non-British owners and manufacturers – Toyota, Nissan, General Motors, Ford, Tata, Mercedes-Benz, etc.

▪ Engineering strengths

As befitted the pioneers of the industrial revolution, engineering has long occupied pride of place in British educational institutions and led to 19th century dominance in the manufacture of ships, vehicles, armaments, tools, railway bridges, dams and great architectural edifices in London, India, Singapore, Malaysia, Shanghai and elsewhere. Now British engineering degrees are being outnumbered by those attained in Germany, Japan, the United States, China and Korea. Britain's focus on financial services has led to serious losses in her manufacturing base.

▪ Class system

The feudal and imperial origins of status and leadership in England are still evident in some aspects of British management. A century has passed since Britain occupied a pre-eminent position in industry and commerce, but there still lingers in the national consciousness the proud recollection of once having ruled nearly half the land area of the globe.

The class system persists in England (though less in Scotland, Wales and Northern Ireland) and status is still derived, to some degree, from pedigree, title and family name. In today's world, this feature is rapidly becoming a derailer, especially when dealing with Americans and democracies such as Australia, Canada and the Scandinavian states. There is little doubt, however, that the system is on its way to becoming a meritocracy, owing to the emergence of a very large middle class.

▪ Insularity

If the class system derailer is about to be eliminated, the lingering insularity of the British is a more tenacious feature. Like the Japanese, French and Spanish, Britons perform poorly with foreign languages, but their insularity extends further than that. Their self-deprecatory attitudes, type of humour, coded speech, regional parochialism and island defensiveness often set them distinctly apart from other peoples who, without disliking them, find it difficult to understand them. The Brits themselves, divided into four nations with four football teams, geographically nearer to Europe than to the Anglo-Saxon powerhouse of North America, nevertheless talk of a "special relationship" with the United States, though such a belief is often weakly reciprocated. The English language facilitates business with the USA, Canada, Australia, New Zealand and South Africa. It helps less in European countries like Spain, Italy and France, who all prefer their former imperial tongues. Britons communicate well with Scandinavian countries, the Netherlands, Swiss, Belgians and Germans, but are not much better than the Americans at understanding or trying to understand the intricacies of European cultures. Ironically, they get on better with the Japanese with whom they share insular and other features (modesty, understatement, reticence, manners, royal families, golf, rugby, similar geographical locations, reserve, historical ceremonies, clubs).

Although British delegates at international meetings frequently distinguish themselves by their poise, charm and eloquence, they often leave the scene having learnt little or nothing from their more successful trading partners. As such conferences are usually held in English, they easily win the war of words, which unfortunately increases their linguistic arrogance. Insularity, though a military and perhaps artistic advantage, is definitely a derailer in a time when electronic communication devalues maritime agility. Though slow on the uptake, British companies are at last beginning to study foreign cultures to enable them to benefit from their hard-won contracts in the imperial era.

Summary

The British are extremely fortunate in that an obscure dialect spoken on a rather small, foggy island offshore the world's second smallest continent has morphed into the lingua franca of the planet. As 500 million people are at any time learning English, it behoves British corporations to use their inbuilt linguistic advantage to offset their traditional cultural myopia.

*   *   *

This seven-country analysis of the effect of nation-state cultural traits on corporate behaviour drives home the point that in six of the seven countries chosen (Britain is the exception), national cultures are so well defined and innately powerful that they dominate the thinking and goals of executives who design corporate culture. Swedish corporate culture has to be democratic and human rights-oriented. Japan and Germany place a premium on hierarchy and discipline. French and Italian corporate cultures must be seen to give social considerations priority over material ones. US corporations must support the American Dream.

One could extend this analysis to over one hundred and more cultures, though this book would be too lengthy as a result. Attention has been concentrated on those cultures of major states that exercise the most pervasive influence on the way they do business. Japan, Germany, France and Sweden are the best examples and indeed all need to consider seriously the derailing elements in their business strategies that the nation-state cultures have injected.

Similar in effect are Communist cultures; that is to say that, though China, Russia, Vietnam and North Korea have wildly different philosophies, they all dominate business methods in their respective areas. All will have to adjust their business cultures for optimal effect, especially when dealing with Western enterprises. The giants – Russia and China – went about reforms in a diametrically opposing fashion: Russia dismantled the (Soviet) political system and allowed commercial practices to develop freely; China introduced creeping capitalism yet maintained the political system so that it continues to control business. Vietnam copied the Chinese model; North Korea remains completely dictatorial in all negotiations with foreign entities.

It is too early to say how doing business with Communist countries will develop. Certainly a lot already goes on, what with ubiquitous Chinese exports and Russian opulence and trade in oil and gas. In these areas, globalization is a reality. Vietnam, with its *doi moi* policy, makes steady progress with some certainty that close governmental control, at least in the three Asian countries, constitutes a derailer. Commercial growth would suggest that this derailer can eventually be eliminated, though foreign executives doing business in China and Vietnam complain of being constantly hampered by governmental or regional interference, China often asserts that one-party control over the economy brings benefits of clarity and unity, thus making it an enabler. In any case, Chinese entrepreneurial traditions are gradually eroding central controls. Ho Chi Minh (Saigon) businesspeople demonstrate more independence than those in the Hanoi area.

As the nation-states diagram (Diagram 3.1) shows, there are a certain number of countries where business traditions have developed in freer, more explora-tory circumstances, where building a corporate culture or creating habitual methods of doing business fell less under the influence of national values. The freer the society, the more democratic its institutions, the less likelihood of nation-state control. Britain, as we have shown, is one of these societies. Other Anglo-Saxon countries, perhaps taking their cue from Britain, display equal freedom and diversity. Canada, Australia, South Africa and also India have all types of companies, often characterized by risk-taking and originality of purpose. Such countries, more immune to derailing traits, demonstrate fre-quent agility and flexibility to correct imbalances. Finland, Denmark, Holland, Belgium, Switzerland, Malaysia, Hong Kong, Singapore, New Zealand and Estonia fall into this category. Consequently, they are of less concern to the authors of this work. They seem to be nimble enough to adapt strategies in a timely manner.

Ultimately, shrewd and timely business strategies will not be activated by countries or governments, but by insightful executives, chairmen and boards of corporate bodies who should keep a close watch on market trends, best practices and developing features of global trade and to what extent powerful national cultures will facilitate, hamper or impede their own plans for the foreseeable future.

4

Introduction

This chapter provides the essential overview of the Cultural Dynamic Model®. First, we examine how embedded values impact work practices, and through this influence the artefacts and espoused values and thus ultimately impact behaviour. We complete the Cultural Dynamic Model® by introducing the central concept of a cultural dynamic. This explains how the individual parts of the model interact, and over time may cause the corporate culture to change without anyone intending it to. Finally, we show how you can identify and verify the deeply embedded values and ways of thinking that may be invisible within the organization.

In the detailed Austin Motors case in the second part of the chapter we use this insight to explore how the national traits that helped accelerate Austin's growth in the embryonic period turned against the company and derailed the strategy in the growth period. As we show in the subsequent cases, this dual nature of national traits is often most visible when a company moves from one lifecycle phase to another or a major event or disruption takes place that upsets the strategy and culture balance.

Let's look at a real life example of what we mean. SAP, a major German technology company, was contemplating how best to deploy a new software development methodology called Agile in order to accelerate the pace of innovation in software development. Agile is an interactive methodology, based on the developer's trial and error interaction with the users – typically used by start-up companies. The engineers will develop a sketchy software solution based on a rough description of the requirements with the users, through rapid prototyping. The user reviews the screens and functionality as they are developed, and together they improve the solution in what is called quick development sprints.

Agile contrasts to the more traditional Waterfall software development methodology, where customer requirements are collected and described in minute detail. It is then translated into a fully specified software solution, screen by screen, where every last functional detail and field is documented, and signed off by the customer before being fully developed. Only once developed, which can take months or sometimes years, will the user know if it actually delivers the expected solution. Waterfall was the mainstream technology used by all SAP's traditional competitors.

However, Agile had become very popular with a new generation of fast growing American entrants in their market – in particular in the Cloud computing space where the release cycles are very fast. The methodology suited the action and results orientation of American software start-up companies. Therefore, the new competitors commanded a shorter time to market for new functionality and could respond more quickly to customer requirements.

The CEO of SAP was convinced it was wise to invest in educating the software engineering organization to fully embrace Agile, despite it being a costly and significant multi-year effort. Ultimately, he was proved right. The results were impressive and in two years the company managed to reduce time to market, in a company with more than 19,000 software developers, from 15 months to seven-and-a-half months on average, showing that even large corporations can learn to be agile and adapt new work practices.

This dilemma goes to the heart of our book: how a company can navigate the complex dynamics of lifecycles, work practices and national culture in order to gain a sustainable competitive advantage. It proves the point that, with enough effort, derailing traits can be overcome but this requires leadership from the top and persistency.

The static cultural dynamic model® – bringing it all together

The embedded values and beliefs from the business realities and the national culture

As discussed in Chapters 1 and 2, the *business influencers* and the *national influencers* lay the foundation for the values, beliefs and assumptions that underpin corporate culture. These values and assumptions are embedded in the organization by the leadership and the employees. The two influencers have different characteristics; values embedded by national influencers tend to be fairly staid, and difficult to change in the short and medium term. In contrast, cultural traits and values rooted in business influencers are more transient and you, the management, can influence them more easily. Importantly, these *deeply embedded assumptions and associated values*, beliefs, thoughts and perceptions are often invisible to the organization as they are taken for granted and not up for debate. They are the water you and your leadership colleagues can't see!

Espoused values and *artefacts*, such as the management philosophies, the observed behaviour and habits, are what an external observer can discern, and are implicitly or explicitly communicated by the organization through its advertising, physical premises, rituals, myths, habits, structure and processes. The *work practices* are where the corporate culture dimension meets the business strategy and execution dimension. Combining these two perspectives results in the static Cultural Dynamic Model® shown in Diagram 4.1.

To better understand the implications of the model, we will first take a deeper look at the work practices and how they relate to national culture.

However, before we start, let's quickly rehearse what we mean with these different terms. In Schein's classical model, he divided culture into three levels. At the root of culture are the underlying assumptions and embedded values. At the next level, the espoused values are derived from these basic underlying assumptions, and are the espoused justifications of strategies, goal and

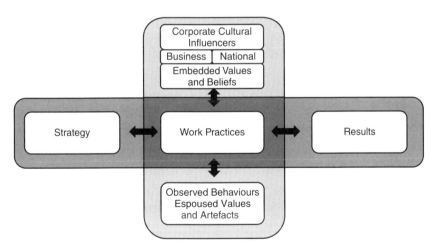

Diagram 4.1: The static Cultural Dynamic Model®

philosophies. Thus, they represent the ideology of the organization. Finally, at the top level are the "artefacts", the "visible" yet hard to decipher organizational structures, processes, routines and habits.

The observed behaviour is at the artefact level, wherein particular *habits* are of interest to us. Most complex living creatures have the capacity to form habits based on actions that repeatedly provide a desired reward. They are critical for our survival and reside in the oldest parts of our brains. Habits are learned and are used to offload the brain, so that the brain can concentrate on more immediate challenges. However, once learned, they are hard to change. At the organizational level, habits are central to the formation of hard-to-change enabling and derailing behaviour based on business and national influencers. *A key component of any cultural transformation is changing deeply rooted habits that have a derailing effect and promoting those with a benevolent effect*, based on an understanding of whether they are rooted in staid national influencers or more easily impacted business influencers.

Work practices are mostly at the artefact level, and include processes central to the organizations and the operational routines and habits that have been established to run the company. Decision making processes are obviously heavily influenced by the espoused values and corresponding justifications.

Work practices

The work practices include:

- The organizational structure and hierarchy (formal and informal)
- Decision-making processes
- The organizational skills and capabilities
- Workflow processes
- Performance management, reward and compensation systems.

Each of the five factors on its own is complex; yet the simple point we suggest is that national cultures profoundly impact organizational work practices, whether for a subsidiary or at the company headquarters.

Organizational structure and hierarchy (formal and informal)

Organizational structure is deeply rooted in national traits. The ways of handling power in a country tend to be rooted in the belief in large sectors of a population as to the proper way for authorities to behave.[1] The number of layers in the organization chart may give an indication of how important status is and the power distance in the company. Will people work in teams or are they organized more individualistically? Is there a matrix or is the business managed through single lines of command and control? What is the role and authority of the boss? These are some of the questions you may ask to gain an insight into the organizational structure.

In the 1980s the Danish hearing aid company Oticon was struggling in competition with larger more resourceful players such Siemens and Philips. A new CEO, Lars Kolind, decided to pursue a strategy of innovation and introduced the concept of the "Spaghetti Organization". The simple idea was to abandon traditional formal structures and physical barriers to spur innovation and radically change the workflow processes. Employees could choose which projects they would work on and would not report to a formal boss.

A new building was designed to support this novel idea, where the personal desk and the personal space would be eliminated, though there were enough desks available for everyone. The employees would move their rolling drawers to join the other members of their virtual project team in a temporary workspace as and when required.

In most countries this may have resulted in chaos, yet for the Danes, with their low tolerance and respect for authority, it worked and helped Oticon regain its position as the innovative leader. However, a few years later the "Spaghetti Organization", once it had served its purpose, was reversed to a more traditional organizational structure. After all, most people, even Danes, benefit from having a boss! Interestingly, the idea of the rolling drawer and no personal desk has been widely adopted by many other companies, though often for the different reason of cost saving!

In Thailand a new executive from Europe could not understand why it took so long to take delivery of his new company car. He had asked for a rather modest car, instead of the expensive German limousine of his predecessor, to communicate his focus on prudence in financial matters and Northern European work ethics. After querying the delay several times, it eventually emerged that the car had never been ordered. The executive's assistant who handled the purchase had felt it did not send the right signal for a senior executive and was embarrassed by ordering it. Only then did the executive understand the

[1]Hofstede G., Hofstede J., Minkov M. (2010) *Cultures and Organizations*, 3rd Edition. McGraw-Hill, pp. 75–76.

importance of this cultural signal and ordered an appropriately big black German car. In some cultures communicating your status in the hierarchy is important to maintain authority and respect!

Decision-making processes

Decision-making is often a reflection of national values. Decision-making at Anglo-Dutch Unilever was impacted by the different dispositions of the British and Dutch. The meritocratic, communal and independently minded Dutch believed in a direct and open debate before making a decision. However, they often found themselves going into a meeting, expecting it to be the beginning of such a good debate to find the best solution. Disappointingly, they would find that the British counterparts had already discussed the issue and agreed upon a shared perspective that the Dutch then found it difficult to influence. Thus, over the years the Dutch often felt they were outmanoeuvred by the Brits when making major decisions.

Westerners working with Japanese companies sometimes marvel at how decisions are made. It is often impossible for non-Japanese to understand how the group-oriented Japanese make a decision. To outsiders, it can best be compared to a school of fish, that in the flick of a second seemingly unprompted but finely coordinated, all move in a new direction. The Japanese in the organization instinctively understand when there is enough pertinent data for them to make the decision without anyone actually making it. They just know as a group and individually! But to anyone else, what happens and what the tipping point might have been is completely opaque.

In multi-active Latin countries, it is not unusual to see employees following a leader throughout their career. Essentially, the leader becomes the "family" head and the fortunes and prospects of the employees, his/her "family", will be closely linked to his/her progress. There is a symbiotic sense of relationship and shared sense of responsibility and loyalty between the leader and their organization. If he or she moves up, the "family" moves with him! This relationship orientation can rub against the Anglo-Saxon focus on individual and meritocratic performance metrics, and where personal performance is considered more important than relationships.

Organizational skills and capabilities

Countries create particular platforms for companies as a result of their educational systems and leadership practices.

The elitist French educational system ensures a uniquely tight integration between the public and the private sector. It has produced a cadre of intellectually highly capable and hardworking leaders who are all tightly networked. They all have been selected through a highly competitive school system and attended one of the exclusive Grandes Ecoles. In 2003 60% of all CEOs of the top 100 French companies came from this background.[2] However, when compared to executives from similar countries, relatively few have become CEOs in international corporations headquartered outside France.

In Korea employees are often seen to be disciplined, execution oriented and willing and ready to loyally follow a leader. Despite the urgent execution focus, they also often have a long-term orientation in their perspective on life. A major Korean company went through a phase of internationalization, hiring multiple international executives to broaden its capabilities in key areas. However, the typically Western executives complained that it was difficult to attract the best Korean employees to their organization. They preferred to work for a Korean leader who they thought would be there for the long term, and who they would benefit more from building a close, loyal, long-term relationship with. A few years later, the same company changed strategy and a new CEO purged all Westerners from the organization within a few months!

In England, it may be difficult to adapt to Lean in the manufacturing sector; however, the financial services industry has thrived and London is the financial centre of Europe for British as well as many European and American banks. The sector demands many of the capabilities inherent in English culture; the creativity, the pragmatism, the independence, the action orientation and the wing-it approach to life. Some of these traits may, however, also have been culpable when people accuse the local financial services sector of having been unable to self-regulate during the early 2000s. In our terminology, a "wing-it" cultural dynamic, deeply rooted in the English culture's reluctance to employ process discipline, may have contributed to derailing the industry. The strength of the financial services sector in England also originates from its cultural fit to English national traits, and not simply because London is an attractive place to live. However, if the industry becomes less entrepreneurial and more dogmatic, with stronger regulation, process orientation and governance, it may lose its appeal to the English!

[2]http://www.telegraph.co.uk/expat/4190728/Frances-educational-elite.html.

Workflow processes

Some countries prefer to work in teams; others have a more individualistic approach to getting the job done. Some countries are more process oriented, some are more people oriented while others are more results oriented. These preferences will have a deep influence on the design and effectiveness of their work processes.

When Toyota opened their first American production plant in the 1980s, their long-term orientation and unique production concepts would lead them to invest significantly in training new employees. The factory would not be fully run in for three years, and Toyota expected it to take up to 10 years to train a non-Japanese manager to react instinctively in "The Toyota Way". In "The Toyota Way", every problem is seen as an opportunity to learn. Even when a minor issue is identified – such as a scratch in the paintwork – the work group will stop and discuss the situation to better understand the root cause.

Each employee has the authority to stop the production line, and thus potentially the entire factory. If a problem is identified, such as a panel not fitting to the prescribed standard by even a millimetre, the employee has the authority to stop the work by pulling the "Andon Cord". Results-oriented American employees may have instinctively concluded that "we must meet the production quota today, so let's not stop production for a minor incident" and therefore would let the small variation pass. However, Toyota expects the production team to view it as a symptom of a potentially larger process issue and expects them to identify the root cause rather than letting it pass. The rationale being that the earlier in the production process a quality problem is identified, the cheaper it is to fix, compared to later having to recall a car that has been delivered to the customer.

The performance management, reward and compensation systems

Many American companies have been frustrated when Europeans and Asians have pushed back on what they perceived as being individualistically-oriented compensation systems, and requested a more group-oriented approach. Compensation systems not surprisingly are deeply rooted in national culture and practices. The conventional wisdom has it that in the USA, it is more accepted that leaders and CEOs are highly paid with a ratio of CEO salaries to workers of up to 400:1. However, recent analysis indicates that while this may have been correct in the past, after 2000 the differences, when correcting for company size, have been largely eliminated in the large economies.[3] The reason may be that the increased fluidity of leadership talent has created a global market, and thus price, for leadership talent. The increased ownership of companies by private equity firms has also helped increase top management pay significantly, in particular in linear-active-type countries. However, below the top, and across countries in the West, there are still significant differences in pay systems and philosophies. In multi-active and reactive economies, these differences are further exacerbated with their different perspectives on individual versus group contribution, equality and risk.

In recent years many global corporations have adopted a performance management philosophy, to define, monitor and reward performance. The key performance indicator (KPI) concept was originated by McKinsey in the 1960s to align performance with strategy. It has become a popular mechanism for translating group objectives to individual objectives.[4] Furthermore, popular ERP (enterprise resource planning) systems often support these KPI hierarchies and thus help institutionalize them over other softer measurements. However, work practices across countries are different and to be effective a compensation system should reflect and respect those differences. Implementing an American, German or Chinese-designed KPI system in a different culture may not deliver the expected results.

Work practice across borders

A study of engineering practices compared German engineering practices with American for a particular problem. The study concluded that the two groups were equally effective in achieving the objectives but would work in two fundamentally different ways. The Americans would experiment and fail, learn from it and try again, four times on average. The German engineers would spend more time upfront debating the best way to solve the problem before agreeing on how to solve it. However, if you wanted the two groups to work together on an engineering task, they may not have been able to agree on how

---

[3]http://denning.law.ox.ac.uk/news/events_files/USCEOsPaidMore_2012_05_21_(2).pdf.
[4]http://www.helium.com/items/1086171-how-do-key-success-indicators-or-kpi-work.

to organize it and thus would be less effective than either of the individual groups using their culturally rooted work practices.

Mixing incompatible work practices can have a significantly negative effect on the overall effectiveness of an organization. In the 1990s, many European and American companies saw the outsourcing of IT and services to India and other lower cost countries as a way to save cost. However, many of the same companies soon realized that they had underestimated the impact of the cultural and work practice differences. They experienced that the process of outsourcing was not smooth, and resulted in significant friction. This reduced the agility, increased communication costs and caused regular and expensive misunderstandings, leading to costly delays that often far exceeded the expected cost savings. Hence, today there is a trend towards a more balanced outsourcing strategy, taking into account the real cost of the effect of this cultural distance. Mixing work practices from different cultures without careful consideration of the real cost of integrating them can be a very costly strategy.

In 2011, the Norwegian giant Statoil realized the risk of mixing national work practices, when constructing a huge platform off the Korean coast. Using Asian labour (cheaper than Nordic), the combined workforce included Koreans, Thais, Norwegians and Indians (designers based in Singapore, therefore Tamils). Intelligently, Statoil initiated cultural pre-training for the Norwegian managers to familiarize them with the work practices and likely attitudes of the Asians involved. A much smoother and cost-saving operation was the outcome.

Decoding observed behaviours and vision statements

An organization may reveal significant information about its embedded values from observable artefacts. Is the boss in a large corner office? Can you identify someone's status in the hierarchy from the size and position of their desk or office or the type of their car? Are the headquarters in a modest building in an industrial area or is it an iconic building on a prominent plot in the centre of town? This type of information about the company and its people can give you a hint about deeply-rooted beliefs.

The work practices and the operational habits themselves are artefacts and will provide further insight. You will gain further insight by understanding the myths in the organization involving the founders, the employees and its

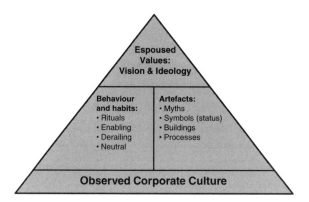

Diagram 4.2: The observed culture

history. The handling of an existential crisis or a heroic effort may also shed light on deeply held beliefs. In one Nordic company a close encounter with bankruptcy was caused by a lack of liquidity, too much debt and an unwilling bank. This led to an embedded value of always being liquid and never relying on banks. This was a belief that was not up for discussion; whoever tried to would be brushed off and slowly it became an invisible embedded value.

An equally important area to understand is who the formal and informal heroes are. Was it a leader or a worker who took an extraordinary action or someone who simply made a particularly good deal for the company? Is the hero an individual or a group of employees? Are the stories focused on long-term strategic thinking or are they hailing pragmatic urgent action? These elements are summarized in Diagram 4.2.

In the case of FLSmidth, the global cement plant producer, the early heroes were the engineers who ventured to faraway places and often had to overcome great difficulties such as getting a heavy 40-metre oven into a remote site with poor transportation. If you read the employee magazines from the 1920s and 1930s, the stories that were recounted were all about people, cement and accomplishing difficult engineering and logistical tasks in inner China, in the Indonesian jungle, in Brazil and in Russia. It portrays an organization of practical people, who pride themselves on solving practical problems under difficult circumstances and constructing cement plants that would help build cities and modernize the infrastructure.

All such aspects are important data to help you identify the embedded values. The information can be found in articles about the company, anniversary reviews, employee newsletters, interviews and books written about the company. Obviously, having access to analysis of the company, such as employee engagement studies, and cultural studies, will add further detail and insight. However, the most reliable source is through personal observation, being part of meetings, and seeing how decisions are made and how people interact.

Mission and vision statements

In general the more influential the company has been in producing a piece, the more critical one has to be when reading it. What companies communicate about themselves is what they want you to hear, and therefore only one part of the story! Leaders often speak about their company culture at the firm-wide and aspirational level. However, this may not reflect the reality at the operational level, and may lead to cultural cynicism. A company's *vision, mission and values statements* usually fall into four categories:

1. **Aspirational values:** lofty, but achievable goals and sometimes not so achievable. A truck company may say: "We want to be the global leader in logistics." Or Google's: "We will do no Evil." Or Steve Jobs on Apple: "We want to make insanely great products."
2. **Fashionable values:** current popular ones include being green, embracing CSR (corporate social responsibility) and a focus on diversity. These types of values may display prominently on banners and in advertisements, but are not always embraced by the organizations and embedded in the values.
3. **Actual values:** these often include the cultural traits and behaviours that are supported throughout the organization, and observable. These articulate the unique cultural enablers and central aspects of the core culture of the organization in the company's own language.
4. **Corrective values:** these are the important values that seek to lessen the impact of implicitly or explicitly recognized culturally derailing traits, e.g. emphasizing team work and collaboration in American companies to help counter the unintended consequences of a highly individualistic culture. Or emphasizing creativity and independent thinking in a Korean company!

It is important to categorize each value statement correctly, to help identify the underlying embedded values.

The observed organizational behaviour may also give significant insight into the embedded values of the organization. Some behaviour may immediately be identified as *enabling behaviour*. When Korean workers at Samsung work 24/7 to complete a major project, this is clearly enabling them to achieve their personal mission and the company's strategic objectives. The top management at GM stopped listening to the customers and primarily focused on internal issues and analysis during long management meetings in the 1970s. This is an example of *derailing behaviour*. *Neutral behaviour* may not immediately be classified as either derailing or enabling, but still gives insight into the values that drive behaviour. For instance, a Danish company preferring to move an individual who is not performing to their standards to a new position, rather than firing him. This in other cultures may be seen as being soft. Or the quarterly focus of an American company compared to the long-term focus of a Japanese company. However, as they interact with other cultural processes they may develop unintended consequences by reinforcing derailing or enabling behaviour.

Identifying the values, assumptions and beliefs underpinning the "cultural universe"

While one can't directly interpret the embedded values from what an outsider observes, this can often give significant clues to them. This is where the art and science of cultural analysis meet. In the linear-active West, it is not unusual to meet the perspective of "if you can't measure it, it doesn't exist". While great strides have been made in terms of identifying the dimensions of both national and organizational culture using statistical analysis, it has proved more difficult to predict performance. There are simply too many interdependent variables, and too much statistical noise from variables that are difficult to identify and measure.

A critical element of the cultural dynamic methodology is to identify the small handful of embedded and often invisible beliefs that underpin the corporate culture and make the organization unique. We call this the organization's "cultural universe". In Chapter 9, we discuss how to handle a crisis, and will further explore how you can use this insight to identify potential cultural accelerators and derailers as your company transforms itself responding to a crisis.

As you will see in several of the cases, the cultural universe is often underpinned by staid national values, and thus difficult to change in the short term. Consequently, during a transformation, it is advisable to accept the existence of these beliefs and make them work for you rather than trying to change them. Medium and long term, these beliefs may be possible to change, but only with a significant effort of time and money.

The last step is to identify and verify the embedded values underpinning an organization. To ensure you have identified the embedded values that best explain the observed behaviour you should:

1. List the key behaviours that best characterize the observed and often unique organizational behaviour. These should include enabling, derailing and neutral behaviour, work practices, decision-making processes and other cultural observations. It is advisable to focus on those which are directly linked to management behaviour and organizational performance.
2. Select a small group (4–6) of embedded values that have the best correlation to the central observed behaviours in this list and influence central cultural dynamics.
3. Verify the identified embedded values:
   a. Experienced cultural analysts should independently arrive at the same embedded values. It is advisable to seek their assistance for this analysis to overcome the "Fish can't see water syndrome". Doing it internally may politicize the process and thereby make the results unreliable.
   b. Experienced employees and leaders who know the organization well and have an open mind will often be able to verify these directly.
   c. Cross-check with the results of existing cultural analysis to ensure the embedded values are consistent with the results.

In the example in Diagram 4.3, the four identified key embedded values in the "cultural universe" are: 1. Elimination of waste, 2. Teamwork and learning is the key to success, 3. Scepticism to outsiders, and 4. Long-term orientation. It is not unusual that the identified embedded values are known to the organization, but not necessarily described as values, since they are often implicitly assumed. It is also often possible to identify the national culture they are most likely to come from. Usually the embedded values will be a mix of national influencers and business influencers. In the example above, the elimination of waste is a business value, which, however, is deeply rooted in Japanese culture. "Scepticism to outsiders" is a national characteristic in many countries and often strongest in rural communities. The long-term orientation is normally a national value, while the embedded value "Team work and learning is key to success" in many cases will be a business value, yet may have some rooting in a national culture.

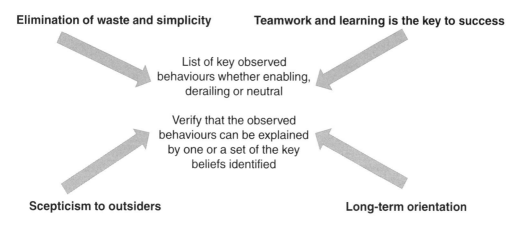

Diagram 4.3: The four identified key embedded values in the "cultural universe"

The subsequent cases will generally focus on one or two embedded values that we have been able to identify through secondary sources and analysis combined with personal observations when possible.

This completes the discussion of all the key aspects of the static Cultural Dynamic Model®. In the next section we will discuss how the model becomes interactive by introducing the concept of a cultural dynamic, before presenting the full Cultural Dynamic Model®.

A cultural dynamic and the full cultural dynamic model®

A change of strategy may start a domino effect of changes in the work practices, which over time dynamically impacts the corporate culture. *A cultural dynamic describes a sequence of reinforced effects where the work practices, corporate culture and results dynamically interact to either reinforce a culture or change it!* Our interest will, in particular, focus on the unintended consequences, often rooted in national traits, when this happens.

When GM changed its focus from market share to profitability, the board and management did not intend the organization to adopt an insular and increasingly bureaucratic and clubby culture that over time distanced itself from the customer. It simply happened by itself as changes in the organizational focus, work practices and leadership slowly impacted the corporate culture and started interacting with the work practices and decision-making processes. Aspects of American national values played a major role in this dynamic. This cultural dynamic was reinforced by perceived success early on and later by repeated bursts of American short-term optimism, with management believing that the newest strategy or major initiative was working, only to be disproved by the market the following year.

Throughout the book you will note that if you attempt to transform the corporate culture of a company against deeply-rooted national traits, you may run into trouble. We are by no means arguing it can't be done. You can change behaviours and work practices rooted in national traits. What we are saying is that it will not be successful without a significantly high level of continuous management attention and substantial investment in training. You can implement "Lean" manufacturing processes in independently-minded England, and you can make a Japanese company open to outsiders and creative, and, yes, you can make an American company less individualistic, less hierarchical and more team oriented, but not without a significant effort and continued management dedication – and not without risking unintended consequences, which you have to monitor carefully, as we will now show you in the Austin Motors case!

This concludes our discussion of all the key components and enables us to present the full Cultural Dynamic Model® (Diagram 4.4).

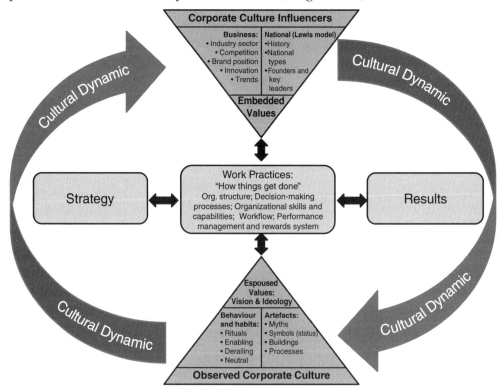

Diagram 4.4: The full Cultural Dynamic Model®
© Kai Hammerich, 2012

Case study: Austin Motors

Let's bring our framework to life by looking at what happened to the British motor industry through the lenses of the Austin Motor Company. This case is somewhat longer, due to duplicated information, than the following cases, as we use it to show how to use all the elements of the Cultural Dynamic Model®. First, we will tell the brief story of the company and the strategic dilemma it faced by 1960. We will then use that information to populate the Dynamic Model, identify two central cultural dynamics and finally discuss the conclusions. In later cases we will generally seek to avoid repetitive information.

A brief 70-year history of Austin Motors[5]

Austin Motors was one of many small car manufacturers established in the UK during the embryonic period of the British car industry. The founder, Herbert Austin, was an industrious, hands-on, production engineer and innovator, with a vision of producing cars for the masses. The early years were turbulent. After some initial success making cars, WWI broke out in 1914, and production at the main plant at Longbridge, near Birmingham, was converted to military purposes.

Following the war, Austin returned to car production. It competed with the other British car companies to gain a stronger position in the market (most of its competitors ultimately went bankrupt and disappeared). Austin was also at one point on the verge of bankruptcy. According to legend it was saved when Herbert Austin flipped a coin to decide to stay in the business rather than inviting the administrators in. To help the company through this crisis, he personally asked employees to work for free for a period in exchange for a lifetime job at the company. As late as in the 1970s there were still employees at Austin (by then British Leyland) under this work-for-life guarantee. The hugely popular Austin Seven from 1923 was designed by a teenage apprentice with Herbert Austin, and helped Austin gain a strong foothold in the mass market, as did the Austin 10/4 in the 1930s. By the end of the inter-war period, Austin and its main competitor Morris had emerged as the two leading volume car manufacturers in England.

---

[5]A main source of cultural information for this case is from Sharratt B. (2000) *Men and Motors of 'The Austin'*. Haynes.

In 1938, Leonard Lord arrived at Austin after quitting as general manager of Morris, to take over the leadership from Herbert Austin. He was an equally industrious, hands-on, hard-working and very effective production engineer. When WWII broke out, Longbridge was again converted to support the war effort.

After the war, a frenzied period followed, focusing on the export of cars of uneven quality, to help bring foreign currency to England. In 1952, Austin and Morris merged to form BMC, adding the Morris, MG, Riley and Wolseley brands.[6] However, BMC kept the competing brands and dealer networks intact and paid little attention to integrating the now fragmented manufacturing operation and company cultures.

In 1961 Lord retired. Though the new leader, Harriman, was also a production engineer, he does not appear to have had the same personal drive, detailed understanding of the operation and respect that Austin and Lord had. He essentially co-led the company together with the idiosyncratic designer and innovator Issigonis, the creator of the Mini.

By the early 1960s, BMC was less export oriented than its European competitors like VW with its Beetle, mainly focusing on the home market. The quality of cars and the reputation of Austin engineering had declined and there was a lack of cost control. This led to the very successful Mini being sold at a loss for the first few years. Rumour had it that it was Ford UK engineers, not Austin, who found this out when they took one apart and cost analyzed it. However, the cars were still very innovative with the ground breaking low-price, front-wheel-drive Mini and the subsequent front-wheel-driven Austin models. In the late 1960s and 1970s, the company was criticized in independent strategic reviews of the industry for not having a long-term product and corporate strategy nor adequate business processes to support a large business, which by 1970 had grown to producing close to a million cars per year.

In 1966, BMC acquired the Jaguar Group. Two years later, in 1968, the UK government forced a merger with the smaller Leyland, a commercial vehicle company (buses and lorries), with a small car division and two brands, Standard Triumph, which was acquired in 1960 and Rover, which was acquired in

---

[6]http://en.wikipedia.org/wiki/British_Motor_Corporation.

1967.[7] Stokes, the general manager of Leyland, was chosen as the new CEO of British Leyland (BL). He had a background in sales of commercial vehicles and was known as the salesman of his generation. In 1975 BL was finally nationalized to save jobs. During the period 1968 to 1985, over £3 billion of taxpayers' money was spent on rescuing BL.

Now let's apply the Cultural Dynamic Model® to Austin Motors as it would have appeared in the early 1960s to gain a deeper insight into the challenges of the company:

The strategic imperatives at Austin in 1960

Diagram 4.5 illustrates how a significant external event will drive a change in strategy that upsets the existing harmony between culture and strategy.

Austin had successfully applied a consistent strategy for 50 years, when the environment suddenly changed and the automotive industry became more mature. The increasingly affluent middle-class population in post-WWII Europe demanded a functional and reliable car they could afford. VW's Beetle led the way with a simple design, which lasted from 1938 to 2003. During its lifetime over 21 million Beetles were produced. This allowed VW to increase efficiency and scale and thus drive cost down. Compare this to the numerous models that Austin and Morris introduced in the 1940s–1960s to support their multiple brands. Each model would be produced for a few years and then

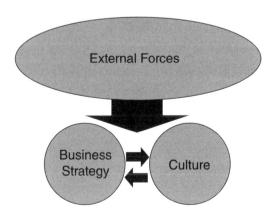

Diagram 4.5: Harmony between culture and strategy upset by a significant external event

[7]http://en.wikipedia.org/wiki/Leyland_Motors.

changed for a new design, which meant the factory had to sit idle while it was expensively retooled.[8] Austin obviously believed it was better designing and building multiple new models, rather than mass-producing a single model in volume over a long period.

With hindsight, Austin probably should have changed its strategy with a broader geographic coverage to gain scale, while focusing on fewer models and longer production runs to compete with the likes of VW. To complement this new strategy, Austin should have changed the culture to be more process and long-term oriented and introduced more sophisticated business management tools and a stronger managerial regime. Using the business semantics of today, this new strategy and culture balance may have looked like that shown in Diagram 4.6.

Clearly, the company needed to change dramatically to compete, but change did not come from within!

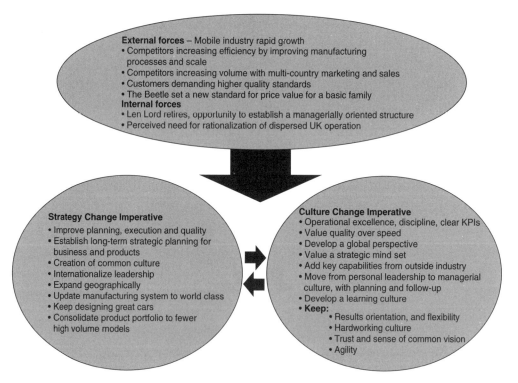

Diagram 4.6: Austin competitive situation by the early 1960s

[8]http://en.wikipedia.org/wiki/British_Motor_Corporation.

The English national influencers

Austin was an English company. As Lewis[9] says about the English: "In general, however, the country's democratic record, her exploratory instincts, her industrial and administrative creativity, her bouts of invention, her sense of humour and willingness to 'muddle through', inevitably led to nation-state traits characterised by liberalism, individualism and freedom of choice." UK business-people are not told how to run companies or given a set of norms or standards to conform to. It would be hard to define "a typical British corporation". This national "muddle-through" perspective is often accentuated with short-termism and pragmatism in business – why plan if you can "wing it"?

The business influencers

Austin, in addition to these national traits, was a Midlands-based (an area around Birmingham) car and engineering company, with a rural, no-nonsense, hardworking and meritocratic perspective on life.

The company anecdotes from the embryonic period were all about creating great innovative cars for the masses and getting new models ready for production in the nick of time. It embraced an insular apprenticeship culture, favouring on-the-job training over formal qualifications. Motor people grew up from within the car industry and stayed there for their whole career. Few people were hired from the outside. Commercial and strategic matters were less important than building great cars. There was limited and inconsistent focus on exporting.

The company was used to dealing with volatility, having twice been converted to war production, and hence had embedded a value of being flexible over having rigid structures and processes. This was ingrained in the company's psyche and accentuated by English pragmatism. Austin had modern manufacturing plants and applied the newest production methodologies until the late 1950s, though these smaller-scale plants gradually started to fall behind the effectiveness of the competition with their larger, more efficient production plants. In the 1920s Austin was one of the first companies in the UK to introduce cost accounting, but this system was abandoned during the war production years.

[9]Lewis R.D. (2006) *When Cultures Collide*, 3rd Edition. Nicholas Brealey, pp. 194–197.

The leadership

Only two people led the company for over 50 years – Austin and Lord. Both were strong leaders, English and production engineers and had a huge influence on the culture and strategy. They were both highly respected and hands-on, involved in the daily operations often seen on the factory floor. They were in close contact with the workers and considerate of their needs.

Companies that transition from strong founder leaders often need to establish a new managerial regime with more processes and become less reliant on personal leadership. This transition did not appear to happen at BMC after Lord retired. Instead a weak dual-CEO structure was chosen.

The work practices

The organizational structure

The Austin manufacturing operation set the tone for the group culture and the company ethos during the first 50 years. All main operations were based in the UK, with limited international influence. The structure was that of a divisionalized and functional organization. After the mergers, the independent companies were allowed to exist as brands, physical entities and distinct subcultures, which created significant tension and resistance to change, ultimately leading to suboptimization.

Decision-making processes

The two leaders appear to have been omnipresent during the first 50 years and involved in most major decisions. Herbert Austin was interested in modern business management methodologies, but that focus appears to have lessened after Lord's arrival. Informal systems could overrule and supplement weak processes. An experienced workforce knew how to get things moving and understood the consequence of most daily operational decisions, while at the same time the CEO and senior managers could and would overrule operational decisions.

The organizational skills and capabilities

The workforce was made up of engineers and craftsmen, combined with lower skilled labour. There were relatively few formally trained managers, with most developed from within. Austin was considered to have excellent practical mechanical engineering capabilities, and twice successfully converted its plants to the manufacturing of complex war equipment. However, it lacked a managerial culture.

Workflow processes

With both Austin and Lord being production engineers, the manufacturing processes at Austin were considered modern; however, the divisionalized nature created a fragmented rather than integrated manufacturing system after the merger with Morris. There were strong relationships between middle managers and the production floor staff.

The performance management, reward and compensation systems

Neither Lord nor Austin are described as being wealthy or displaying wealth. They appear to be car people who thrived on producing new exciting models. A piecework system (pay-for-results) for the workshop employees had supported getting things done. However, after the early 1960s, unions became increasingly hostile, thereby reducing productivity while they attempted to introduce compensation systems that were not based on the piecework philosophy.

Artefacts, rituals and communicated values

Austin was a modest, task-oriented company. The buildings and factories were simple. Herbert Austin's office was next to the entry gate to the factory and used as the CEO office until the 1950s. Status was ascribed through someone's contribution to the common objective of building great innovative cars. The designer Issigonis became a hero with the innovative Mini, despite its leakages and early uneven build quality. There is little internal material about the corporate values and company culture. This was a company that spoke about itself through its products. In his book *Men and Motors of "The Austin"*, Barney Sharratt[10] portrays a company of enthusiastic people who had grown up together in a new exciting industry that expanded dramatically in the first half of the 20th century, sharing a passion for this new great consumer product, the car.

---

[10]Sharratt (2000).

Observed behaviour at Austin

There was a very positive and constructive fix-the-problem, bias-for-action attitude at Austin, which helped the company beat the local competitors. There was a clear ambition – coming from both Austin and Lord – they wanted to create a big successful motor company, and didn't shy away from exploring growth opportunities. They were prudently bold. Top management and the CEO made the key decisions. Most were good decisions; however, the company failed to put in place a managerial culture to support a large company producing over 300,000 vehicles per annum at the Longbridge facility alone, when Lord retired.

From second-hand sources it appears that emotional decision-making was accepted and often applied by both senior executives and the CEO. This may indicate that the company was culturally and managerially stuck in the embryonic lifecycle period.

The 1960 Austin corporate culture, and some of the identified embedded values, either originating from national or business influencers thus, can be summarized as:

- A practical and tactical orientation combined with short-termism (English)
- An insular apprenticeship culture with on-the-job training (Business)
- Flexibility favoured over rigid effectiveness and tight processes (English and Business)
- A "wing-it" pragmatism favoured over planning and processes (English)
- Innovation being more important than analysis and responding to customers (Business)
- Divisional structure favoured over integrated operations (Business)
- Good historical relationship between employees and management/owners (Business)

Lacking personal observations, we have too little information to make a full map of the cultural universe at Austin and to identify all the central embedded values with certainty. However, this list is a good starting point. It is important also to note that the culture described above is of Austin proper rather than the wider BMC group.

The results

By 1960, BMC had a 36.5% share of the UK production of cars and was the leading local manufacturer of cars – American Ford and GM (Vauxhall brand) also had significant manufacturing operations in the UK. BL would peak at 40% of new car registrations in 1971, only to decline to 18.2% by 1980.

In 1955, Britain produced 4.1 vehicles per employee per annum versus 3.9 in Germany. By 1970 Germany had leapt to 7.5 cars per employee while Britain had progressed more slowly to producing 5.6 cars per employee, a 35%+ difference in productivity. This was the result of a higher level of investment in new technologies and bigger plants, as well as better management systems for financial control, combined with stronger industrial relations.

One enabling cultural dynamic – "the bias-for-action"

A central and enabling cultural dynamic at Austin was the *bias-for-action* and problem-solving focus as depicted in Diagram 4.7. It is rooted in English pragmatism and its entrepreneurial short-termism. Austin had a practical engineering business culture and two strong long-serving leaders with empathy for

Diagram 4.7: The bias-for-action and problem-solving focus at Austin

the employees. They created an organization with clarity of purpose and a shared commitment to building great cars for the masses. Employee dedication, enthusiasm for cars, flexibility and trust from a stable workforce reinforced this.

Despite an amorphous organizational structure, Austin established a problem-solving bias-for-action attitude in the organization. Heroes were those who solved problems in time, and informal status was given based on it. The company succeeded in solving many of its engineering problems this way, and did it better than competitors. As a result, sales and market share increased, thereby reinforcing this pattern of behaviour and the underlying embedded values. In essence Austin thereby created an organization that was more agile and effective than its competitors. Success can reinforce a cultural dynamic and help create a virtuous cycle!

Obviously, a key ingredient in the strength of this dynamic was the trust between the leadership and the employees. Companies that are successful over a long period of time often will have a trusting relationship between management and the employees. Fear can give you wings – but only for a short while – trust works better, yet is easily compromised.

The potentially derailing short-term wing-it cultural dynamic

A somewhat more dysfunctional trait was the *lack of strategic thinking and short-termism*. Interestingly, the English pragmatic, short-term muddling-through traits that fuelled the bias-for-action cultural dynamic also fuelled the wing-it cultural dynamic, thus showing the power of the same national traits to be enablers and derailers at the same time. Austin had the ability to fix problems in the nick of time. As the company became more successful, this behaviour was reinforced, to the extent that it may have redefined all problems to be short-term problems. This would have made it difficult to introduce the needed long-term planning of new models and recommend processes to support a larger organization.

The wing-it approach was reinforced by Austin being asked to completely turn to war production twice by the British government. These experiences probably reinforced the view that agility and flexibility were more important than rigid processes and careful strategic planning. An insular management team that had narrow skills and a local outlook further reinforced this. They were trained and recruited from within their industry, and had limited formal education and thus preferred to deal with the tangible over the abstract and strategic.

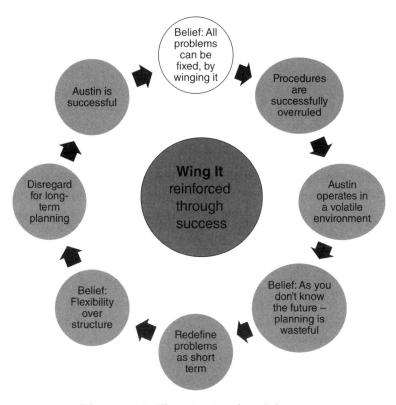

Diagram 4.8: The wing-it cultural dynamic

After WWII, in order to raise revenues, the British government introduced new car taxes at regular intervals, which significantly impacted the demand for individual models, making long-term planning for the product line-up and the production schedule less meaningful. Thus, the world around Austin reinforced the company's belief that a tactical orientation was the most suitable approach to navigate its challenges.

In graphical form the wing-it cultural dynamic can be summarized as shown in Diagram 4.8.

Conclusion

BMC faced two key challenges in 1960. It was in need of a new strategy as it entered the scale-and-efficiency phase in its corporate lifecycle, and this existential crisis coincided with the last founder leader retiring. Austin was not well prepared for these challenges, and the key question is how, having the clarity of hindsight, should the company have responded?

The key moment was the leadership transition after Leonard Lord. If the company had understood the challenges and installed a stronger managerial regime, favouring a more process-oriented, international and strategic focus, it may have fared better. Instead the board decided to take an evolutionary path by choosing a weak leadership set-up with two leaders, both from within the company and the industry, who weren't well trained and prepared for the new challenges.

In his authoritative book *The Rise and Decline of the British Motor Industry*, Roy Church[11] concludes that the failure of the British motor industry to transform itself into an internationally competitive enterprise is explicable on account of *historically rooted weaknesses in corporate structures and management, which for so many years obscured the need for systematic planning and organizational change.*

Was Austin an isolated case or is this a symptom of a deeper issue? One could argue that Austin was a unique company in special circumstances. However, the same happened for the British motorcycle industry, where Japanese competitors outmanoeuvred the local industry players in less than 10 years. The symptom is further reinforced by the general demise of the engineering and manufacturing sector in England over the past 40 years. Does this mean you can't have manufacturing in England? Of course not – but the government, management and shareholders are well advised to carefully analyze how these dynamics and national traits may prevent success. The instinctive response may be to just wing it and hope it will go away, but what is needed is probably a comprehensive programme to more effectively deal with the issue!

Chapter closing

In the following chapters, we will take you through each step of the lifecycle, and analyze how global companies from different nations navigated their particular challenges. We will use the Cultural Dynamic Model® as the framework and focus on how national values impact the strategic response when a company transitions from one lifecycle phase to the next.

---

[11]Church R. (1994) *The Rise and Decline of the British Motor Industry*. Economic History Society, p. 129.

Part II

CASES: THE LIFECYCLE OF A COMPANY FROM INNOVATION TO CONSOLIDATION

5

In this and the following two chapters, we will use the lifecycle model from the introduction to structure the discussion of our eight cases. They are organized to cover the three main periods shown in Diagram 5.1, with some of the cases spanning several phases.

A transformation point indicates where a company needs to transition its skills and capabilities to navigate the challenges of the next phase. This is a critical point where a company may stumble.

In this chapter, we discuss the embryonic period and the national and business traits that may enable or derail success. In the Austin Motors case, we showed how the embryonic period has a disproportionate influence on a company's embedded cultural universe. In this chapter we discuss three cases: first, Finnish Nokia that, in less than 10 years, became the king of the mobile industry, speeding through the innovation, geographic expansion and product-line expansion phases. After a strategy change, it reached the scale and efficiency phase as Nokia 2.0, when it was hit by an existential crisis caused by technology disruption from Apple and Google. We finish the chapter with two cases describing the global expansion of Finnish KONE, and finally American Walmart's fascinating international expansion into Germany, China and South Korea.

In Chapters 1 and 4, we illustrated the deep influence founders have on the embedded values. So let's first start with a quick look at the American tech industry and how the personality of the founders embedded distinct values in three well-known US companies, during their formative years. Apple, Microsoft and Dell were all led by their founders for at least 20 years, and are among the highest valued companies in their industry.

The tech industry is a young industry. It is global and many of the founders are still active. They all grew up in linear-active America. The business cultures

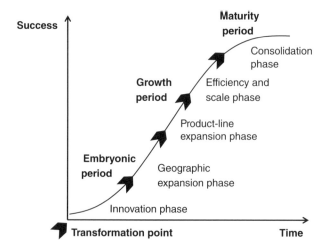

Diagram 5.1: Three main periods used to organize cases

of these three American companies are different, but they all share the competitive, ambitious and confident American national values of the 21st century and while now mature global corporates, they still retain many of the key traits established during the embryonic period.

Values embedded during the early years: Apple, Microsoft and Dell

Apple

Kai Hammerich worked at Apple for six years from the late 1980s. From early days Apple had a culture of a creativity and focus on the user experience, reinforced by both Steve Wozniak's and Steve Jobs' hands-on attention to detail and appreciation of design. It had a stronger appeal to, and interest in, consumers than in business customers. Apple did not believe in open models, it believed in controlling its technology and its ecosystem, to ensure a great user experience. Steve Jobs, a dominant genius, would still personally review the design of new products up until his untimely passing. Steve Jobs' strong personality helped to create a strong cultural universe centred on him – some even called it a parallel distortion universe – that, as an executive, you either had to accept or leave the company. In this universe, the rules and the logics were different compared to the world outside. It was Jobs' logic that ruled, and as he was successful it prevailed. However, the company lost its way as a force of innovation after Steve Jobs was forced out in 1985 to found Next, bringing with him the next generation Macintosh operating system.

Apple had already adapted to a post-founder managerial culture, hiring in top executives from outside, when Kai Hammerich worked at Apple. However, being in a highly innovative and dynamic industry, it was too early for Apple to lose its power of innovation. Kai recalls a pivotal moment when a CEO announced that Apple's goal was to become a $10 billion company, an ambitious goal for a managerially led corporation. But Apple was still a young company with young employees. Many, like Kai, had joined Apple because of Jobs' dream of "changing the world". As a goal it was therefore inappropriate and not motivational and, for many, it felt like "having the air sucked out of you" when they heard it.

Apple's market share rapidly declined once Jobs' creative influence waned and by 2001 revenues had dropped to $5 billion annually and a rebased share price of $8. Only after Steve Jobs came back in 1997 did the company rediscover its creative ethos for making "insanely great products"; the iPod, iTunes, the iPhone and the iPad – the rest is history. By 2012 Apple passed $150 billion in sales with a stock price of over $600. Some say that Apple's luck was that the world moved into a strategy of consumer focus and simplicity, and that Jobs brilliantly exploited this. However, when the world moves on, as it always does, a natural question is whether Apple can prosper without the influence of a technological visionary like Jobs. Has it inculcated a culture of innovation and strategic agility in its work practices? This is the big question that the board and investors must carefully consider.

Microsoft

Microsoft has an unusual dual-personality culture, which has served it well: Bill Gates gave Microsoft the traits of the intellectually brilliant, technically detail-oriented, visionary and self-confident engineer. These traits were successfully combined with a more aggressive and competitive sales culture: traits that came from Steve Balmer's equally intellectual, brilliant and competitive personality. Unlike Apple, which was ahead of Microsoft in the early 1980s, Microsoft believed in an open model, working with multiple partners to popularize its technologies, in particular in the corporate market. This strategy, combined with its effective dual-personality culture, successfully propelled Microsoft to become the world's most valued company by 2000.

However, in the recent decade, Gates has been less visible internally, and a cultural dynamic appears to have emerged where the competitiveness at times has overshadowed customer insight and innovation. A work practice known as "stack ranking" – a program, perhaps more in the spirit of competitive Balmer, that forces every unit to declare a certain percentage of employees as top performers, good performers, average and poor – may have hampered Microsoft's ability to innovate. Employees indicate that "it leads to employees focusing on competing with each other rather than competing with other companies".[1] The Windows operating system (OS) is the core product for Microsoft's domination. Vista, a version of the OS launched in 2007, is an example of a Microsoft technology developed at great expense over many years that was not cherished by customers, yet was sold very hard by the sales organization. The subsequent versions, Windows 7 and Windows 8, recovered some ground, yet was not seen as being on par with Apple, particularly for consumers. By 2012, Apple had over twice the value of Microsoft, which, however, was still in the top 10 in terms of market capitalization.[2]

Dell

Dell started its amazing growth trajectory in the late 1980s. Michael Dell invented the direct model, selling out of his college dorm. With this model, Dell could price its products keenly with short product cycle times in an industry where component prices dropped weekly, combined with offering customers high levels of customization. Michael Dell is a founder who has a real passion for getting the detail right and for product technologies. Customers report that he can still competently discuss the individual components of a product and clearly enjoys this over many other topics. Numerous employees have found themselves getting emails from Michael at 3am, querying a faulty webpage he had visited or the printer connect rate for a specific PC model in a remote country.

Dell has a confident Texan attitude, combined with rationality, coming from the many former Bain executives they employed in the early growth years. It

[1]http://www.vanityfair.com/online/daily/2012/07/microsoft-downfall-emails-steve-ballmer.
[2]http://en.wikipedia.org/wiki/List_of_corporations_by_market_capitalization, Q3, 2012. Google market capitalization.

is extremely data driven and short term oriented. The company grew up in a low margin business, dictated by perishable components margins – so at Dell it is all about an unrelenting swift execution focus. The simple logic being: if you miss the sales target today, you miss the week! If you miss the week, you miss the month and if you miss the month, you will miss the quarter. And missing the quarter is not acceptable!

Dell has a modern American, tough, you-compete-to-win perspective. Early on results were more important than people at Dell, but today it has evolved a more paternalistic approach. However, the company has had difficulties evolving beyond the direct model. The model lost its competitiveness as the price of all-inclusive PCs and laptops dropped below $1000 and customization became less important. In parallel, competition has successfully copied key elements of Dell's supply chain efficiency. Its supply chain, manufacturing and customer services processes are still world class, while other systems are less developed. Yet, Dell has struggled outside the USA, pursuing the original successful direct business model developed for the USA, although it has been tactically aligned to meet local needs of multi-tiered distribution and partnering in places. Consequently, Dell may have fallen into the trap of being so tactically focused on the short-term execution that it hasn't developed the required strategic orientation and the transformative skills to evolve or even revolutionize its original business model.

These are not average founders and these are not average corporate cultures. These are extreme cultures that have been shaped by the persistent personalities of their founders, with both their personal strengths and weaknesses on full display in the companies they created. The work practices and cultural traits reflect their beliefs, values and preferences. Each company also developed a cultural dynamic that it has found difficult to navigate and which may derail its success in the next business cycle. Naturally, the key question for all three companies is what happens with them and their respective cultures, once the founders ultimately step down. The transition to a managerial regime is never easy, as we saw in the example of Apple in the 1980s and it has to be timed well.

Like many other influential founders, these were all different personalities and cherished different "games" to play. A game that played to their own personal strengths; whether that meant being the most brilliant engineer, a perfectionist designer, ambitious and competitive or detail oriented. They all had a desire for overt or implicit domination and a confident American belief in their own abilities and ideas. They defined the "game" internally so that they could win it, and because their game also won in the external marketplace it reinforced their leadership dominance and the associated values and beliefs.

Traits that enable success over the business cycles

So what are the characteristics of a successful culture? Diagram 5.2 outlines key corporate traits and capabilities that commonly are seen as having a positive impact on success across national cultures. Traits helpful during the embryonic period are highlighted with dots. As we will observe in the following chapters, the cultural profile of a successful company tends to move to the right as the company grows through the various phases.

However, let's start with a few words of caution. First, it is important to note that some of the traits and scales may have specific national interpretations and not be opposites in the traditional sense. For instance, the opposite of "bias-for-action" or urgency is hesitation. Organizations will hesitate for a reason, and often for a cultural reason. In linear-active cultures, it may be based on rationally analyzing the issue; in reactive cultures, the hesitation may be because other wider issues of systemic harmony are taken into consideration, while in multi-active cultures it may be because the effect on relationships is taken into consideration. Equally, the opposite of being open is being closed. However, being closed can be caused by multiple cultural factors including dogmatism, scepticism to outsiders, nationalism, or arrogance.

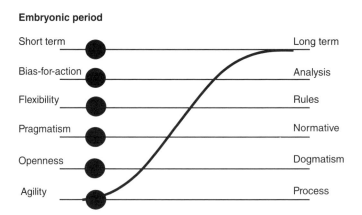

Diagram 5.2: Key corporate traits and capabilities that have a positive impact on success across national cultures

A second important point to note is that to be effective, a company may need to nurture different traits at each of the three levels of the organization; the front line, the middle management and at the corporate level. A mature company, for instance, may need a long-term and strategic perspective at the corporate level, while it also requires a tactical and short-term bias-for-action in the front line. However, the front-line empowerment will often be restricted through the rules and processes of the mature company. The art of leadership is to manage these dichotomies of opposing cultural and operational require-ments at the three different levels. In the cases we will primarily discuss the systemic requirements at the corporate level.

Lastly, companies tend to hire employees with skills and capabilities that match the challenges of the phase. As the company transitions to the next phase, these employees define the legacy traits and capabilities that it carries along, and which may become a hindrance to establishing the necessary organizational capabilities required for success in the new phase.

We have not included traits that are mostly dependent on the national types, rather than performance, such as the masculine–feminine dimension, the power distance and individualism versus collectivism – though they cer-tainly impact how a company is organized and its corporate culture – the same way that German and Brazilian football styles are different, but equally effec-tive. The only trait for national types we have included is the time orientation, which does appear to have an impact on the performance of companies over the various phases.

As you will note in many of the cases, *successful founders often have personal traits and values that can help neutralize or eliminate potentially derailing national traits*. Hence, the list above is directional rather than dogmatic.

The embryonic period

The innovation phase

The innovation phase is, by its nature, volatile. Not all ideas are good and not all ideas can be successfully commercialized. The art of venture capital requires having the patience to identify the business model that can make an innova-tion successful. Often a start-up company will go through several iterations before it finds the right model, though frequently it won't find it. The failure rate in this phase is high.

A small and intimate team works long hours and the founder is omnipres-ent. The core group is usually made up of engineers, scientists or technical experts in their field. Every potential client is precious, and the products are often customized to win a deal. Projects have a tendency to go wrong, with adversity overcome by heroic efforts in the nick of time. The tension and employee motivation runs high. Taking risks is a simple necessity and the difference between success and failure is often razor thin. During this phase, enabling business traits will centre on:

- Creative thinking
- Hard work and persistence
- Teamwork and collaboration (in small teams)
- Agility, pragmatism and a short-term orientation
- Risk taking, empowerment and trust (within the team)
- Building relationships externally.

National traits that tend to enable or derail during the innovation phase

Naturally, the industry in which a company competes will impact both the business traits and the national traits that are most critical for success. A services company will need to focus on the quality of the delivery processes sooner than an innovative products company. A company that needs to grow its employee base significantly during this period to succeed, e.g. in retailing, will have to focus on the people side of the business and people processes earlier. However, across industries, the following national traits at the strategic level are often seen to enable or derail the success of a company:

- Bias-for-action/urgency over perfectionism
- Pragmatism and flexibility over dogmatism and structure
- Creativity over rules orientation
- Results focus over process discipline
- Short-term orientation over long-term orientation (though founders often have a long-term vision).

The geographic expansion phase

During the geographic expansion phase, the company meets the wider world and starts interacting more closely with customers. For many companies the initial expansion is in their own country, where they establish a dominant position that creates a financial platform for further expansion. This is often followed by an expansion into familiar neighbouring countries. A delicate balance has to be struck between customizing to win the deal and getting a volume of standard products that cost less to produce. During this phase, the engineering and product organizations are supplemented by the sales, marketing and partnering organizations with their different professional cultures. This can create internal friction that needs to be managed. As the company grows, the need for some processes and managerial discipline becomes apparent and this may create friction with the previous, more flexible and pragmatic philosophy. However, being agile and flexible is still important. Most of the virtues from the innovation phase are still critical, though new capabilities start to become more important, including:

- Building longer-term relationships with customers and commercial partners
- Balancing pragmatism and flexibility with some processes discipline
- Timeliness/promptness versus simply winging it
- Balancing engineering (technical) with sales and marketing (customers).

Successful leaders are usually visible and lead from the front during this phase. At Sony, the CEO, Morita, would focus his attention on the international sales and marketing side. He was a truly global CEO, managing to be efficient when travelling constantly. He moved his family to New York for a period, as the American market grew in significance. He had four secretaries – two in Japan and two in America – and seemed to recover easily from trans-Pacific flights.[3] He had seemingly boundless energy. His management style was very personal and based on friendships. In essence, he created Sony in the image of a family with independent fiefdoms, reporting directly to him, the paternalistic father figure, and possessed the personal charisma and energy to keep this web of entities together.

National traits that tend to enable or derail during the expansion phase

The key national traits that support this phase are centred on dealing effectively with the wider world and balancing the entrepreneurial spirit with the

---

[3]Morita A. (1984) *Made in Japan*. Dutton, p. 120.

increasing requirement for more processes. However, those processes often have the hallmark of flexibility to suit a company that is still in the embryonic period. Key national organizational traits that are seen to support success or derail it in this period include:

- Openness and listening over being closed and insular
- Balancing short-term results with longer-term process orientation
- Balancing pragmatism with some process discipline.

When the crisis hit

A crisis can strike at any time, but the risk increases as the company transitions from one phase to the next. A new trait required to succeed may prove difficult to acquire as it rubs against deeply rooted national traits. If a company faces a transition involving a significant strategy change combined with a profound cultural change, you, the management, need to be aware, as this can be the precursor to a life-threatening crisis.

Let's now examine how Nokia fared as it raced through the initial phases in the embryonic and growth period, elegantly navigating the chasm between the individual phases, until Apple and then Google challenged its fundamental business model.

Case study: Nokia

Nokia is truly a phenomenon. The company revitalized an entire nation. It inspired people across the globe that the improbable can happen; the underdog coming from nowhere can achieve global dominance in a new industry. What the leadership team at Nokia achieved after 1991 is simply astonishing. In less than 10 years it became the largest technology company in Europe and the No. 1 global mobile technology company. This is the stuff Silicon legends are made of. But Nokia is not your typical Silicon Valley company; it originates in a rural region of Finland.

The Finnish culture

Nokia was founded in 1871 as a pulp mill company on the banks of the Nokia River near Tampere in southwestern Finland. It is a Finnish company with a culture based on strong Finnish rural values of honesty, integrity and hard work. The scepticism to outsiders, normally found in rural communities everywhere, had been accentuated by being under foreign influence for long periods, first by Sweden and later Russia, before Finland gained independence in 1917.

There is a unique Finnish quality called *Sisu*. *Sisu* is a combination of perseverance to overcome adversity combined with a long-term perspective. This was best exemplified during two brutal winter wars against Russia in 1939 and 1941, where Finland displayed true *Sisu* and also showed its capability of going-it-alone, its love of freedom and fierce individualism. Finns have a strong national pride, yet are humble. They are warm hearted, yet will not attempt to charm.[4]

The Finnish language has Asian roots and is not part of the Indo-European language group. Thus, the Finnish culture includes Asian traits of reflection, desire for solitude, emotional distance and sensitivity to losing face. While a Finn can act alone, he frequently takes refuge in a group and may, at times, only reluctantly engage in proactivity. No one has described this better than Richard D. Lewis, who is a fluent Finnish speaker, in his book *Finland, Cultural Lone Wolf*.[5] In the Lewis model, Finland is somewhere between the linear-active Europeans and the reactive Asians. At Nokia these national traits were combined with a classic engineering products culture with its factual, analytical and introverted mindset, the latter reinforced by the national tendencies for introspection.

Finns love good design. They are also creative, as seen in the popular mobile phone game Angry Birds and at Nokia, where Finnish engineers originally invented the SMS (Short Messaging System) technology.[6]

The embryonic period of the new Nokia 1.0

Over the years, Nokia evolved into a diversified conglomerate with activities in forest products, consumer electronics, television sets and PCs, rubber tyres, rubber boots and a small telephone business. By 1990, it was in poor financial shape after the collapse of the Soviet Union, Finland's main trading partner, in 1989.

---

[4]Lewis R.D. (2006) *When Culture Collides*. Nicholas Brealey, p. 331.
[5]Lewis R.D. (2005) *Finland, Cultural Lone Wolf*. Intercultural Press, Nicholas Brealey.
[6]Hakkarainen A. (2011) *Behind the Screen*. eBook, Amazon.

However, it had a young, ambitious and capable CEO, Jorma Ollila. He was appointed at the age of 39 in 1991. In 1992, he recommended to the board that Nokia should focus on mobile phones and infrastructure equipment, and thus Nokia 1.0 was created. From Jorma Ollila, the new Nokia would get its traits of competing to win, a global outlook and ambition.

Ollila attracted a golden generation of highly capable and ambitious executives: Matti Alahuhta, Pekka Ala-Pietilä, Sari Baldauf, Olli-Pekka Kallasvuo, Pertti Korhonen, Anssi Vanjoki and the designer Nuevo. They were all Finnish nationals. Together, they created a culture with an international outlook, ambition and strong Finnish roots. They were masterfully led and worked well together. They were swifter and more agile than the competition in their decision-making and able to translate a strategic decision into action quickly and cohesively.[7]

The mobile industry was about to take off. Nokia was the new kid on the block, competing with mature and slower moving companies who had grown big making fixed wire equipment. Nokia had a fresh and different perspective, which was appreciated by the new mobile operators. Nokia was ready and simply went for it!

With the new GSM standard, mobile phones quickly reached attractive consumer price points that would dramatically expand the market in Europe. The emerging markets soon after took off and Nokia was quick to expand into China, Asia and Latin America. The established competition was slow to react. Nokia used its Finnish design traditions, innovative and creative mindset and its experience with consumer electronics and retailing to design good-looking, durable and user-friendly handsets that soon became popular with consumers.

The Nokia brand was further accentuated when Nokia launched the hugely popular "Connecting People" campaign. Nokia was fun and friendly and helped the world connect from the businessman in New York to the farmer in India. Nokia empowered the global village to communicate before the Internet had arrived. When Nokia 1.0 quickly expanded geographically to Asia, China and Latin America, the subsidiary culture would adapt to the local culture, though there were significant efforts to promote a consistent Nokia culture, based on its Finnish virtues. Not all employees were Finnish by birth, but all new employees were proud of being part of Nokia with its unique values of

---

[7]Kosonen M., Doz Y. (2008) *Fast Strategy*. Wharton School Publishing.

personal respect, trust and empowerment. These early "Nokians", as they were affectionately called, were an eclectic mix of energetic entrepreneurs and people with management experience from the IT industry.

The work practices at Nokia 1.0

In the decentralized Nokia 1.0 organization, the sales-oriented country heads were encouraged to take sensible risks when making deals with the new operators while Nokia HQ maintained tight financial control. Empowerment and risk taking was expected and forgiveness granted if the intentions were right.

Nokia was still a relatively small company. Decision-making was informal and quick, while the tight financial controls ensured that employees did not go off-piste for too long. The engineering organization was still relatively small, with small teams organized around each new model introduced, and most often produced at a single factory. Thus, product design, engineering and manufacturing were all part of a simple process where key people in each function knew each other and could call each other if a problem occurred.

The top group around Jorma Ollila was physically together at the head-quarters in Helsinki, and would make major decisions swiftly and in unison. This enabled Nokia to create a fast, agile and assertive culture, compared to its more traditional competitors.[8]

Thus, national Finnish values and a new emerging industry, combined with the competitive spirits and leadership skills of a highly talented young group of world-class leaders, created the formula that quickly established Nokia as a world-class company. It soon developed a distinct, agile, hardworking, customer-oriented yet humble attitude and a resulting "we-can-do-it" cultural dynamic, with the executives leading from the front.

Nokia 1.0 brought out the best in Finnish culture. Many of the enabling traits were rooted in the Finnish psyche: hard work, honesty, sticking together to overcome adversity (*Sisu*) and facts orientation over emotions. Potentially derailing traits were neutralized: the Finnish go-it-alone instinct, which is connected to the scepticism vis-à-vis outsiders, the lack of emotional engagement, reluctance to engage proactively, as well as the reflective introversion. This enabled Nokia to develop a classical challenger profile and grow beyond what any other Finnish company had achieved before. Nokia was agile in the front line, quick in executing decisions at group level, customer centric and had

---

[8] As described in Kosonen, Doz (2008).

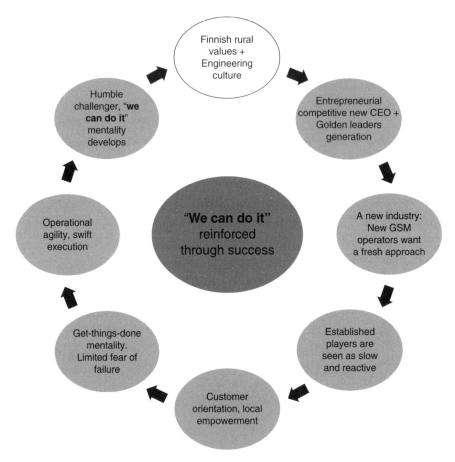

Diagram 5.3: The "we-can-do-it" cultural dynamics at Nokia 1.0 in the 1990s

simple shared objectives.[9] Nokia, true to its humble perspective on life, was also surprised by its own success and the ethos of Nokia 1.0 also reflected this.

The success reinforced the "we-can-do-it" cultural dynamic in a virtuous cycle, and Nokia's market capitalization grew 20-fold to €20 billion by end of 1997, from under €1 billion in 1990. In Diagram 5.3 we have sketched the "we-can-do-it" cultural dynamic.

However, not everything was perfect in the engine room. Fast growth and empowered entrepreneurship challenged the organization. Nokia relied on its "small company" informal network to get the task done, bypassing whatever process was in place when required. This prompted the leadership to fundamentally review the organizational structure and Nokia 2.0 was born.

[9]Kossonen, Doz (2008).

After a logistics crisis in 1995,[10] Nokia realized that its systems and work practices were no longer adequate for a rapidly growing multi-product line global business. It decided to pursue a strategy of becoming the most efficient supply-chain company in the consumer electronics space. Over the next 24 months, Nokia would create an unparalleled and complex organization that could concurrently design, manufacture and sell over 100 different phone models, marketed in over 150 countries, to over 500 operators, with each operator demanding the phones to be customized to work on their particular network.

Thus, Nokia had reached a classical transformation point, moving quickly through the embryonic period to reach the later stages of the growth period and the scale and efficiency phase. Nokia had to learn to master the processes, complexity and scale of a large corporation. These new work practices would slowly impact the culture and in time create two distinct cultural dynamics that no one had foreseen.

Nokia 2.0

Nokia became the low-cost producer in the industry, with strict financial controls in place and integrated end-to-end product creation, manufacturing and marketing processes. As with all large complex and process-oriented organizations, the complexity also increased the requirements for analysis, planning and disciplined cooperation. To help manage this complex organization, Nokia began hiring more MBAs and managers from global blue-chip corporations. The more entrepreneurially inclined Nokia 1.0 managers of the embryonic period left over the next few years. The top team began spending more time managing the complex interdependencies and governance requirements in a large global business and over time became less visible in the front line.

As these fundamental work practice changes took place, Nokia continued to out-execute the competition. First, the 2001 recession was overcome. Then Motorola challenged Nokia with the Razr and for a brief period threatened to overtake Nokia's dominant position. The strategic threat from Microsoft's Windows Mobile operating system was eliminated through the Symbian partnership. By 2000, its market capitalization reached €200 billion and after 1998 it would hold the No. 1 market share position in the industry for over 10 years. Nokia now employed over 100,000 employees globally.

---

[10]Hakkarainen (2011).

Slowly, a belief emerged that Nokia could fend off any challenge, by applying a dose of Finnish *Sisu* and utilizing its global scale advantage, the "Nokia System" as it anonymously was referred to, would prevail! The analytically inclined Finnish engineers and their newly hired colleagues trained in running large corporations thrived on designing and running a global complex matrix organization. Managers became increasingly focused on achieving their own narrow objectives without recognizing the systemic consequences of their decisions. Nokia became more bureaucratic, more process oriented and more hierarchical.

Culture change often lags behind a strategy change by three to five years, as we discussed in Chapter 1. During a transformation, success will be seen as proof of the effectiveness of the new work practices. Combine this with the simple observation that 'success has no memory' and it is easy to see how companies get into trouble. Success will reinforce the work practices present at the time of the success, as management will attribute it to their immediate actions, even though the actions and culture of the previous period may have enabled the success. This way, the negative influence of the new culture only appeared some time after the strategy change.

Slowly, the agility of Nokia 1.0 gave way to simply following the process and avoiding taking risks. There were fewer decision-makers. The complex nature of the organization required systemic insight into the interdependencies when making decisions and therefore many decisions were deferred upwards.

Fed by its success, the "we-can-do-it" challenger attitude gave way to a more arrogant and less proactive "we-are-the-best" derailing cultural dynamic as shown in Diagram 5.4. Nokia 2.0 had become more arrogant and more complacent.

In parallel, Nokia also became less customer and partner centric. Operators and suppliers increasingly complained about Nokia's arrogance, not listening to their perspective as it flexed its muscles. Customer centricity started to morph to the more introverted and analytical "Customer Remote" perspective, fuelled by Nokia's more confident attitude (Diagram 5.5).

These changes were reinforced by Finnish traits that had been neutralized earlier in Nokia 1.0, e.g. the reluctance to engage emotionally, while the go-it-alone traits, scepticism to outsiders and national pride, further reinforced the "we-are-the best" cultural dynamic. Thus, in effect, the "Nokia system" created a virtual distance between Nokia and its customers and stakeholders.

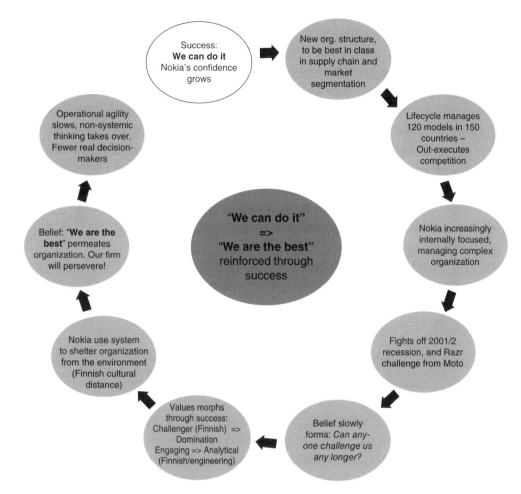

Diagram 5.4: The morphing of "we-can-do-it" to "we-are-the-best"

Obviously, these two cultural dynamics were not planned for, but simply the consequence of the complex changes in work practices necessary to support the new strategy. This is often what happens after reaching a transformation point! The unrelenting daily operation running a complex global organization makes it difficult for leaders to elevate themselves and take an outside-in perspective. Consequently, the two derailing cultural dynamics were not fully recognized or debated at the time. Instead they were reinforced by the success.

In 2006, at the peak of its market dominance, Jorma Ollila who was already chairman chose an internal successor as CEO, the CFO Olli-Pekka Kallasvuo. The executive leadership team continued with a majority of Finns and three non-Finns.

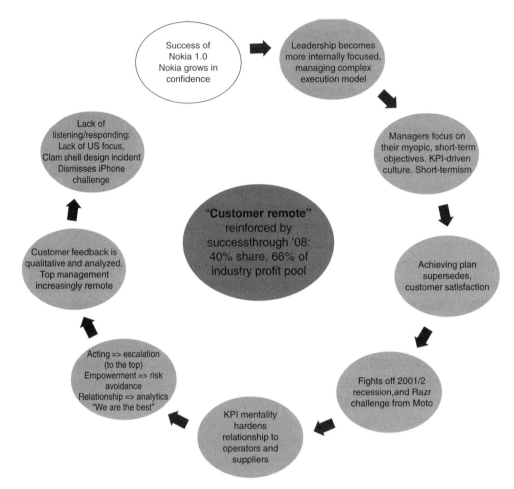

Diagram 5.5: The morphing from "Customer Centric" to "Customer Remote"

Nokia 3.0

In 2007, Apple launched the iPhone, and the year after Google launched Android. Nokia was at its peak of success when it suddenly faced two new formidable competitors. Essentially, Apple challenged Nokia's basic strategic game: Why have a hundred different models when you can have one insanely good one that comes with thousands of applications and exciting content? Compared to Nokia, Apple and Google had a significant advantage in architecting complex software and building a content ecosystem with skills which were more readily available in Silicon Valley than in Finland.

Nokia at first dismissed the iPhone, "it is not a good phone", and technically they probably were right. Nokia was then hit by the 2008/9 recession and was slow to react to the new competition. By 2010 it found itself in a challenging competitive situation with Apple and Google taking share in the profitable high-end smartphone segment and Asian competitors in the low-end segment. It also became increasingly clear that the core Symbian operating system was outdated. By Q1 2011, Nokia's market share had dropped from 40% in 2007, to 25.1%[11] – the level they had in 1997 and at the end of the year the market cap had dropped to €14 billion. Nokia 3.0 was about to be born.

In September 2010, Nokia hired their first non-Finnish and external CEO, Stephen Elop, a Canadian national with a strong track record in the US technology sector, including running the Office Products division at Microsoft. After reviewing the options, he launched a new strategy, announcing a strategic partnership with Microsoft. Windows Mobile would become Nokia's primary smartphone strategy, and the two companies would use their combined capabilities and assets to strengthen the Windows Mobile ecosystem.

Elop launched the new strategy by publicizing a now infamous "Burning Platform" memo – comparing Nokia's situation to that of a man waking up in the middle of the night on a burning oil platform. The message being: "You sometimes have to jump into dark, cold and icy waters to survive . . ." This fundamental change in strategy would also require a cultural transformation, as he said in the memo: "We, too, are standing on a 'burning platform,' and we must decide how we are going to change our behavior." Nokia had reached a crisis point where dramatic action was required. Only the future will tell if Nokia can once again reinvent itself and become a relevant challenger in the global mobile industry! It certainly has done it before and the national traits will support a period of hard work and perseverance to achieve this. Never discount the Finns!

However, whatever happens in the future, and the first Windows mobile phones have been successfully launched, Nokia has spawned a plethora of young and innovative companies that have benefited from the new skills and global perspective that Nokia has brought to Finland. This should not be underestimated at the national level. With Nokia, Finland has become stronger and more competitive as a nation.

[11] http://www.mobilenewscwp.co.uk/2011/05/nokia-market-share-slips-to-lowest-in-14-years/.

Now that you are familiar with the Finnish culture, let's have a look at another Finnish company, KONE, and how the founder influenced a different but very successful internationalization strategy.

Case study: KONE – agility and humility

KONE is a Finnish manufacturer of lifts and cranes – the third largest in the world in its cluster. As in the case of Nokia, many eyebrows were raised at the prospect of a modest-sized company from a nation of 5 million inhabitants securing a dominant position in a major world industry. How did they achieve this feat in a rapid surge in development between the years 1967 and 2010? What was their business strategy? How were they able to change their corporate image (surely Finnish culture is relatively unknown to many) in order to synchronize rapid change and cultural imperatives?

KONE's business strategy from 1966 was international growth through acquisitions. American companies beat all-comers making acquisitions mainly through financial muscle. What was remarkable about KONE's purchases was that they started acquiring rivals considerably larger than themselves and in major manufacturing countries such as France, Germany, Italy, Spain, Belgium and the USA. How did they get away with this and why were good relations quickly developed with the French, German, American and other managers?

Richard Lewis, based in Finland in the early 1970s, got to know the KONE management just when they embarked on their ambitious expansion. As he became involved with their cultural and linguistic training, he realized that their board consisted not only of more than a dozen exceptionally forward-looking individuals, led by the legendary Pekka Herlin, but also that it was one of the most diversified groups he had worked with and consequently was admirably equipped to combine worldviews and perspectives. It was an agile, multi-cultural team in itself with German, French, British and Australian members to add spice to some outstanding Finns and Finn-Swedes whom Herlin had assembled.

KONE's acquisition programme was extremely ambitious. They devoured big names such as Westinghouse Europe, Montgomery USA, UK Lift Company, Fuji Elevator, Havemeier & Sander and Asea-Graham in rapid succession, acquiring not only manufacturing units, but entire staff and management systems steeped in the national cultural traits of France, Germany, the USA, etc. The business strategy was clarion clear – rapid growth, integration and consolidation, economies of scale and satisfactory profits. The cultural clashes, nearly a dozen different ones, loomed ominously.

Pekka Herlin, though renowned for his strong will and resilience, declared as early as 1972 that "there is no way that problems spread all over the world can be solved from Helsinki". The far-seeing chairman made it a principle from the first acquisitions that Finnish teams moving in should give considerable leeway to local management. Finns, known for their common-sense and humility, had a healthy respect for the positions and achievements of companies belonging to countries bigger than Finland. This respectful approach maintained much of the touch and feel of the best cultural features of acquired companies and consequently minimized customer flight. "Local excellence backed by global resources" became KONE's slogan. The KONE corporate culture during the 33-year period of acquiring 26 companies changed from being stubbornly Finnish (small-but-good, rural values are best) to truly international (multi-faceted, adaptable, tolerant). The cultural change preceded the implantation of strategic imperatives, or at the very least took place in tandem with them. Finnish humility and relaxed management traits obviated the multiple conflicts, misunderstandings, tension and gaffes that occurred because of lack of preparation in the case of Walmart. Matti Alahuhta, KONE's current CEO, himself a relaxed and genial senior executive, now presides over the KONE far-sighted philosophy in its service and maintenance division, with the slogan "CARE FOR LIFE".

Changing corporate culture in time requires nimbleness and agility – often easier to find in small nations such as the Netherlands and the four Nordic countries than in bigger ones with cumbersome structures and more complex cultural baggage.

Case study: Walmart – an American business tackling foreign markets

In 2004, Walmart was the biggest business in the world with sales of 220 billion US dollars, comfortably ahead of Exxon Mobil ($196 billion), General Motors ($177 billion) and BP ($174.2 billion). Indeed, its turnover exceeded the GDP of most countries on the planet and would have ranked 21st – just behind Belgium and ahead of Sweden and a host of powerful state economies such as Poland, Norway, Turkey, Saudi Arabia, Indonesia, Iran, South Africa, Singapore, Hong Kong, Pakistan and United Arab Emirates. In many ways,

Walmart was the ideal prototype of a US corporation – huge, ubiquitous, aggressive, successful, profitable, possessing a formidable brand and meticulous national organization. It owned 3800 stores in the United States alone and dwarfed the biggest non-American stores such as Tesco, Asda, Sainsbury's, Kaufhof, Metro, Carrefour and Stockmann. It was only natural that such a retail giant would seek to expand its operations into other countries, especially those with strong economies and/or massive populations.

The business strategy beckoned crystal clear. It remained to be seen if Walmart would find cultural acceptance in its target markets. Two obvious ones, for different reasons, were Germany and China. Germany, since reunification, boasted a healthy population of 80 million, most of whom were consumer oriented and with cash to spend. Their main stores, Kaufhof and Karstadt, were busy and profitable. The disastrous merger of Daimler and Chrysler (combined global sales of $150 billion) had highlighted the deep rift between German and American cultural habits and business aspirations, but one could also recognize that the two nations had several commonalities. These included a driving work ethic, a cult of efficiency, a linear approach to tasks, punctuality, disciplined agendas, results orientation and emphasis on competitive prices and reliable delivery dates.

These are business behaviours and work practices. Would cultural styles align in similar fashion? Would Walmart change its corporate culture and image in time to appear acceptable in the German environment?

In the 1990s, Walmart bought two German store chains – Wertkauf for $375 million (21 stores) and Interspar for $750 million (74 stores). It set about Americanizing these establishments. One thing about the Walmart cultural image in the USA is that it is intrinsically American (not unsurprising in view of it having been founded in Arkansas): straightforward, intensely friendly, classless, pushy, engaging the customer the moment he/she comes through the door ("How are you today, sir? How can I be of help? Let me show you . . . We have a great new line in . . ."). The attendant attaches himself to the customer, intending to walk him round the store. On leaving, "Have a good day!" follows the client on to the street. American customers expect, accept and are agreeably lulled by these pleasantries. British customers find them over the top; Germans see them as intrusive and inane. How a German feels today is his own business and he does not wish to be quizzed about it. He will construct his own "good day". Above all, he does not wish to be followed all over the shop.

Unfortunately, paying little attention to variations in greetings cultures, Walmart foisted the American version on the German public, compounding the error by instructing its attendants (who varied in nationality) to accompany these cheerful inanities with a wide, Hollywood-type smile, irrespective of the reaction. This approach works well in the United States – the very size of Walmart proves this. The considerable cultural change required for German customers was not effected.

Walmart, confident of American methods (and freewheeling culture), persisted in trying to remake Wertkauf and Interspar in its own image. In fact, Walmart was not experienced in the area of acquisitions and mergers. The founding company had been built ground-up in the USA and Canada. It therefore lacked managerial skills needed to create synergy between themselves and the staff of non-American acquired companies. Often, top management refused to acknowledge the differences in customer behaviour in other countries. German customers are not similar to American or Canadian customers. For instance, Germans like to see advertised discount products up front, without having to query store attendants. Such discounted products in Germany are placed at eye level, facilitating readiness to purchase.

Walmart in Germany, however, used the American merchandise display custom of keeping premium priced products in the foreground and discounted prices less visible, on higher shelves or in the bottom racks. German shoppers were irritated by this. They also liked to carry out their own search for marketing and do not wish to be influenced by sales talk during their own foraging. Top management at Walmart consistently failed to give adequate acknowledgement to German habits and preferences. The first head of German operations was an expat from the USA, with hardly any knowledge of German culture. He actually insisted that all business operations be carried out in English. It is hard to imagine senior executives in the United States failing to appreciate the value of working in the language of the country! Walmart had shown much wisdom in its marketing in the United States, but blatantly neglected the necessity of making concessions to another culture – even one as important as the German.

This neglect led them to commit many of the same cultural gaffes that Daimler had done with Chrysler executives in 2004/5 (for a full account see *When Teams Collide* by R. Lewis, NB Publishing, 2012, pp. 28–37). Not all were so obvious and objected to in the same way as the greetings episodes, but by 2006 it was apparent that Walmart faced relative failure in Germany (with cumulative losses in the billions of dollars and Walmart Germany losing over $150 million annually) and it was decided in the summer of 2006 to sell the stores to Metro at an apparently good price of $750 million.

Here again cultural issues intervened. Walmart utilized American GAAP (Generally Accepted Accounting Principles) when providing information to Metro during the negotiation process and Walmart reporting an apparent gain. The purchasers, however, conducted the transaction according to HGB – the German version of GAAP. The final purchase and sale agreement specified German GAAP as the standard for determining any purchase price adjustments. German GAAP allows for the accrual of a greater number of contingency reserves than US GAAP. A year after the sale, when all purchase price adjustments created by Metro were proposed, the result was Metro requiring an adjustment to the purchase price which in effect resulted in Walmart paying back to Metro the entire purchase price.

Some time later, in an internal meeting, Mike Duke, then CEO of Walmart International, was asked how he felt about the pace of Walmart expansion worldwide. Duke replied that they had learnt from mistakes made in Germany and that Walmart was slowing the process of Americanization of international stores accordingly. For instance, stores that Walmart was buying in Latin America were to be allowed to trade under their own names. Similarly, in London, where Walmart owned 100% of Asda, the British store was allowed to continue to trade under the Asda name.

Walmart in China

In late 2007, Walmart purchased an interest in Trustmart, a small chain of stores in China. Walmart was operating in China at the time, but growth acceleration was desired. Walmart bought less than 50% but had a right to buy the balance of the chain over time. Again, serious cultural considerations had not been examined. It turned out that the former owners of Trustmart and all of the store managers were not PRC Chinese but Taiwanese. Apparently, the Taiwanese had some income tax issues in China related to their Chinese wages. Walmart was uneasy with this situation but, in its usual hurry, went ahead with the purchase. As a good American company, it decided they would regularize things and become compliant.

Walmart hired a third party to help sort out these issues. Unfortunately they found out they had to deal with many local jurisdictions on these tricky issues. The locals were uniformly uneasy. Had the authorities been complicit or incompetent regarding these irregularities? Many difficult meetings followed. Subsequently, whether related or not, Walmart found it problematic to obtain permits to open new stores for the Trustmart business. They had envisaged opening thousands of stores in China over time (among a population of 1.3 billion). Ultimately, the Walmart China CEO resigned. This is another case of business strategy being executed ahead of cultural adjustment.

Walmart in South Korea

Walmart were also unsuccessful in Korea after entering the Korean market in 1998. Despite being firm US allies on the political and military fronts, Koreans, with their traditional Confucian ethics and tightly-controlled business practices, were alienated by the effusive "greeters" and the naïve Walmart ploy of calling all employees "associates". Walmart withdrew from Korea in 2006, selling all its 16 stores to Shinsegae, a local retailer, for $882 million. Shinsegae rebranded the stores as E-marts.

Walmart cultural adjustments

Fortunately, Walmart executives, still headed by S. Robson Walton (chairman), the eldest son of Sam Walton, and the perspicacious CEO Mike Duke, have shown their ability to learn from past mistakes and adapt to nation-state cultures in the countries they have expanded into. In 2012 the organization had grown impressively, with 8500 stores in 15 countries under 55 different names. It began to realize that the Walmart name did not always bring with it the best connotations. First, it was modified: Walmex in Mexico. In the UK, when Walmart bought Asda it wisely kept the name, as Asda was already a household name in Britain. A similar policy was adopted in Japan where the name Seiyu was retained. In India, Walmart decided to operate under the name Best Price. In Canada, where the 122 stores of Woolworth Canada were acquired (now 300), the first three stores, opened in 2006 in Hamilton, London and Aurora, Ontario, were called Supercentres – note the spelling in Canadian English! Even in the United States, in towns like Houston and Phoenix, where Hispanic customers are numerous, stores opened in 2009/10 were called Supermercados de Walmart.

In terms of modernizing their corporate culture, Walmart has responded positively to regional and international concerns, providing rapid help to victims of the Hurricane Katrina disaster in 2005, donating $20 million in cash, 1500 truckloads of free merchandise and food for 100,000 meals. In an initiative to become "a good steward for the environment" goals were established in

2005 to reduce greenhouse gas emissions by 20% in seven years and reduce energy use in stores by 30%. Three more experimental stores were designed for southern states such as Texas with wind turbines, solar panels, water-cooled refrigerators and bio-fuel-capable boilers. Steps were taken to ensure Walmart would become the biggest seller of organic milk and the biggest buyer of organic cotton in the world. Encouraged by a group headed by Michelle Obama, Walmart announced a programme to improve the nutritional values of its store brands, gradually reducing the amount of salt and sugar and eliminating trans fats.

In a new approach to China, Walmart bought a 51% shareholding in Yihao-dian, a Chinese online supermarket, noting, however, that the expansion was subject to Chinese government regulatory approval. As Walmart had previously struggled to try to export its rigid model overseas, it now makes attempts to adapt to local tastes. For instance, in China it found that Chinese consumers preferred to select their own live fish and seafood, so its stores have begun to install fish tanks, leading to higher sales.

Finally, realizing that the cultures of potential new markets must be scrutinized in advance, Walmart appointed the German retailing veteran Stephan Fanderl as President of Walmart Emerging Markets – East, to explore business opportunities in Russia and neighbouring states.

Chapter close – preview the growth period

In each of our three cases it is evident that every company will need to find its own way as it navigates the various phases based on its national cultures and strategic imperatives. Navigating a transformation point from one phase to the next is a critical moment in every organization's life. It is essential for the management to understand the perils well in advance and not to take success for granted. As in the Nokia case, the immediate change of work practices to overcome a transformation point may be successful; however, the subsequent changes in culture and the creation of new cultural dynamics are rarely considered in advance. In the case of Walmart, blindly believing that the formula which was so successful in the home market can be easily exported proved to be a costly assumption.

In the next chapter we will venture to a new continent, and look at how two Asian companies, Sony and Samsung, fared as they took two different routes to compete in the global consumer electronics industry.

6

In this chapter, we will discuss the growth period, when the company continues its geographical expansion, often beyond the more familiar neighbouring countries. As it expands the number of product lines and the number of customer segments the company addresses, it becomes a more mature corporation needing global processes. It will need different skills and capabilities to be successful, and different national traits will impact its success, compared to the embryonic period.

While the transformation from one phase to the next often appears evolutionary, the requirements for different work practices combined with a new mix of national and business influencers can be disruptive. We will use the case of Samsung versus Sony to compare and contrast the fortunes of these two global consumer electronics giants and study the perils of globalization as national and business influencers impact the execution of the strategy.

A typical example of this is the important decision that non-American companies have to make when contemplating how to expand in the USA. Should they hire a local leader or relocate an expat? Or should they acquire a local company with products that are better suited to the local needs? Companies often mix these strategies over time, as they realize that each has its own pitfalls. A familiar case study of a European company entering the USA may look like this:

> "Company X – a market leader in Europe – comes to America to open new markets and compete on the larger stage. Egalitarian European executives, unable – or unwilling – to rationalize the high salaries top US talent expects, hire less expensive, and often less skilled, candidates to run the US outpost. That team, made up of 'B' and 'C' players, underperforms relative to their 'A' team competition. The home country executives

start to lose confidence in their American colleagues. When those colleagues then begin asking for product or service modifications to suit American customers – often costly but almost always necessary – the Europeans refuse them due to a lack of confidence in the team, a lack of understanding of the customer or a combination of both. The company underperforms further as customers choose competitive products more tailored to their needs. A trusted European is sent over 'to clean things up'. That executive usually does not understand the local market in detail, and performance deteriorates even further. Headquarters makes a clean sweep of US employees and tries to start all over again, repeating the same pattern of hiring on the cheap and then compounding the talent issues with cultural missteps.

Sometimes, a European challenger will try to 'buy' their market positioning by acquiring a US firm but, inevitably, get derailed by the same issues: They acquire on the cheap, and the firm underperforms relative to competitors with higher market caps. Home country executives lose confidence in the company and reject its strategic counsel. The company further underperforms, and the vicious cycle of deteriorating performance gains intensity until the European company pulls the plug on what it sees as an ill-fated venture or simply accepts a lower share.

It does not have to happen this way. By giving more credence and a higher priority to conducting due diligence upfront, establishing robust people processes and 'Americanizing' their initiatives, European companies *can* position themselves for success in the US market."[1]

Let's now look at the two new phases in this period: the product line expansion phase, and the scale and efficiency phase. *The growth period is all about balancing the opposing needs of the innovative and flexible embryonic organization with the needs of the more disciplined mature company* as seen in Diagram 6.1.

The product line expansion stage

Description of this phase

In this period, a company often dramatically expands its product portfolio. Sony's first products included a transistor radio and a tape-recorder, and at

---

[1] Adapted from Hoover B., Hammerich K. (2009) Building the "A" Team in America. White paper. Russell Reynolds Associates.

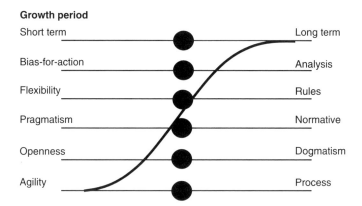

Diagram 6.1: The growth period

Samsung Electronics, they included DRAMs and TVs. Both went from a couple of lines to mastering virtually all product categories in consumer electronics in less than 15 years. In the case of Sony, they even invented a couple of them: the portable transistor radio and the Walkman.

As the company expands its geographic coverage beyond the familiar neighbouring countries, it often finds that the products need to be localized to accommodate differences in consumer preferences, product standards and distribution channels or for legislative reasons. Companies often find that even seemingly insignificant differences can have a big effect on their success.

In his first job, Kai Hammerich was a marketing manager at HP – responsible for a small line of computer systems in Denmark. There had been a sticky issue with printers, which were designed in the USA, as they did not print the three special Danish characters, æ, ø and å. Considering the complexity of a printer, this was not considered a big issue by product marketing; Denmark being a tiny market in the overall scheme of things. However, for the Danish customers it was a problem, and severely impacted the success of the product line. Imagine printing English text, without having the letters "a, o and t", instead having the characters ";, + and &" printed. The sentence "That looks pretty awful" would thus be printed: "&h;& l++ks pre&&y ;wful".

Over several months, there had been a dialogue about the problem with product engineering in Palo Alto. This didn't happen directly, but through the European product marketing group, which managed the interface between the country offices and product engineering, but to no avail. However and by chance, one day Kai's manager Lars Ole Hansen was in Palo Alto and coincidentally bumped into the engineer responsible for the printer and explained the issue. The engineer listened carefully and smiled: "Oh is that really an issue? I can fix that easily for you; I just need to change the character table settings." The next day the issue was fixed for all the printers.

This small example exemplifies the realities a company faces, as it increases the geographical coverage while expanding the number of products. The complexity goes up exponentially and so does the need for processes and systems to deal with this complexity. This is where the agility of the embryonic period meets the bureaucracy of scale. Small issues that could have been resolved through personal contacts become big issues. National cultures will play a big role in how a company establishes these new work practices and resolves these inherent conflicts of objectives. The original culture from the embryonic period will still be visible; however, as the new processes start to guide behaviour, the corporate culture may change. Enabling business traits in the product-line expansion phase include:

- Disciplined/evolutionary innovation
- Process and discipline; mastering planning, budgeting and execution
- Balancing agility with a control and quality orientation
- Longer-term and more strategic orientation, while still being agile.

National traits that tend to enable or derail during the innovation phase

- Innovation (creativity, openness) versus managing the system
- Instilling processes, structure and discipline versus action-orientation
- Empowerment versus rules based and disciplined decision-making
- Balancing the long and short term.

As we saw in the Austin and Nokia cases, the national traits supporting innovation (individualism, agility, creativity) and efficiency (discipline, processes and organization) may rub against each other and create significant conflicts and unintended cultural dynamics.

The scale and efficiency phase

As the industry matures, there is a drive towards more efficiency often through sheer scale and the desire for a stronger global market position. This phase is often characterized by the creation of strong global processes, more discipline and a short-term execution and results focus. While the root culture, myths and rituals from the embryonic period may still be present and publically revered, the increased focus on processes to drive scale and efficiency will start placing a permanent and often irreversible mark on the culture. A new breed of employees is hired. They are often better trained and better qualified to manage complexity, but also less entrepreneurial.Companies from countries with strong individualism and an innovative creative bias, which thrived during the embryonic period, may well struggle now. Countries like Denmark and the UK have a high proportion of small and medium enterprise (SME) companies. Larger nations, in particular those with a history of organizing at scale at many levels of society, often thrive during this phase, though not always. This is the phase where Austin stumbled and Toyota thrived, as we shall see in the next chapter, and where execution-oriented and disciplined Samsung Electronics rose to become the largest consumer electronics company in the world. Key enabling business traits include:

- Managing complexity and process discipline
- Balancing risk, revenues, costs and margins
- Long-term relationship building; partnering and collaboration with equals.

During this period, a company often moves beyond the direct influence of the founders and establishes a managerial regime. As this happens, it will often display national traits that have become closer to the national root culture, however, now without the founders present to neutralize potentially derailing dynamics.

In both phases, urgency is still important. Getting there first with a new product will enable you to gain experience to patent critical intellectual property and get to economies of scale and thus lower cost first. However, companies may lose this simple insight, as they trust the "system" to deliver against competition and allow the instinctive hesitation of its national culture to prevail.

National traits that tend to enable or derail during the scale and efficiency phase

- Results versus strengthening processes, structure and discipline
- Controlled empowerment and risk taking versus rule-oriented decision-making

- Flexibility and pragmatism versus a normative orientation and dogmatism
- Long-term orientation versus short-term.

As the managerial system starts to gain a life of its own, the risk of invisible and derailing cultural dynamics increases. The disciplined work practices will start influencing the corporate culture and reinforce new habits, sometimes with the unintended consequences of a cultural dynamic.

In the case of Sony and Samsung you will notice how the reactive national culture played very different roles in the two companies. Both companies had reached the scale and efficiency phase when they had to deal with a technology disruption as industry differentiators moved from analogue (mechanical) to digital (semi-conductors and software).

Case study: Sony versus Samsung Electronics

Sony

The Japanese national culture

As discussed in Chapter 3, unique Japanese nation-state traits that may enable or derail success for Japanese companies include:

- Poor linguists
- Face protection, honour
- Ultra-courtesy
- Age-based hierarchy
- The company (*kaisha*) is sacred
- Long termism.

In this case we will examine what effect these traits had on Sony's strategy execution and how this was different from the influence of the Korean national values at Samsung Electronics.

The history of Sony

The embryonic period

Sony is a family company created by two men: Masaru Ibuka, the original founder, and Akio Morita, a charismatic and energetic leader, yet better known internationally. Masaru Ibuka was a brilliant engineer and Morita's senior by 13 years.[2] He was well connected being the son-in-law of Tamon Maeda – a right-hand man to Prince Fumimaro, a former prime minister of Japan. Ibuka and Morita first met in the navy's technical labs during WWII. In 1946, Ibuka set up a company on the outskirts of Tokyo, known as Totsuko,[3] and soon Morita joined Ibuka and his 12 employees. The vision for the company was to be "an innovator, a clever company that would make new high technology products in ingenious ways"[4].

Morita was Sony's CEO for more than 40 years. He too had a privileged background coming from the Aichi prefecture, where his family had owned a successful sake brewery for generations. His family had an unusually international mindset and interest in the arts – in particular music. Morita learned English at a young age and as a young teenager was fascinated by electronics and built an early crude electric phonograph and a radio. Later he gained an engineering degree.

Like most start-ups, the company would make anything to survive. The company's first commercially successful product – after failing to design an automatic electrical rice cooker – was a tape-recorder. In 1948, Ibuka travelled to the USA, to study tape-recorder manufacturing, and there learned about a new small device called the transistor. This inspired Sony to get the technology licence for transistors from Western Electric. Ibuka's engineers greatly advanced the transistor manufacturing process and discovered the diode tunnelling effect, which later earned Esaki, a Sony researcher, a Nobel Prize in 1973.

The transistor laid the foundation for Sony's first successful consumer product, a pocket transistor radio, in spite of the advice from Western Electric that the transistor could only be used for small consumer products such as hearing aids and not for radios.[5] In 1958, the company changed its name to Sony, combining the word *sonus* meaning sound in Latin and *sonny*, a nickname for a small boy.[6]

---

[2]Morita A. (1984) *Made in Japan*. Dutton, pp. 16, 30.
[3]Tokyo Tsushin Kogyo K.K. (Tokyo Telecommunications Engineering Corporation), also known as Totsuko (http://www.sony.net/SonyInfo/CorporateInfo/History/history.html), Nov. 2012.
[4]Morita A. (1984), p. 50.
[5]Morita A. (1984), pp. 60–70.
[6]Chang S.-J. (2010) *Samsung vs Sony*. Wiley, p. 10.

The growth period

Over the next two decades Sony would amaze the world with a string of products based on their innovative capabilities, thereby redefining the global consumer electronics industry. First came the Trinitron TV, where Sony greatly improved the existing cathode ray technology. Then came the immensely successful Walkman in 1979, selling over 100 million units. Sony created entirely new product categories such as video tape-recorders, CD players, camcorders, digital video disc players and the 3.5″ floppy disc. These were the pinnacle years for Sony. In short, Sony successfully combined mastery of analogue technologies with innovation, miniaturization, an understanding of customer trends, a global perspective and high-quality products that were technologically cutting edge. This period reinforced the belief that Sony on its own could create proprietary technology and world-class, consumer electronics products.

Sony also diversified into music and entertainment, with mixed commercial success, taking full control of its 1968 joint venture with CBS records in 1988, under the name CBS Sony Records, and in 1989 it acquired Columbia Pictures. This acquisition was a strategic response to the Betamax failure, a failure that created a deep wound in Sony's psyche and became embedded in its business values. The competing VHS video format had won, despite being technically inferior, in Sony's eyes, to its Betamax standard. More manufacturers embraced the VHS format. The larger installed base made it more attractive for movie companies to use when releasing movies on video and thus Betamax ultimately failed. Following this, Sony always strived to make its proprietary technology the standard, as exemplified by the 3.5″ floppy disc and the Blu-ray technology used in DVD players, and accelerated Sony's strategy of owning entertainment software, as it called content.

The industry transitioned from analogue to digital. However, as the world moved from the analogue into the digital age, Sony struggled to keep up. In 1995, Nobuyuki Idei became the president of Sony, the first non-engineer and salaryman, a Japanese term indicating he was not a founder or closely related to the founders. He had a vision of "The Digital Kid" that correctly predicted a networked and digital content-driven future, linking all their devices in home entertainment on a single platform. However, he and Sony ultimately proved unable to deliver fully on it. Sony's only notable success in the digital era so far has been the PlayStation, created by the maverick engineer Ken Kutaragi.

When Apple introduced the iPod in 2001, Sony was well positioned and had many of the skills and capabilities necessary to compete, but diluted its focus and didn't exploit its unique strategic advantage combining devices and content. Sony had planned the introduction of two digital music players from different divisions that did not cooperate: the Memory Stick Walkman from Personal Audio Products division and the Vaio Music Clip from the IT Products division. Equally significant was Sony's sensitivity to the copying of music, having its own record label. Consequently, its audio products came with cumbersome digital rights management software known as "Open MagicGate". Furthermore, when Sony introduced the unsuccessful Network Walkman HD-1, the company made it incompatible with the popular MP3 format, in contrast to the competing iPod. Thus, instead of benefiting from the ownership of both content and devices, Sony found itself in a perpetual conflict of interest between the two.

Sony, intellectually, was aware of the need to transform its capabilities and that software was a key factor for success in the digital age. In an analysis from 2005 to determine what Sony's strategic options were, it was noted that while Sony had 300 "true" software engineers who could architect and build modern software, Microsoft had 30,000, of which 3000 were working on consumer electronics software. Sony also recognized the need to shift the culture from one of being "closed" to becoming "knowledge intensive" – sharing, partnering and cooperating with others in contrast to their ingrained proprietary focus. However, despite being aware, Sony proved slow to react to its own insights, often a sign that a derailing cultural dynamic is at play.

The founders and the values they embedded

Akio Morita

Richard D. Lewis lived for five years in Japan in the late 1960s and knew Akio Morita: "Under Morita, Sony was a star amongst the Japanese corporations," Richard explains. "Morita was the most Westernized CEO of any Japanese company. He had an open mind and wasn't particularly Japanese. He had an engaging and charismatic persona. He networked constantly to promote Sony and had an open door policy being accessible to people he met, whether Japanese or Westerners. He would often give them his personal phone number to call if they needed him."

Richard further reflected: "He understood how to balance the Japanese culture with the needs of a global business. In Japan one's position is fundamentally based on tenure. If you have 1000 Japanese managers you will have 1000 rungs on the ladder." Morita then explained to Richard: "it can be difficult to promote young talent over more experienced employees". He circumvented this elegantly by identifying a small group of talented individuals, the leaders of the future, which he would groom personally, such as the later president Ogha. They would have his personal attention and his phone number, but he could not promote them ahead of their time and make them boss of an older person. But he would send them on international assignments for development purposes and discuss their ideas directly with them, approve them, which would then give them the confidence to execute them.

Morita outlined his Japanese philosophy on management in his memoirs: "The most important mission for a Japanese manager is to develop a healthy relationship with his employees, to create a family-like feeling within the corporation, a feeling that employees and managers share the same fate."[7] He would address new employees telling them: "We did not draft you. This is not the army, so that means you have voluntarily chosen Sony. This is your responsibility and normally if you join this company we expect you will stay for the next twenty or thirty years."[8] He believed in forgiveness and that Japanese companies were better than American ones in balancing long-term interests with short-term, often willing to sacrifice short-term profits for long-term gains.

Morita focused his attention on international sales and marketing. He was a modern global CEO, managing to be efficient when travelling constantly. His management style was personal and based on friendships with the executives reporting to him, which he (reluctantly) would fire if necessary. Unlike many Japanese companies, he would let local people run the local operations quite independently; Americans in America and Europeans in Europe. This led to the creation of a web of siloed fiefdoms, dependent on his personal charisma and energy to keep the entities together, but also to increase frictions once Morita's presence faded.

Masuru Ibuka

An engineering genius, Masuru Ibuka directed the development of many of Sony's successes. Ibuka was a traditional Japanese leader, and the culture in the engineering and products organization was markedly different from the

---

[7]Morita (1984), p. 130.
[8]Morita (1984), p. 131.

culture in the international organization directed by Morita. It was more traditionally Japanese, more hierarchical and deeply respectful of Japanese societal values. Most of the engineering and research employees were Japanese, and were based in Japan.

Both men were almighty, and no one dared to go against them. They were fast decision-makers and even when Sony grew big and complex, the company's decision-making structure did not change: Morita and Ibuka made all the big decisions.[9]

Work practices and leadership post-Morita

Morita and Ibuka formed their inner circles based on their personal relationships. Ohga, the successor to Morita, met them both when he was young. In 1989, he became CEO of Sony and in 1994 he succeeded Morita as Sony chairman, marking the end of Morita's reign. Ohga's behaviour and decision-making patterns were similar to those of Ibuka and Morita. His management style was autocratic, and people described his tenure as president and chairman as "the tyranny of Ohga". The members of the inner circle were expected to be loyal and committed, and some exercised considerable power while manipulating their personal relationship with Sony's founders.[10]

Before a stroke hospitalized Morita, he told Ohga to find a successor among his engineers. Ohga had trouble finding one and Morita gave him permission to appoint a non-engineer. Later, Ohga would publically admit that choosing Idei was a mistake. Idei lacked the support from the engineers, did not have Morita's charisma and had not been trained to be a CEO of a Fortune100 corporation. Consequently, the power position of Idei was weak.

To strengthen his power position, Idei reformed the governance structure – adapting a Western philosophy in 1999, with a board of independent directors and a simpler management structure, and less dependence on complex personal relationships. He reduced the size of the top leadership team and reorganized the 19 independent divisions into four independent business units. He would reorganize Sony on a regular, if not annual, basis, which can be an early indication of a failing corporation.[11] Idei's attempts to restructure

[9]Chang (2010), p. 138.
[10]Chang (2010), p. 140.
[11]According to Collins J. (2009) *How the Mighty Fall*. Random House.

and reform Sony along Western management principles may also have over-looked the fact that Sony's management practices and employee base were fundamentally Japanese, as Sea-Jin Chang concludes in her book *Samsung vs Sony*.[12]

In 2005, Howard Stringer, the former president of Sony Pictures and Sony America, replaced Idei. Stringer, a British national, who had a 30-year career at CBS, starting as a journalist, ultimately became president of CBS Inc., before joining Sony in 1997 as head of America. He was the first non-Japanese CEO of a major independent Japanese company. Soon after taking over, Howard Stringer noted: "It's not about the absence of great engineers, or the absence of great ideas. It's about the orchestration of the engineering groups and deploying them effectively." He also admitted that Sony needs "better integration between our services and device portfolio".[13]

Financial results

In the fiscal year ending 31 March 2012, Sony had yen 6.5 trillion ($82 billion) in sales, down 10% on 2011. Since 2008, Sony has had four years of increasing operational losses and its market capitalization had dropped to less than $15 billion by 2012.

In early 2012, Stringer stepped down as president and CEO, replaced by Japanese Kazuo Hirai, a Sony long-timer, and became chairman of the board of Sony. As Stringer stepped down, he noted[14] that what he had found particularly difficult was: "That the urge for consensus often would conflict with the need to change", a critical disadvantage, as Sony faced Korean Samsung – a new formidable competitor.

Samsung Electronics

The South Korean national culture

Korea's last dynasty, "The Choson", was established in AD 1392. The Choson adopted a new extreme form of Confucianism as the basis of both government

---

[12]Chang (2010), p. 149.
[13]Chang (2010), p. 18.
[14]http://www.bbc.co.uk/news/technology-16832990.

and society. It divided people into classes, and began the process of establish-ing a system of etiquette and ethics that prevailed for the next 500 years, based on sex, age, social class and official position. It conditioned people to be obsessed with making sure that others treated them with formal courtesy and respect. This created the national character that continues to distinguish Koreans to this day. Following a brutal battle with Japan in the late 16th century, Korea was sealed off for 300 years and became known as the Hermit Kingdom.

Ironically, it was also Japan that demanded that the kingdom end its isola-tionist stance and opened up Korea to the outside world in 1876, just as the Americans had ended the isolationist Japanese Shogun period in Japan a few years earlier.[15] From this time Japan extended significant influence over Korea, and from 1910 to the end of WWII, Korea was a part of the Japanese empire. During the Korean War, Korea became divided into a highly militarized North and a South, with the perceived threat of an imminent attack always present. We refer to the cultural traits of South Korea in this chapter.

An overreaching goal of Confucianism is to structure society in such a way that it ensures harmony. The etiquette and division in classes ensures everyone understands what appropriate behaviour is. Personal relationships are very important. However, the intricate structure of etiquette may also deprive the Koreans of the opportunity to think and act as individuals. It can suppress creativity and innovation, and for a long period kept Korea in a time warp where nothing changed for generations. Koreans are still class and behaviour conscious, and though there is little overt discrimination against foreigners, there is a distinct scepticism to outsiders combined with national pride. Korean companies are often reluctant to have foreigners in their leadership teams and boards.

Arrogance is not well accepted, reflecting a primary principle of Confucian-ism of the value and importance of humility – from the king to the lowest subject.[16] Foreign people have noted that the emotional content of loyalty generally overrides the logical content. Face saving is prevalent and a strong influence on behaviour.

In Richard Lewis's book *When Cultures Collide*, he summarizes some of the core South Korean national traits that influence business behaviour:

---

[15] De Mente B.L. (2004) *Korean Business Etiquette*. Tuttle, pp. 8–10.
[16] De Mente (2004), pp. 56–57.

- Confucian ethics, observance of protocol, respect for elders and protection of *Kibun* (inner feelings)
- Toughness, competitive spirit and tenacity
- Nationalism, suspicion of neighbours, dislike of foreigners in general, willingness to suffer hardship for the good of the country and adaptability.

The history of Samsung electronics and its strategic imperatives

Samsung Electronics, headquartered in Seoul, Korea, is the world's largest electronics company. It is the flagship subsidiary of the Samsung Group, with over 150,000 employees. In 2009, Samsung overtook Hewlett-Packard as the world's largest technology company. In 2011, Samsung Electronics reported $164 billion in revenues and profits of $16 billion, with a market capitalization exceeding $160 billion. In early 2012, Samsung Electronics' mobile handset division overtook Nokia as the world's largest handset manufacturer.[17]

Lee Byung-chull founded the Samsung Corporation, today the largest Korean chaebol, in 1938. Since then the Samsung Group has diversified into a wide range of businesses from foods and textiles to shipbuilding, financial services and consumer electronics. Samsung Electronics, the largest subsidiary of the Samsung Group, was established in 1969.

The embryonic period as a challenger

In the early years, Samsung Electronics' revenues grew significantly, catching up from a position of having limited technical capabilities to one of being on a par with the Japanese, though still relying on advanced Japanese components. From the early 1970s to the early 1980s, it made great strides in learning to master modern manufacturing and went from basic black-and-white TV production to manufacturing colour TVs with fully automated plants. Their main products, home appliances and TVs, were mostly sold as OEM (original equipment manufacturer) products to be rebranded and served as loss leaders for large American retail stores like K-mart, Sears and Walmart. Its products at the time were perceived as being low quality and cheap.

The key to understanding Samsung Electronics lies in the spectacular growth of its semiconductor division, manufacturing DRAMs, SRAMs and

---

[17]http://www.bbc.co.uk/news/business-17865117.

flash memory. After WWII, the Korean industry remained heavily dependent on Japanese know-how and Japanese components. In 1974, Lee Byung-chull and his son Lee Kun-hee, decided to enter the semiconductor business, seeing the technology sectors as a means of survival for the Korean economy with its limited natural resources.

Ten years later, Samsung Electronics announced it had successfully developed 64K DRAMs, less than a year after announcing its entry into the DRAM business through the "Tokyo Declaration". However, it was still four to five years behind the USA and Japan. Over the next 10 years, Korean engineers steadily decreased the gap for each generation of chips. By 1992, it gained global leadership by developing the first 64Mb DRAM![18] By 1995, DRAM chips accounted for 35% of Samsung Electronics' total sales and 50% of profits.

The memory business is a battle with time because a company can enjoy a high price premium only for a brief period until another competitor catches up. The business requires huge upfront investment in manufacturing capacity that must be recouped early to secure profitability. As Lee noted in 2004: "Pre-emptive investment is critical to success in the chip industry since missing the timing for an investment will generate huge losses."[19]

It set up the first DRAM production facility in 1984 in six months, against an industry norm of two to three years, by planning, designing and constructing the facility all at the same time. The employees would stay in barracks during the construction period only returning to their homes once a week to change clothes. They would work around the clock to improve the efficiency in a new plant to increase yield and quality. Thus, speed of execution and hard work became core corporate cultural traits, supported by strong national influencers of work ethics and obedience.

The growth period

From the mid-1990s, Samsung Electronics applied the same formula of aggressive investment and speed to enter the flat panel business, used for computer and TV screens and the mobile phone business. Initially, Samsung had a high defect rate but then outflanked their Japanese competitors through aggressive investment in next generation technology. Samsung's emerging mobile phone

[18]Michel T. (2010) *Samsung Electronics*. John Wiley & Sons, p. 23.
[19]Michel (2010), p. 20.

business, focusing on cheap phones, thrived in the same period as they could complete the design of a new product within three to six months compared to 12 to 18 months for Nokia and Motorola.[20]

In 1996 Yun Jong-yong was appointed as CEO of Samsung Electronics after having served as president of the consumer electronics business. He was a 49-year-old long-serving engineer. Unusually, for Korean CEOs, he also had a Western perspective and was a great admirer of Jack Welch. He was a strong believer in constant restructuring of a business in order to progress it.[21] In 1996, Samsung's sales fell for the first time, as competitors had caught up with its lead in the DRAM business and in 1997 the Asian crisis hit Korea hard.

The 1997 crisis and Samsung's response

Eric Kim, an American CMO of Korean origin, who was instrumental in defining Samsung's global consumer brand, observed: "I think it was the financial crisis in 1997 that literally put Samsung on the edge of dying, which forced them to rethink everything. Yes, initially there was a major resistance . . . there was also the view there was no other choice."[22] The crisis challenged the chaebol structure at the core of Korean business life, where a family would control a huge conglomerate such as the Samsung Group, through a web of intercompany ownership and strategic investment. All chaebols had financed their expansion though debt. Yun streamlined the company and made operations more effective to repay the crippling debt. A positive side effect of the crisis was the depreciation of the Korean won by 50% versus US$, helping a swift export-led recovery.[23]

Its products were still regarded as cheaper and lower-quality imitations of leading brands such as Sony while, in their own market, LG electronics and Daewoo Electronics were successfully chipping away at their market share. To counterbalance the cyclical memory chip business, Yun outlined his strategic imperative: "We want to become the best in terms of digital convergence and core components." For Yun and Samsung, digital convergence meant using the same microchips to provide the various electronic functions in one single product.

[20]Chang (2010), pp. 54–56.
[21]Michel (2010), p. 25.
[22]Michel (2010), p. 6.
[23]Michel (2010), p. 31.

This was a very different interpretation of convergence compared to Sony's "Digital Dream Kid" vision. As Yun explained: "The IT industry is heading towards convergence. TVs, camcorders, mobile phones, PCs and other digital devices are being connected together through networks. We make all these products and we make the chips needed to operate them. We are better placed than any other company in the world to enjoy the benefits of digital convergence."[24] Samsung's new strategic focus included mobile phones, flat-screen TVs, PCs, CD and DVD players and camcorders.

Yun set in motion processes to refresh the organization. In a 1999 address to all employees he said: "Timing and speed will determine life and death of a company in the digital era. Thus we must take the initiative in eliminating the 'Five Ills' of complacency, habitual practices, formality, authoritarianism and egoism, and equip ourselves with sound management fundamentals represented by speed, simplicity and self-regulation."

The golden years

From 1997 to 2007, Samsung Electronics quintupled revenues from $13 billion in 1997 to $67 billion and rose to global prominence. By 2002, it had become the world's largest supplier of flat-panel monitors, as well as DRAM chips, and the third largest supplier of mobile phones. In 2005 it overtook Sony by market capitalization and as the more valuable consumer brand.

The founder and the values he embedded

Chairman Lee Byung-chull was born in February 1910 to wealthy landowners. Lee studied at Waseda University in Tokyo in the 1930s and had a Japanese wife. He founded Samsung in 1938. As a young businessman trading in Masan, he showed his competitive spirit and technique for outclassing competition. Noting that his competitors all used slow ox carts for distribution, he bought a motor truck – and soon left competition in the dust.

When Lee Byung-chull founded Samsung Electronics in 1969, he was already the richest man in Korea. However, he was at odds with Park, the South Korean president, who had come into power in 1961, and had to negotiate his return to Korea after a six-month exile in Japan, by surrendering his

[24]Michel (2010), pp. 35–36.

ownership of most of the Korean banks. Throughout his later career, he had a tense relationship with the authorities. In 2007, the Samsung Group accounted for 20% of South Korea's GDP, and thus its fortunes are intricately linked to those of South Korea.

In a 1976 article *Time* magazine described him: "Outwardly (he) is mild-mannered and looks a bit professorial behind gold-trimmed spectacles. He clearly enjoys wealth. His home is a palatial retreat . . . and he has a world famous collection of ancient Korean pottery. His greatest pleasure, he says, comes in meeting 'the challenge of making money'."[25]

The leadership style of chairman Lee has been referred to as "Emperor Management". With full managerial control, decisions were being made quickly and decisively. He made large bets, the two most important ones being buying a life insurance company in the 1950s which became the financial centre of his chaebol – life insurance companies have significant positive cash flow, which could be used to fund the group's other businesses – and the decision to invest in DRAM manufacturing in 1983. He also empowered his direct business managers, and did not attempt to micromanage.

Samsung's external directors were mostly members of the inner circle and until recently the company had only relatives of its founders on its board.[26] The global management team of the Samsung Group is all Korean and even the US Samsung Group management team, as late as 2011, was made up of Korean executives with long time careers at Samsung.[27]

When he founded the Samsung Group, Lee Byung-chull specified three missions:

1. Contribute to his nation's economic development
2. Pursue economic rationality
3. Value human resources.

Sea-Jin Chang, in her book *Samsung vs Sony*, observes: "This original business culture of economic rationality and efficiency has influenced their results-

---

[25] Chang (2010), pp. 52–53.
[26] Chang (2010), p. 164.
[27] http://www.samsung.com/uk/aboutsamsung/management/boardofdirectors.html; http://www.samsung.com/us/aboutsamsung/management/usexecutiveteam.html.

oriented culture of today."[28] She continues: "Samsung has always had an execution-oriented culture, with a high degree of loyalty, and with an emphasis on integrity and can-do spirit. Samsung Electronics employees are highly disciplined and try to achieve their mission, however difficult it might be. Although the Korean culture's emphasis on hierarchy and rote memorization may facilitate swift, effective strategy execution, this same emphasis may obstruct expression of creative or dissenting opinions."[29]

As Sea-Jin Chang also noted: "Samsung Electronics' corporate culture – its base for success in the memory business – has been a potential liability in the non-memory business." Unlike Sony, however, Samsung, now a market leader in itself, lacks the ability to develop new technology and products when there is no clear trajectory or another firm for it to benchmark.

The embedded values of making money and making South Korea successful thus appear to be two of the main driving forces behind Samsung. However, while rebuilding Korea is a strong motivator for Koreans, it is less so for international employees, while making money has a broader appeal.

Work practices and leadership post-Lee Byung-chull

Lee Byung-chull spent considerable time deciding which son should be his successor. In the 1960s, he shocked his family by firing two of the three sons, both of whom were Samsung managers. They were not fit to hold executive positions, he explained, and he worked closely with his third son Kun-hee to groom him. After his death in 1987, the Samsung Group chairman role passed to Lee Kun-hee. Lee continued his father's style of not attempting to micromanage everything. He articulated his own vision for the company in the early 1990s. Believing that the Samsung Group was overly focused on producing massive quantities of low-quality goods, it was not prepared to compete in quality, Lee famously challenged the organization stating "Change everything except your wife and kids."[30]

In 2007, Lee Kun-hee began the process of transferring his wealth and power to his son Lee Jae-yong. Some considered this act controversial as it highlighted the governance issues of the family controlling the group, through relatively small strategic stakes in critical units. In June 2012, Kwon Oh Hyun,

[28]Chang (2010), pp. 126–128.
[29]Chang (2010), pp. 99–100.
[30]http://en.wikipedia.org/wiki/Lee_Kun-hee.

head of its display and chip business, became chief executive officer, while Lee Jae-yong became vice chairman a few months later.

Up until recently, nearly all male recruits within the Samsung Group were graduate recruits. With compulsory military service in Korea, this meant having graduates as old as 28. Thus, most of the managerial staff at Samsung have military training before joining and are used to and comfortable with the command-control management of an authoritarian and hierarchical system, which some outsiders have described as being based on fear management. The women employed at Samsung follow a different recruitment track. Their roles are limited to temporary employment, as South Korean women tend to leave upon marriage.

Korean cultural values of harmony, unity and vertical social relationships strongly influence Korean firms and their human resource practices. These values can be a catalyst for change yet, at the same time, a bond preventing change. At Samsung the assertiveness of the Lee family has enabled the company to overcome significant crises and embrace change on more than one occasion.

Conclusion on Sony versus Samsung Electronics

Sony is a Japanese company, albeit an unusual one. Many of the virtues of Japanese culture and society exist in Sony's corporate culture:

- *The importance of the company.* The lifetime job philosophy is good for loyalty, but may backfire if a new skill set and urgent change are required. Sony appears at times to engage only reluctantly in restructuring to become more competitive
- *The long-term perspective over short-term profits* allowed Sony to invest in long-term R&D and product development, but also at times got the better of the company, e.g. when it suffered continuous losses at Sony Pictures due to overly independent American leadership. It may also feed a cultural dynamic of lack of decisiveness, as hope for future prosperity overrides the short-term need for dramatic action
- *The respect and status of age and the principle of tenure-based promotion* meant that the senior engineering managers often had the skill set and capabilities of the past. During the transition from analogue to digital, this clearly conspired against Sony, as it lacked software and architectural skills and leadership to compete with Apple, Google and Microsoft

- *Courteous behaviour and insular hierarchical thinking.* Western managers who have recently worked at Sony will tell how Japanese executives at Sony will "politely beg you for your support to a plan and later thank you for obedience", indicating that Sony may have lost some of the openness from the Morita era and has become more Japanese. They also observe that the opaqueness of decision-making, combined with centralization of executives in Japan, made it difficult for them to have real impact, though English is mostly well spoken in Tokyo at the executive levels. The insular perspective may also have led to Sony embracing a proprietary technology focus for too long, instead of partnering with other companies

Sony was hit by three existential crises at the same time, which it struggled to navigate effectively:

1. The transition from the founders to a managerial regime after Ohga
2. The transition from the analogue to the digital era, and
3. New competitors in the shape of Samsung and Apple, with more relevant capabilities, to which they reacted slowly and ineffectively.

For all three, the courteous and respectful Japanese culture may have derailed Sony's ability to respond effectively and swiftly. If one existential crisis can threaten you, then three at the same time need to be dealt with assertively.

So how did Samsung succeed in taking the global leadership in consumer electronics from Sony? It has the same technological capabilities as Sony. In some areas they may even have been inferior. A senior official from a Japanese research institute came to visit Samsung a few years ago. When asked about the purpose of the visit, he implied that he didn't perceive Samsung as having access to superior technology, but added: "I wonder why, although Samsung's overall technology level is still behind Japanese companies, how is it that overall output is superior to ours." An American executive commenting on Samsungs success, may reveal the simple reason for this dichotomy: "When Samsung wants to get things done, the decision comes down from the top, and everybody moves with lightning speed to do it."

In the analogue era, the technological gap between Sony and Samsung was insurmountable. Sony was often able to patent-protect their analogue products, having control of most of the components and manufacturing processes in-house, thereby gaining a longer-lasting competitive advantage for the products. In the digital world, three trends worked against that strategy: first, digital technology will nullify technical gaps when the technology standardizes;

second, modularization means that it is more difficult to innovate at the systems level; and last, the shortening of product lifecycles combined with often weekly price deterioration of components means that disciplined and urgent execution is necessary to stay competitive.[31]

Sony's response to those three challenges was to become even more creative and innovative and pursue a vision of mastering the complexity of a digital world with content, hardware, software and networking, just as they had mastered the complexity of the analogue world better than anyone else. Sony succeeded with PlayStation, but that platform was simply not broad enough to bankroll the entire company. The wider aspiration of linking all their consumer platforms from TVs to cameras has so far failed, exposing it to fierce competition for standalone products in TVs, audio systems, cameras, camcorders, mobile phones and DVDs.

Samsung Electronics, in contrast, early on invested in one big risky bet in the fiercely competitive global DRAM business. This hard-earned success became the foundation for its business culture, based on strong Korean values and heritage, and implicitly understood by everyone: a focus on swift and disciplined execution, centralized decision-making, the founders' focus on making big pre-emptive bets on the next generation technology and on making money.

These principles were combined with the unrelenting pressures of operating in an always-on commoditizing components business. Little was invested in integrating technologies across the product lines, except for using the same chip components, product management processes and manufacturing techniques. No grand vision existed or exists for Samsung Electronics. Yet, Samsung proved that you don't need a sophisticated grand vision if you execute better than the competition.

Like Sony, Samsung is organized in a complex matrix structure. However, unlike Sony, Korean expatriates fill virtually all the important positions abroad with decision-making highly centralized, and often conducted in Korean. The policy of relying on internal recruits, especially Koreans, has led to a lack of diversity but also facilitated the swift execution. However, at times this has also undermined Samsung's ability to respond sensitively to local market demands. Historically, local managers were not empowered. Important decisions had to be communicated back to the head office in Korea – in Korean. Korean expatriates would grab the phone and tell HQ what they needed and consequently lower ranked Koreans were often more powerful than their

---

[31]Chang (2010), p. 43.

locally hired bosses. There are signs that Samsung has become aware of this and attempted to attract more senior executives locally and provide them with more empowerment, though not always successfully. Old habits die hard.

Like Sony, Samsung uses a variety of Western KPIs such as EVA (Economic Value Added), cashflow and earnings per share to judge the performance of employees and managers. Samsung is more individualistic in its approach than Sony, giving ample room for individual employees achieving significant bonuses, sometimes exceeding the fixed pay. Samsung managers are fiercely competitive, which together with the compensation system may have exacerbated a tendency to silo the individual business units, though there is also ample evidence that businesses within the group will assist each other, having a strong sense of belonging to the same chaebol.[32] Sony, in contrast, and in line with Japanese group orientation, has a less individualistic and more tempered approach to compensation and competition. The consensus orientation at Sony that Stringer referred to is in sharp contrast to the command and control culture at Samsung.

Both Samsung and Sony were blessed with the influence of a consistent founder for nearly 50 years. However, Sony is an older company and thus the transition to a managerial regime happened earlier. Samsung has uniquely managed to maintain family control for two and possibly three generations. The critical transition from founder family dominance to a managerial regime has therefore not yet fully taken place at Samsung Electronics, and clearly did not go smoothly at Sony.

Sea-Jin Chang comments that[33]: "The major decisions made by Sony and Samsung Electronics during the past decade did simply not originate from differences in these firms' strategic content. They were deeply rooted in their organizational processes and their executives' political behaviour", and these we hasten to add were also deeply rooted in the national cultures.

Samsung's spectacular rise also shows that diversity may not always be the only recipe for success, possibly a politically controversial observation, but worth considering, if your company plays a consistent strategic game. However, in the next round of the consumer electronics game, diversity of thinking may well play a more important role for Samsung than for Sony. Sony has already embraced some diversity of thinking, with a non-Japanese CEO and international executives – as well as three non-Japanese members of the board.

---

[32]Chang (2010), pp. 129–130.
[33]Chang (2010), p. 22.

Samsung Electronics became successful as the fastest follower in the consumer electronics industry and is now the biggest company. In the future, Samsung may have to become the innovation leader, rather than just following. This will present an entirely new challenge for the company, where its Korean roots may not be as benign as they have been hitherto. Furthermore, because of its outstanding performance and the worldwide adulation it is receiving, hubris is reported to be growing within the organization and may undermine the company's ability to look critically at itself and correct its mistakes. This arrogance reminds some observers of Sony 10 years ago, Sea-Jin concludes.[34]

The next few years may well prove to be more challenging for Samsung Electronics. In the future, Chinese companies could out-execute Samsung with lower costs, and the consumer electronics industry may move from a focus on components to one where the winners will be companies that create a technological proprietary architecture and ecosystem for content such as Apple, Google and Microsoft are currently doing. Likewise, if Sony can rediscover its creative culture, learn to master digital and software, and become more assertive it could bounce back, as it still has a formidable global organization, and highly relevant skills and capabilities.

Chapter close

The two cases highlight the challenges that the global company faces in the growth period. It needs to balance operational agility with execution discipline and often has to navigate a significant crisis point. It carries with it the organizational skills and capabilities as well as habits of the earlier phases. A growth organization will often benefit from taking an outside-in perspective to identify potentially derailing cultural dynamics; however, these companies are successful and therefore may be reluctant to engage in introspection. In both cases, the national culture played a significant role in defining Sony's and Samsung's response to changes in their environments and how they chose to navigate crises.

In the next chapter we will discuss the maturity period through the lenses of three companies: Japanese Toyota, Danish FLSmidth and American P&G.

---

[34]Chang (2010), p. 173.

7

In this chapter we discuss the maturity period. This period includes the latter stage of the efficiency and scale phase and the ultimate consolidation phase. We examine it through cases from three different continents: Japanese Toyota, Danish FLSmidth and American P&G.

As an industry matures, there is a drive towards more efficiency, often through sheer scale and a desire for a stronger market share position with its consequent higher profitability. Consolidation is the end game of an industry, with only a small handful of global or regional players in the segment. This period requires different capabilities from the earlier periods and again different national traits will impact success.

As we have observed earlier, a crisis can strike at any time of the lifecycle, and may take many forms. The mature company is set in its ways and hence change does not come easily, as evidenced by IBM in the 1990s. In our terms, this means that the embedded values have been solidly inculcated and reinforced in the work practices for a long period. The culture is now well defined, succinctly articulated and communicated and supported by all the substitute leadership mechanisms of the large corporation. However, the risk of an existentially derailing cultural dynamic also increases, as the long-established work practices in a well-organized mature company will reinforce the existing corporate culture.

The company is often protected by its strong market position and profits and therefore the board and the management may not recognize that a serious derailing cultural dynamic is at play. General Motors (GM) steadily declined, yet at first only slowly, from being the leading industrial company in the world to bankruptcy. But it took almost 50 years before the same US government, which had threatened with breaking it up in the late 1950s, bailed it out. Its decline was interrupted by multiple short-term bursts of American leadership optimism. Major initiatives were launched to great fanfare to change the direction, such as the Saturn car, veiling the downward projection of the long-term trend.

It is also a period where companies can find unusual sources of differentiation. In the Toyota case, we will examine how Toyota, over a 30-year period, applied some very Japanese principles to create a business system that competitors found difficult to copy in its entirety. Through this, Toyota created a sustainable competitive advantage that propelled it to become the No. 1 global car manufacturer.

While mergers and acquisitions can be a key activity for a company during this period, we will only discuss these briefly and indirectly in the cases. The subject of mergers and cross-border cultures is inherently complex. It merits a separate in-depth discussion, if not an entirely new book, taking into account the effect of pairs of national cultures as well as their lifecycle status. For P&G and FLSmidth, however, it was a central part of their recent growth strategy, while at Toyota acquisitions did not play a significant role.

The maturity period consists of the latter stages of the scale and efficiency phase, which we discussed in the previous chapter, and the consolidation phase as shown in Diagram 7.1.

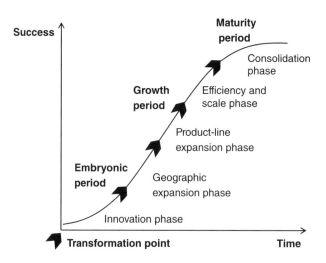

Diagram 7.1: The consolidation phase

The consolidation phase

Description of the consolidation phase

The consolidation period signifies the end game of an industry. The financially stronger players will take over the weaker as the industry consolidates. It can carry on like this for a long time, depending on the external forces of disruption, the speed of change and the economies of scale dynamics in the industry. The car industry, given its importance for employment in many countries, has proven resistant to pursue consolidation, while many consumer product categories, such as nappies, detergents and beer, are further along being consolidated. The book publishing and newspaper industries have been mature industries for decades if not centuries. However, with the advent of the eBook and the ubiquity of news on the Internet, both were severely disrupted in the past decade and may not survive in their current form.

The period is typically characterized by slow organic growth. Consequently, there is a stronger focus on mergers and acquisitions often with large successful companies from different nations. While a merger may make sense from an industrial structural perspective, significant integration challenges, often based on deeply rooted national and corporate cultural issues, frequently hamper the value creation for shareholders.

A mature organization is often a well-oiled execution engine, organized to execute the strategy and plan with discipline. The skill set and capabilities required to succeed are well recognized both at the corporate and individual role level. Successful companies usually master all key capabilities from evolutionary innovation to planning, execution and quality. However, companies still occasionally need to adapt to smaller or bigger changes in consumer behaviour or technology, and thus need to stay somewhat agile.

The main friction during this period is between the focus on effective execution through well-defined systems and processes, and the need to continuously adapt the organization to changes in its environment – and the ever-present risk of complacency fed by success. Given the size and scale of these organizations, changes usually take longer to implement than in a smaller organization and thus a mature company that faces a period of more rapid change in its environment may find itself flat-footed, always one step behind, as was the case for General Motors.

In a mature industry like the newspaper industry, the genes of strategy change were long forgotten, being largely irrelevant for success for decades.

The focus was on making great newspapers, through journalistic excellence, finding a good story and getting it out first. Thus, even if the board and the management intellectually understood the need for change in the Internet era, most did not have the experience and capabilities to deal with it.

Even if a company recognizes the need for change, it will face the classical dilemma of how to change while keeping the legacy business ticking over to fund the new strategy. If you, as a board member or a senior executive, face this dilemma, it has to be taken seriously. This is where big companies or even industries stumble and shareholders lose money. Just look at Kodak, Polaroid, RCA, Zenith, the European TV industry, the European mechanical watch industry as well as many of the excellent examples in Jim Collins' book *How the Mighty Fall*[1] or in Clayton Christensen's book *The Innovator's Dilemma*.[2]

The traits that typically enable or derail success during the maturity period include:

- Strategic orientation: managing complexity in a global scale business
- Commercial orientation: mastering all aspects of running a complex multi-line global business and its key disciplines: quality, manufacturing, sales, marketing, R&D, supply chain, etc.
- Process orientation: focus on systemic efficiency and cost control
- Mastering change: integration of acquired entities
- Mastering continued innovation.

In short, the capabilities that characterize this period are centred on the longer-term perspective, discipline and following the standard processes that have been developed over many years. Innovation and disruption are rare. Companies are analytical and often dogmatic, and will drive their operations using a well-understood set of key performance indicator (KPI) measures.

National traits that tend to enable or derail during the maturity period

National rooted traits tend to become more distinct in the maturity period (Diagram 7.2). Global companies usually have acquired some level of international veneer, enabling them to employ and motivate people globally and

---

[1]Collins J. (2009) *How the Mighty Fall*. Random House.
[2]Christensen C. (1997) *The Innovator's Dilemma*. HBS Press.

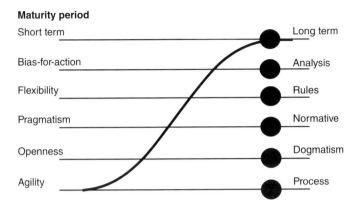

Maturity period

Short term	Long term
Bias-for-action	Analysis
Flexibility	Rules
Pragmatism	Normative
Openness	Dogmatism
Agility	Process

Diagram 7.2: The maturity period

partner with other companies. However, these mature companies are financially successful, with a high level of self-confidence. They will often fully display their national identity without perceiving the need for adapting to the environment. During a crisis, the company will tend to revert to its core national culture and instincts.

Companies rooted in a linear-active country may have a shorter-term time perspective than is ideal for the period, which can lead to suboptimization. Companies rooted in countries with an agile and pragmatic approach to life may struggle during this period where they need to enforce the process discipline and hierarchy necessary to manage a large organization.

For American companies the national traits of ambition, individualism, the do-what-it-takes to get results, the drive and perseverance to succeed and agility underpin the embryonic period. However, in the maturity period, American corporates are influenced by the equally strong masculine elements of the American culture such as using the power of position and success. The focus is on results over people concerns and processes, and the power distance is accepted. American companies tend to become more control and command oriented, more hierarchical and more bureaucratic as they grow bigger. Command-and-control systems are after all a highly effective methodology to rein in individualism, and will often be supported by simple KPIs. Those companies become more uncompromising and assertive during a crisis, with little capacity for listening, as reported by European employees from more "feminine" and collectivist countries. There are more rungs on the ladder and the symbols of power and status are often visible. However, the complex power structure may also slow down decision-making, which could also explain why American corporates have a fascination with the strong leader who can straighten things out in a time of crisis!

For a large Japanese corporation, decision-making becomes even more centralized and more Japanese. Most large Japanese corporations have all-Japanese senior executives and all-Japanese boards. Danish companies often struggle in this period. Their feminine and collectivist traits emphasizing inclusion in decision-making, individualism and compassion for the people can make Danish companies less efficient in designing and running a globally disciplined execution processes.

National traits that enable or derail success during this period include:

- Bureaucratic and disciplined decision-making versus front-line empowerment and agility
- Balancing the long- and short-term perspective
- Openness and strategic orientation at the executive level versus disciplined execution at the operational level
- Nationalism and dogmatism versus openness.

Let us look at a few cases, where we will highlight a unique point in each, rather than doing a full cultural analysis. Large corporations are complex from a cultural perspective, as we will see in the FLSmidth case. Companies need to decide if they want to pursue a strategy of cultural dominance in their organization or apply more of a hybrid strategy allowing for strong local influence on the culture. Both Toyota and P&G pursued a cultural dominant strategy, while FLSmidth, coming from a small pragmatic country, implicitly chose a cultural hybrid strategy.

Case study: Toyota

The Toyota story is a powerful example of how work practices steeped in national culture enabled Toyota to gain a sustainable competitive advantage and take the pole position in a global industry. The case illustrates how Toyota, with its Japanese long-term orientation and embedded beliefs, patiently transferred its principles to its international subsidiaries, in this case the US manufacturing plant in rural southern Kentucky. For a detailed discussion of the reactive Japanese culture, please refer to Chapter 3.

The founder and Toyota's embedded corporate values

Sakiichi Toyoda, who was born in the rural and frugal Aichi prefecture, founded Toyota in 1924. Throughout his life Sakiichi was a doer, not a manager. He was a great engineer and later referred to as Japan's King of Innovation.[3] Having grown a successful business in power looms, he suggested to his son Kiichiro: "Everyone should tackle some great project at least once in his life. I devoted most of my life to inventing new kinds of looms. Now it is your turn. You should make an effort to complete something that will benefit society." This quote tells us much about the Toyota culture. The influence of his father is evident, as well as his calling for creating greater good for society through continuous improvement. Thus, Kiichiro went on to establish Toyota Motor Company in 1924.

Eighty-three years later, in the first quarter of 2007, Toyota surpassed GM in quarterly sales for the first time in its history, selling a total of 2.35 million vehicles. Toyota not only builds great, reliable cars; they revolutionized an entire industry, introducing an entirely new philosophy, including Lean and Just-in-Time production methods while partnering with suppliers, all based on typical Japanese values.

The Japanese rooted values of continuous improvement and the elimination of waste, as discussed in Chapter 1, became core embedded values in Toyota's corporate culture, most clearly articulated in the Toyota Way principles. The Toyota culture also embraces the typical reactive value of harmony, as evidenced in Toyota's philosophy when working with its suppliers.

The Toyota Way and work practices at Toyota

In 2001, Toyota summarized the values that underpin the company culture, called the Toyota Way 2001. It was an attempt to share the principles of the company with non-Japanese employees and stakeholders. It took Toyota 10 years of deliberation and dialogue to agree on how to best articulate these principles. The fact that it is called "Toyota Way 2001" is a reflection of the belief that nothing in life or nature is permanent and that Toyota will always strive to continuously improve its ways and thus also the Toyota Way!

The Toyota Way is pictured as a house, with the roof called The Toyota Way, supported by two pillars, each with a few subcategories to support them, as

[3]Liker J.K. and Hoseus, M. (2008) *Toyota Culture, the Heart and Soul of the Toyota Way.* McGraw Hill, p. 11.

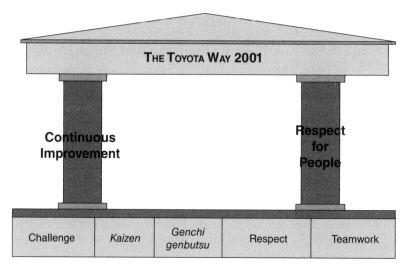

Diagram 7.3: The Toyota Way 2001

the floor of the building. The two pillars of the Toyota Way are their central values: respect for people and continuous improvement (Diagram 7.3).

Respect for people

- Respect – We respect others, make every effort to understand each other, take responsibility and do our best to build mutual trust.
- Teamwork – We stimulate personal and professional growth, share the opportunities of development and maximize individual and team performance.

Continuous improvement

- Challenge – We form a long-term vision, meeting challenge with courage and creativity to realize our dreams.
- *Kaizen* – We improve business operations continuously, always striving for innovation and evolution.
- *Genchi Genbutsu* (Go and See) – We practise Genchi Genbutsu – believing in going to the source to find the facts to make correct decisions, build consensus and achieve goals at our optimal speeds.

Each of the five foundation principles is then described in much deeper detail to show how they should impact the work practices and culture. Under *Kaizen*, for instance, there are three subcategories:

- *Kaizen* mind and innovative thinking
- Building lean systems and structures
- Promoting organizational learning.

The Toyota Way as a source of sustainable differentiation

Toyota is probably best known for its Lean systems, which is included in the *Kaizen* subcategory. Many companies have tried to copy parts of the renowned Toyota Production System (TPS). They may have implemented Lean, Just-in-Time and even added six-sigma processes (not an original Toyota principle). However, most struggled to make a permanent cultural change or reach the levels of productivity of Toyota. The American authors of *The Toyota Culture*, who both worked at Toyota Motor Company Kentucky, the main US plant, argue that this is because other companies failed to understand the culture and values behind the Toyota Way. In the Toyota Way, Lean and Just-in-Time are subcategories under *Kaizen*, which is a subcategory under continuous improvement. Thus, unless you understand the value-system and the result-ing work practices behind continuous improvement, you risk copying the artefacts, but not the cultural DNA – the embedded values.

To take a look at the structure of a "Lean system", we include Diagrams 7.4 and 7.5 representing horizontal and vertical *keiretsu*, respectively. Most of Japan's really big companies are organized as horizontal *keiretsu* – that is to say they are conglomerates linked to and surrounding a big central bank. The Mitsubishi group of companies (Mitsubishi Heavy Industries, Mitsubishi Cars, Mitsubishi Trading, etc.) are financed largely by Mitsubishi Bank. The same applies to the Sumitomo Group, Mitsui and others. There is normally exten-sive cross-shareholding between the member companies, which support each other briskly if one of them starts to fail.

In a vertical *keiretsu* such as Toyota, the central body – Toyota Car Co. – employs a relatively small number of workers, but relies heavily on upstream suppliers as well as downstream marketing organizations. A corporation such as GM in Detroit would have many times more workers on fixed wages, with the concurrent liabilities and far less flexibility.

Toyota's relationship with suppliers also developed in stark contrast to Western car companies that traditionally had an adversarial relationship with suppliers. Toyota's partnership philosophy is to learn together, share the learn-ing and intellectual property and improve together for the long term to create a win–win situation. This is in particular true for the closest group of tier-one suppliers.

Horizontal **KEIRETSU**

(average 31 companies)

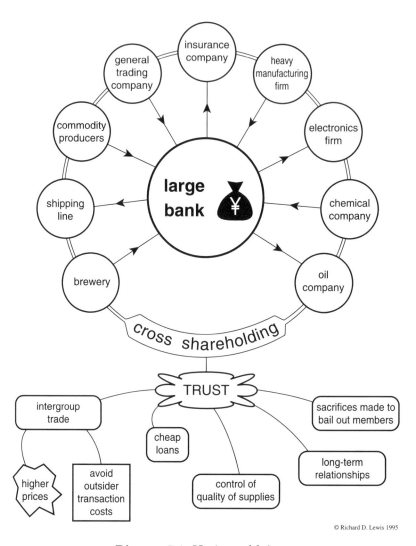

© Richard D. Lewis 1995

Diagram 7.4: Horizontal *keiretsu*

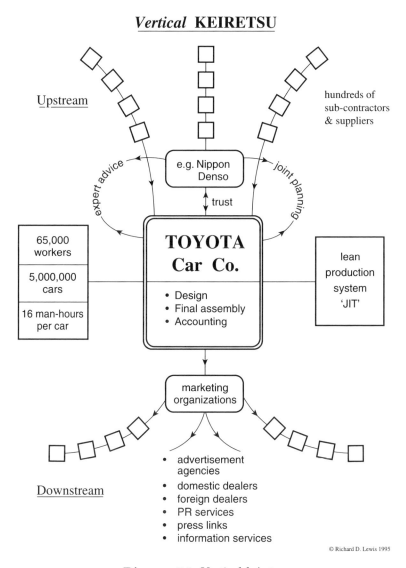

Diagram 7.5: Vertical *keiretsu*

Toyota in America

As Toyota's global sales volume grew during the 1980s it decided to move manufacturing outside Japan. Toyota faced the challenge of building operations in countries that had different nation-state cultures, and were foreign to Japanese values and ways of thinking. In line with their values, the Japanese leadership set a Toyota Way "Challenge" to transfer the essence of the Toyota Production System, while respecting the national cultural context in the USA.

A key challenge was to ensure that the US organization instinctively understood the fundamental principle that *Quality Always Comes First*. This is best exemplified when it ramped up the Camry production in the late 1980s at their newly established Kentucky plant. The initial focus dictated by the Japanese management was simply on safety and quality. After having recruited and trained most of the local staff to run the plant, the plant would build just one car per day. Only when it was verified that the car produced met the Toyota Camry standards from Japan, would the production be ramped up to two cars per day, and only increased as standards were continuously met. It took three years of ramp-up to get to the desired standards and full volume. Only then would Toyota challenge the plant management to improve effectiveness by optimizing the production processes! Contrast this with how an American or European company would have run in a new plant – to get to profitability much more quickly – and the cultural differences become evident.

A particular issue to overcome was obviously the short-term action orientation so deeply engrained in US culture. It took Toyota years to teach each member of the workforce that the desired behaviour was to stop an entire production line for what seemed to be an insignificant issue, such as a dashboard having a 3 mm gap rather than the required 2 mm. Even if this meant that that day's production target would not be met. The key point being that at Toyota understanding and fixing the process is more important than fixing the narrower problem.

The role of a Toyota leader is culturally quite different from the assertive American manager. A strong assumption within the Toyota culture is that managers are leaders and that leaders are teachers: "You need to learn together from mistakes, only this way can you continuously improve individually and as a team." In Toyota's experience it takes 10 years to train an externally recruited (non-Japanese) manager to fully understand the Toyota Way and act correctly when faced with an unforeseen challenge, and to use the situation as a platform for coaching and teaching in his/her production group.

A core belief at Toyota is that "We build people and cars simultaneously." Thus they don't separate the people from the process![4] Obviously, this is where competitors have struggled to copy the Toyota Way. The Toyota Way is the combination of a philosophy, the people and a process; whether it be Lean, Just-in-Time, the use of the Andon Cord to stop the production process or *Genchi Genbutsu* – which requires managers to go and see for themselves what

---

[4]Liker and Hoseus (2008), p. 55.

the problem is – hands-on. Simply copying the processes and expecting it to work will not suffice.

The crisis and conclusion

Over the years, Toyota has refined its ability to export the Toyota Way to other countries. This does not mean that the culture is exactly the same at every plant. The Toyota Way has been somewhat adapted to the local culture, but the essence of the Toyota Way remained intact. As Toyota became more confident, it pursued a strategy of growth to achieve global leadership beyond the 1990s, and appears to have forgotten some of its own long-held principles, in particular the value of patient transferral of capabilities and embedded values to new entities and partners.

It is easy to understand the public humiliation (loss of face) the Toyota leadership felt when faced with public criticism, following a very public problem in the USA in 2009, where a faulty accelerator had caused multiple deaths. It coincided with several costly recalls of millions of cars in 2009 and 2010. This was not just an incident to be dealt with; it was a fundamental process issue, as *Business Week* observed: "As grave as the current troubles are, they are symptomatic of a larger problem at Toyota: it got carried away chasing high-speed growth, market share, and productivity gains year in and year out. All that slowly dulled the commitment to quality embedded in Toyota's corporate culture."[5]

Akio Toyoda, the president of Toyota and grandson of the founder, publically admitted that something was amiss and that Toyota had prioritized growth over quality and compromised its fundamental principles:

> "We maybe slacked in some of our core principles [like the] attention to
> the basics of manufacturing. It was as if we were engaged in car manu-
> facturing in a virtual world and became insensitive to vehicle failings and
> defects in the market. Now we understand the gaps between virtual
> world and real world, and we're working hard to fill those gaps. We want
> to pursue the basic performances in our cars – run, turn, and stop – and
> secure the confidence of our customers."[6]

[5]BusinessWeek, March 2010, quote from IBS Center for Management Research. Case on Toyota, BSTR/385.
[6]BusinessWeek, March 2010.

The Toyota case is an example of how a company achieved global dominance in the maturity period, by embracing culturally rooted work practices. They were possible to copy at the artefact level; however, it proved difficult for the competition to replicate the effectiveness without embracing the cultural values that underpinned them. Toyota carefully and patiently embedded these values in their international subsidiaries. However, after 2000, a derailing cultural dynamic fed by its historical success and a new growth strategy took Toyota's focus away from its core values and led to a deterioration of the same quality processes that had made Toyota so successful in the first place.

Some argue that the impetus to this derailing dynamic may have been sown after the US stock listing in 1999 as noted in a recent case study on Toyota:

> "Toyota's culture changed further in 1999, when its stock was listed on the New York Stock Exchange. From the culture which encouraged every worker to perform better in order to collectively improve the company, it began to adopt the Western culture which rewarded growth. Toyota started to use US accounting principles. However, the low dividends it was paying to the investors became a point of contention for institutional investors. To increase dividends, Toyota went on reducing costs."[7]

Deciding how to internationalize and inculcate your corporate culture in foreign subsidiaries is a critical decision that most companies need to make, but often not consciously. Toyota chose to pursue a conscious strategy of cultural domination, while other companies may choose the looser local culture adaptation strategy or a hybrid between the two. The next case shows how this decision may be accelerated as a consequence of a strategy change.

Case study: FLSmidth

FLSmidth is a Danish publically quoted company with over €3 billion in revenues and 12,000 employees globally. The case is an instructive example of how slowly business cultures will evolve if there is limited external incentive to change. It also exemplifies the ramifications of a sudden change in the employee footprint, from local to international, due to the forces of globalization. The case was developed through a leadership assessment that Kai Ham-

[7]BusinessWeek, March 2010.

merich and his colleagues at Russell Reynolds Associates conducted in 2011 for a new incoming chairman and the CEO of FLSmidth.

The Danish national culture

The Danes are linear-active and belong to the collectivist Nordic region. The foundation culture of FLSmidth is Danish; a small, flat and windswept land in Northern Europe, yet fertile and prosperous. Over the years, Danes have learned to accommodate the greater powers surrounding them – England, Germany and Sweden – while keeping their independence. Key Danish traits include[8]:

- Short-term pragmatism
  - Flexibility, creativity, opportunism and short-term orientation
- Independence and non-confrontation
  - Friendly, optimistic, curious, humorous and non-confrontational style
  - Independence (respect for the individual), individualism
- Low power distance combined with collectivism
  - Team work, group and consensus orientation
  - Meritocratic
  - Power is accepted, if not used overtly
- Scepticism to outsiders[9]
  - Danes tend to stick together
  - "Don't stand out" and be different (Janteloven), i.e. it is advisable to simply "blend into this homogeneous society"
  - "Don't tell us what to do" – stubbornness when threatened as a group.

Jutland is a main agricultural area of Denmark, and geographically closer to northern Germany than to Copenhagen. It is home to many of the largest industrial and consumer companies in Denmark. The Jutland regional subculture, which is one typical of rural areas, adds to the Danish traits:

- Conservative, hardworking rural values
- Humility, honesty and integrity
- Having a sound commercial judgement.

---

[8]See also Lewis R.D. (2006) *When Cultures Collide*. Nicholas Brealey, pp. 350–355.
[9]Re. Janteloven, see also the Thyra Frank case.

A brief history and the values the founder embedded

Fredrik Læssøe Smidth founded FLSmidth & Co. in 1882 in Copenhagen. These were times of crisis and change for Denmark. In 1864, Denmark had lost a third of its territory, economy and population in a war with Prussia and Austria led by General Von Moltke. The national pride was hurt, yet at the same time the loss also signalled a clear break with the past. "What you lose externally you shall regain internally" expressed the sentiment of the time. The Danish industrial revolution was about to take off, with a new generation of young entrepreneurs who would soon establish the companies, several with global reach, that would dominate the Danish industry for the next century, such as Carlsberg Breweries (beer), AP Moeller Maersk (shipping) and FLSmidth.

Fredrik Læssøe Smidth was a practitioner and a "self-made" man, as his two partners Poul Larsen and Alexander Foss would describe him. He was a quick student and understood the known laws of nature in terms of engineering intuitively. The trio complemented each other well. Both partners had civil engineering degrees from the newly established leading polytechnic school in Copenhagen, whereas Fredrik had taken a more practical apprentice training as a machine constructor.

All three grew up in or had strong family ties to Jutland. Together they also represented a contrast to the prevailing public attitude of hopelessness in Denmark at the time: "What can we do?" was the sentiment expressed by many people, while the three partners had an almost modern: "Yes, we can do it" attitude.[10]

This was a period of rapid growth for the cement industry fuelled by the increased urbanization and industrialization globally. FLSmidth was in a growth industry and seized the moment.[11] By 1898, FLSmidth was the leading global company with a 33% market share of the global cement plant equipment market. Ninety-five per cent of revenues came from international customers.

In 1898, Fredrik died, supposedly from hard work – his work day normally being from 6.30am to 10pm. Alexander Foss wrote about him in his memoirs:

---

[10] Riisager K. (1922) *FLSmidth & Co. 1882–1922 (40 years)*. Trykt i Langkjaers Bogtrykkeri Ad, p. 27, "hvad nytter det – ja, det nytter, ville de sige".
[11] Drachmann P. (1932) *FLSmidth & Co., 1922–1932*. Egmont H. Petersens Hof-Bogtrykkeri, p. 15.

"As an autodidact, he was not always clear to the often better educated people around him, but had the ability to do the right things at the right moment." The company benefited from being led by the founders for over 50 years, until Poul Larsen's death in 1935; this established the foundation for a strong and uniform culture.

The partners worked hard, putting in long hours for many years, establishing a culture of hard work, results orientation and a focus on solving customers' problems. The culture was centred on cement and cement people. The mostly Danish employees innovated, designed and installed the heavy equipment in faraway places. The heroes were the individuals who solved a tricky customer problem, or found a way to transport a large heavy rotary kiln to a remote location. It was a firm of doers, where everybody made a difference and received praise for it. Loyalty was high and tenures long.

The next 70 years – disaster strikes – and a new strategy is outlined

Let us fast forward to the present. The next 70 years had limited impact on the culture of the core cement company, being the workhorse in the group that continued to generate cash and profits. By the year 2000 it was still a Danish company. Most managers were Danish engineers with long tenures, and often with experience from international postings, and the employee footprint was dominated by Danish employees.

In the final two decades of the millennium, the cement business financed a financially disastrous diversification into environmental equipment and aircraft services. By 2001 the founder families gave up control and in 2002 a new blunt and effective chairman was hired to restructure the group. In 2004, he hired a new CEO, Jørgen Huno Rasmussen, who was tasked with refocusing on the original cement engineering and turnkey business and the smaller but promising minerals business.

Customer loyalty was still remarkably high; an Asian customer ordered a new cement plant at a site where his family had built the first of now four plants in 1912. When FLSmidth suggested to discontinue the original energy-inefficient line, the gear still being manually greased with a broom and a bucket of oil, he refused on the grounds that: "this line has paid for the other three plants – and it is still working fine".

The new strategy was successful with increasing profits and revenues. In 2007, the company acquired the Canadian minerals equipment company

GL&V. This company was led out of the USA and the employees mostly based outside Europe. GL&V itself was a product of multiple acquisitions of smaller and mid-sized minerals businesses, often founder controlled and managed. FLSmidth generally kept the managers and maintained a loose organizational structure with the independent businesses cooperating in a matrix around specific projects. Over the next four years the minerals business grew to be of equal size to the cement business with over €1 billion in annual revenues, on the back of the boom in raw materials worldwide.

A new footprint challenges the culture and the work practices

After 2000, FLSmidth expanded its business to low-cost India, by outsourcing engineering from more expensive Denmark. It hired over 3000 local employees – equivalent to 25% of the global employee base, and further expanded into China and Russia. It had also acquired a couple of German companies in the products business, and expanded into the post-construction services and maintenance business. Consequently, by 2011, only 12% of the global employees were Danish by birth. Suddenly, FLSmidth was not so Danish any longer!

However, Danish nationals still dominated at the headquarters in Copenhagen and the senior positions. During the leadership assessment, the non-Danish employees in particular observed that the original Danish FLSmidth cement culture might not be appropriate for a new, more global and multi-business FLSmidth. Newly hired or acquired non-Danes indicated they had a poor understanding of the culture, and described it as being:

- Danish and non-diverse
- Headquarters centric, sometimes with unclear empowerment principles
- A small executive team of Danes making all key decisions – the decision-making principles though were seen as neither being clear, inclusive nor transparent to outsiders
- There was a perceived lack of performance management culture and it was observed that performance issues rarely had consequences
- The organizational matrix was considered complex and slow
- There was limited cultural integration between the old core cement business and the new companies in the FLSmidth Group.

The Danish nationals on their side indicated they saw a clear and consistent culture. They generally enjoyed the pragmatic small company orientation.

From this it was apparent that the Danish-influenced corporate culture and work practices were perceived as being less relevant in many parts of the company and, in particular, in three key areas:

- Decision-making; more formality, clarity (rules) and transparency was required
- The perceived lack of performance management and consequence management
- The consensus orientation, where the Danish informality and collectivism was foreign to many and not effective in their cultures.

The "small country" dilemma facing FLSmidth as it moves from 1.0 to 2.0

The new FLSmidth had, in a few intensive years, successfully evolved beyond its original core cement business to a company with a vastly different geographical footprint. Diagrams 7.6 and 7.7 articulate this dramatic change in employees and the national cultural footprint of FLSmidth.

The three cultural strategies options facing FLSmidth

Coming from a small country accentuates the need to respond to this change. If you are a company from a larger nation such as the USA, China, France,

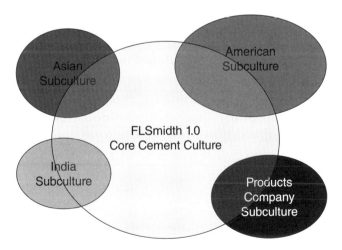

Diagram 7.6: FLSmidth 1.0 – the culture map of FLSmidth before 2000, with a dominant Danish culture, may have looked like this

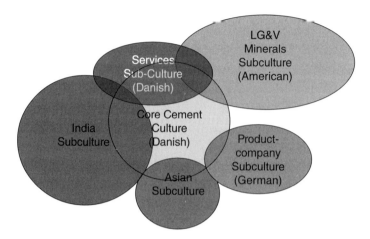

Diagram 7.7: Contrast Diagram 7.6 with the cultural map of FLSmidth by 2012, which visibly is more diverse and with a much smaller Danish core

Britain or Germany, you may find a pool of local employees who have experience in working in a company from your country or industry, and who are dual-language/dual-culture. This makes it somewhat easier to build a local subsidiary culture that is aligned with the national core culture. If a company is from a smaller country, and has grown through acquisitions, it often won't have this option available and typically will have to choose between one of the following three cultural alignment strategies:

1. **National culture domination:** Send home country executives and more junior employees to essentially manage the main functions in the local subsidiary. Invest significantly in cultural indoctrination to adapt the local culture to the global core culture. This can be done through intensive cultural training of local employees, moving executives around the subsidiary system, including spending time at the headquarters. This will usually ensure that the local work practices are tightly aligned with the global practices. However, the disadvantage is that this is expensive and takes time. The company can lose cultural touch with the local customers and not understand the deeper market and dynamics. Asian and American corporations from large countries often pursue this strategy.
2. **The hybrid global/local culture:** Companies following this strategy typically identify specific areas of shared cultural beliefs, values or passions that they can use to build a common culture around; the professional

culture, a passion for cars, a passion for helping people, educating children – the options are endless. The company allows for local flexibility while providing the global cultural glue! Companies will usually hire in conformity with those shared beliefs to ensure a good cultural fit and thus, over time, create a globally consistent culture, which may lead them towards cultural domination. However, this is expensive, time and resource consuming and therefore challenging to short-term-oriented cultures.

3. **Local culture domination:** Hire local people or acquire companies that understand the local business. Ideally establish a couple of tight global processes – typically financial management and operational, e.g. Lean. This is how many Western companies internationalized, in particular those from smaller nations. The advantage is that the investment in aligning work practices is reduced; however, the risk is that the subsidiary and headquarters are not culturally, strategically or operationally aligned. Small companies from small nations seeking a global footprint swiftly often have no alternative to this option.

Epilogue on FLSmidth

True to their national roots, the management and board at FLSmidth listened and respected the various perspectives raised, and used a pragmatic approach to tackle the key issues. It immediately decided to increase diversity in the top leadership group with two non-Danish nationals; it enhanced the decision-making discipline and clarity through a simpler business unit (markets/products)-oriented organizational structure. Finally, as planned, the successful CEO announced his retirement and a German industry expert who had worked for a major Swedish company was hired.

Case study: P&G

This case is a simple reminder of how embedded values are constantly reinforced through the day-to-day work practices in the mature company, and will create rigidity that may become a derailer for change. Most, if not all, business environments constantly evolve, and thus companies also need to adapt. However, changing even a single aspect of a strong culture that has been reinforced over years, if not decades, requires a major leadership effort – by the right leader.

A brief history of P&G

P&G was founded in 1837. The two founders, Procter and Gamble, were religious people whose families had emigrated from Ireland and England to the USA, both ending up in Cincinnati through a combination of chance and adversity.[12] They were honest, hardworking, practical men who involved themselves hands-on in the operations. They reacted boldly and ambitiously to crises and from early on saw a crisis as an opportunity to strengthen their position. P&G was blessed with three generations of extremely capable and hardworking family members who, as CEOs, led the company for almost 100 years, thereby embedding strong and consistent values. From the founders came the honesty, almost to a fault, which can still be seen at P&G today. They had a purist quality about them, combined with American ambition and competitiveness.

Over 150 years, P&G grew to dominate the global branded household goods industry with international category winners such as Ivory soap, Star Soap, Lenox, Camay, Tide, Ariel, Crest, Head & Shoulders, Pantene, Pampers, Pringles, Oil of Olay, etc. Its success was based on both relentless execution and brilliant marketing as well as ground-breaking R&D with the aim of providing real value to customers occasionally through targeted acquisitions. P&G was competitive, and its brand managers would compete as much with other P&G brands in the same segment as with external competitors.

A few central embedded values

P&G is an American firm with strong Midwestern values reflecting its American frontier legacy combined with its founder's personal values. It believed that: "A word is a word", "A man should be judged on his character", "One should never compromise on the quality you have promised the consumer – even if it costs you money short term", "One should not make factually false statements about our products". The founders were also considerate of the workers, introducing profit sharing and staff share ownership long before other companies adopted those practices. Make no mistake, the founders were competitive, enjoyed making a profit and winning over competition and were

---

[12]Schisgall O. (1981) *Eyes on Tomorrow*. Doubleday Fergusson – extensively referenced in this section.

by no means commercially naïve. P&G developed an analytical mindset and over time a strong normative culture as discussed in Chapter 1, best expressed through the one-page-memo.

P&G always had a keen eye on the next generation of leaders and would invest significant resources in hiring the right graduates from the best colleges and later MBA schools at an early age and then hone their talent for a 25-year plus career. P&G had a policy of promoting from within. It also had its "Eyes on Tomorrow" as a book on its history from 1981 was titled. It was given to all employees – a subtle way of sharing embedded values and beliefs and inculcating the espoused values.

The focus on talent may have begun as early as in the 1880s when the third P&G CEO Cooper Procter started to recruit at universities to secure the best future leaders. The founder families believed in further education, sending their sons to the best universities. However, they were also pragmatic people. In the 1930s Richard Deupree became the first non-family CEO. He was a P&G lifer with limited educational background, having joined P&G at the age of 14. At P&G, results and character were always more important than academic credentials, a sign of a meritocratic results-oriented organization. Only the best, in P&G's own definition, came through its development system.

In 1983, when Kai Hammerich worked at P&G as a summer associate, every executive, marketing manager or brand assistant would carry with him or her at all times a big binder called "the Facts Book". This binder – it was before the PC – would hold all pertinent facts about the business: recent market research, detailed product and marketing plans as well as the strategy plans. It would also include key detailed financial performance and market share data and a history of the one-page-memos (see Chapter 1). Shame would fall on anyone who lost the Facts Book. There was a rumour that a brand manager was fired on the spot after losing it. No one knew his name, but he was no longer there and everyone knew the story, whether it was true or not! The Facts Book and the one-page-memos were the intellectual capital handed from one brand manager or executive to his or her successor, as P&G rotated their managers between brands and countries, to ensure a consistent culture and a regular fresh perspective – in the P&G way – on the businesses.

If we look at the key characteristics of a mature company, P&G would be a good fit. It had a long-term orientation in its corporate decision-making, combined with a short-term tactical/bias-for-action focus for the front-line brand managers. Their tactical empowerment was essentially managed through the one-page-memos. It was a highly results-oriented company, intending to win in the categories it played in, relying on facts and thorough analysis to guide its decisions.

The company had developed a rather dogmatic mind set – things had to be done the P&G way – and this was not up for debate. There were well-defined processes and rules for most activities, and little flexibility to change them. People who had grown up in the company oversaw the organization and the systems. P&G did not hire from the outside – on the contrary P&G was considered an academy company, training people for other "lesser" companies – so when you left P&G you were somewhat frowned upon.

P&Gers, who all work long hours, and their spouses often would also spend their spare time together. P&G was like a family for them. However, it was beginning to show the signs of an insular culture, set in its own successful ways, being almost cult-like. Many of the more entrepreneurially inclined young leaders would leave after a few years of training at P&G and go on to become very successful executives elsewhere; this list include, Steve Balmer at Microsoft, Meg Whitman at eBay and HP, H. Jeffrey Immelt at GE and James McNerney at 3M and Boeing.

By the late 1980s, P&G had become a formidable, well-oiled machine, growing globally by expanding its market share and geographic coverage. However, it also had become stiflingly process oriented, lost some of the original entrepreneurial drive and agility, and become set in its own successful ways. Over a 15-year period, P&G had only launched one successful new product – its innovation agility had clearly been compromised. A derailing cultural dynamic was at play.

By the early 1990s, it was clear that P&G needed to reinvent itself as two trends threatened it. First came the rise of dominant and powerful global retailers and discounters like Aldi, Walmart and Carrefour. They had the market power and capabilities to create strong in-house and low-cost brands, and would use their marketing skills and buying power to influence the demand, thereby lessening the value and profits of P&G's more expensive brands. P&G had developed an adversarial relationship in particular to "discounters", who they felt used P&G's brands to attract customers but would then promote their own low-cost products. However, in Walmart they found a company which shared its conservative values and focus on serving the customer. This partnership helped P&G to learn to master being brand focused and low cost at the same time.

Second, it had to become more innovative, given its lacklustre track record of innovation. In 1999 a new CEO, Durk Jager, a tough and direct Dutch national, became the first non-American CEO at P&G. He had an agenda of deep change both in terms of being more globally efficient and in becoming more innovative. He made a point of breaking with P&G's past; however, his reign lasted less than two years. He was poorly connected to the US operation, having spent most of his career in international operations, and did not create a strong following there, though his strategy and ideas were the right ones.

In 2001 a new American CEO, the softer-spoken A.G. Lafley – a Harvard MBA and P&G long-timer – stepped in with a strong US following. His style was less revolutionary – recognizing the value of P&G's past, but despite being softer in his style, he was equally, if not even more, determined to fundamentally change P&G. He continued the drive for efficiency and turned P&G's innovation model on its head. Instead of focusing on protecting its IP, P&G would embrace outsourcing of innovation and include external partners in its innovation processes by sharing its technology and processes. They would also share the benefits of innovations with the partners – in stark contrast to their historical secretive and introvert IP philosophy. In a short period he doubled P&G external innovation.[13]

As a result, between 1990 and 2007, P&G's share price went up sevenfold. At the heart of this transformation was its normative culture – a willingness to ultimately face the truth and act upon it – just as Procter and Gamble had reacted to crises 150 years before. Like all big corporations facing change, it initially engaged reluctantly, as all levels of the organization had to embrace the change and move forward together. However, its sense of shared responsibility for the well-being of the organization (family), and the right leader, ultimately enabled P&G to embrace the deep change.

P&G successfully transformed itself, and is today again a major force of innovation and efficiency. This ability to continuously transform itself is an enviable cultural trait that gives P&G a sustainable competitive advantage. Companies that are successful over several business cycles often have this normative trait at heart, which enables them to ultimately change, even though change is always tough! However, as shown in this case, it is equally important for the board to choose the right leader to lead the organization through such a period of change. In the end, leadership comes from the top!

[13]http://www.businessweek.com/stories/2003-07-06/p-and-g-new-and-improved.

Key lessons from the eight cases

This completes our discussion of eight companies over the three business cycle periods. We hope that we convincingly have illustrated how significant the impact of national culture is on a company's strategy execution over the cycles. The key lessons are:

- A national culture lies at the core of virtually every global organization
- This national culture will impact a company's ability to execute its strategy over the business cycle. Some national traits are better suited for the early phases of an emerging company, while others are better aligned with the later phase of the mature company
  - Most countries will have traits that are particularly strong in one period. In the final chapter we will list those for a small group of countries
  - These national traits can be used as a source of differentiation by underpinning unique work practices that are difficult to copy
- The board and management need to pay particular attention when a company reaches a transformation point, as it moves from one of the five phases to the next. This is when new skills and competencies are required at both the corporate level and in the front line. As seen in our cases, this is often where a company stumbles
  - The skill set and capabilities that a company carries with it past a transformation point are naturally a reflection of the previous phase and may prevent it from moving forward
- A derailing cultural dynamic, rooted in national embedded values, makes change more challenging and will require strong leadership to break. Recognizing when a nationally rooted enabling or derailing cultural dynamic is at play is a key responsibility for the board and the management
- Culture exists at three levels at the same time, the front line, the middle management and at the corporate level
  - The challenge for the leadership is to manage the dichotomy of nurturing opposing traits at different levels of the organization. Most mature companies as an example benefit from some agility and tactical orientation (often called bias-for-action) in the front line, while having a long-term strategic orientation at the corporate level
- Having a strong normative (truth-seeking) culture at the heart of the organization will help a company realize the need for change and also facilitate its ability to embrace change throughout the organization

- Having a strong leader, with the right strategy and cultural fit, will also help facilitate such a transformation
- The successful mature company may over time develop an inside-out and dogmatic perspective on the world and habits that can lead to a lack of openness to customers and stakeholders
- As a company expands during the geographical expansion phase, it should consider its strategy for embedding its culture. The three options are:
  - □ national cultural domination
  - □ hybrid global/local culture
  - □ local culture domination
- Successful entrepreneurs often have personal values and beliefs that neutralize potentially derailing national cultural traits. (Steve Jobs' focus on design perfection in a country known for its price/value focus and throw-away mentality. Moritas global outlook and open mind at Sony.)

At its very best, corporate culture guides judgement and enables people to overrule man-made systems that otherwise would dictate decisions and encourage behaviour, adversely affecting the organization.

In the next chapter we will discuss the golden rules for how linear-active cultures can make themselves attractive to members of reactive and multi-active futures!

Part III

THE MODEL IN ACTION (LESSONS FOR BOARDS, MANAGERS AND INVESTORS)

8

In the previous chapters, we have discussed how the introduction of new business strategies necessitates changing the corporate culture to accommodate them. When it is a case of predicting *internal* strategies – for instance, when an eastern US firm needs to adapt its culture to benefit from new initiatives or exigencies from California – or how Sicilian enterprises have to restyle themselves to satisfy demands of modernization or packaging from Milan – then nationals from different regions will ultimately be able to cope.

When, however, a new business strategy becomes imperative in order to deal with foreign and overseas customers and partners – belonging to different cultural categories – the task of remodelling the corporate culture becomes infinitely more intricate.

This chapter itemizes the areas in which adaptation and concessions must be made. Basically, what follows is a list of golden rules to help linear-active cultures such as Britain, Germany and the USA deal with and make themselves more acceptable to members of reactive cultures (China, Japan, Korea, Indonesia, etc.) and multi-active ones (Latin, Arab, African, etc.).

Whither the West

It has been mentioned in earlier chapters how the centre of gravity of world commerce is moving inexorably east. We say "east" not only on account of the stunning rate of growth of China in the first decade of the 21st century, but also recognizing the maturity of Japan's economy – No. 2 in the world until recently – as well as the brilliant economic performances of the Asian "Tigers" – Korea, Hong Kong, Taiwan and Singapore (Indonesia, Thailand, Malaysia, Vietnam and the Philippines are following in their footsteps). And then there is India . . .

We could also say "south". Latin America has a population of 700 million (Brazil 200 million), Africa one billion (Nigeria 180 million). The populations of North America (350 million) and the EU (500 million) seem small by comparison.

The changing economic prospects for each area are not only a question of population, though obviously China and India will become the world's biggest consumers in due course. Productivity is also significant. The work ethic in Confucian countries (China, Japan, Korea and Vietnam) is superior to any in the West with the possible exceptions of Germany and the USA (where working hours are shorter). The wage structure in China, Vietnam and Indonesia gives these nations a competitive edge which is likely to be maintained for the next two decades at least. Projections show that the West's current (2013) share of 50% of global GDP will decline to around 20% unless trends are reversed.

There are other factors to consider. The developed Western economies (the linear-active societies) have been able to hang on to their lion's share of global production largely on account of the technological gap between them and other countries. The knowledge economies of the USA (Silicon Valley), Britain, France, Germany, Finland, Sweden and Switzerland have been matched else-where only by Japan and to a lesser extent Korea. This gap is now narrowing rapidly as China, India and Brazil share technologies and innovate of their own accord.

The United States, Britain and some European countries have, in the second half of the 20th century, lost their dominance in manufacturing. America and Britain, once the factories of the world, have seen their structure of employ-ment change to US agriculture 0.9%, industry 20% and services 77%. France's industry produces 20% of GDP, Italy 28.9%, Germany 30% and Spain 30.4%. Corresponding figures for industry in the East are China 48.9%, Korea 39.6%, Vietnam 41.5%, Indonesia 49.9%, Iran 40.8%, Russia 39.3%, Thailand 44.4%, Egypt 38.4% and the Philippines 31.6%. In the southern hemisphere Argen-tinean share of industry is 35% and Brazil is 30.1%.

In the Knowledge Age, the services sector is obviously of enormous impor-tance. The largest services output is provided by the West – the USA, Germany, the UK, France, Italy, Canada and Spain hold seven places in the top 10, but Japan is second, China seventh and Brazil 10th. Financial services loom large in the US and British economies, but the sector may weaken in the face of mounting debt, particularly in the USA. The huge or burgeoning populations of China, India, Indonesia, Brazil, Pakistan, Bangladesh and Nigeria will provide billions of consumers for manufactured products for the rest of the century. The 20 largest countries in 2050 are predicted to be India, China, the United States, Pakistan, Indonesia, Nigeria, Brazil, Bangladesh, Congo-Kinshasa, Ethiopia, Mexico, the Philippines, Uganda, Egypt, Vietnam, Russia, Iran, Turkey and Afghanistan in that order, all with over 100 million people. Only *one* of these nations (United States) is linear-active Western! In the other categories there will be 5.3 billion customers!

There is no doubt that the developed West would like to trade with and sell products to this large market of multi-active and reactive people. The maintenance of its own standard of living will depend on it. The decline or loss of the West's manufacturing base will be a minus in this regard, neither are their agricultural sections particularly strong, though potential exists in the USA and Canada. Technological services will be in the forefront of their activity. The West must, however, learn to *sell* to nonlinear societies, by *adapting* to their likes and dislikes, motives, tastes and aspirations. Currently it is not equipped to do this. The cultural sensitivity is lacking, particularly in large countries such as the United States, Britain, France, Spain and Italy. Germany does a little better, though the nations best equipped to trade with the world are small, agile ones such as the Netherlands, Switzerland, Belgium and the Nordic countries.

There is no reason why major Western economies should not adapt their strategies to improve their relations with nonlinear cultures. Historically, however, the USA and Europe are both poor at adaptation. The USA is fixated on the American Dream. European countries have for centuries cooperated rarely with each other. Conflict has been the norm – Greeks against Turks, France against Germany, Russia against Poland, Austria against Italy, Spain against Portugal. The British have fought everybody in Europe except the Portuguese. Denmark and Sweden – now good friends – have been at war for 132 years – longer than any other two European countries.

If Western adaptation to the East is slow, the reverse is hardly any better. China and Japan have never fully emerged from their cultural isolation, are poor at learning foreign languages and have their own versions of uniqueness (and superiority complex). There are Chinese and Japanese Dreams as well as the American one. Their need to adapt to linear cultures is, however, less critical, since they are not chasing a market of six billion. China's focus will soon change from export-led growth to domestic, consumption-led growth and Japan's share of exports is stable. As in Europe, the most adaptable countries have been the smaller ones – Taiwan, Singapore, Korea and Hong Kong.

To restate the West's problem – how do the English-speaking and Western-European linear-active nations mitigate loss of market share and proportion of GDP by cultivating better relations and maintenance of trade with nonlinear states?

Appearance and reality

All cultures are to some extent ethnocentric, that is to say, they consider their own worldview normal and others lacking in accuracy. Western nations are also guilty of this and we talk about people being Norway centred or French centred, etc. Linear-active cultures in general have a list of qualities which they consider positive in nature and would not expect anyone to think otherwise. Such qualities are punctuality, accuracy of facts and figures, job orientation, clear schedules and deadlines, self-determination, result orientation, respect for rules and officialdom, binding contracts, scientific truth, planning ahead, word–deed correlation, transparency of motives and aims and minimization of power distance between colleagues.

In reality, these seemingly *positive* attributes are often viewed *negatively* by nonlinear cultures. Strict punctuality causes concern in Mexico, Brazil and almost all African cultures, where the mood and appropriateness of an encounter is considered more important than the moment it takes place. Facts and figures can be manipulated and in multi-active cultures are less significant than *feelings* about an issue. Deadlines are dreaded by Japanese, who fear loss of face. Job and product orientation count little without the right relationships in countries like China, Italy or Japan. German respect for officialdom is not imitated in Spain or Australia. Self-determination goes against the beliefs of Indians or Thais. In South America a contract is hardly binding, but viewed as an ideal document in an ideal world, while in China and Japan it is a statement of intent. Truth is scientific in linear cultures but contextual in Brazil, ambiguous in China, negotiated in Italy and dangerous in Japan. Word–deed correlation, so loved by Norwegians and Finns, is rarely found in Africa or in cultures that have a tendency towards euphoria. Transparency of goals is a rare feature of business in Armenia or Uzbekistan, or even France. Power distance is paramount in Saudi Arabia, Mexico and India. Careful planning ahead, so typical of Switzerland, is derided by flexible Sicilians.

Interestingly, the reverse side of the coin is when Westerners discern negativity in nonlinear characteristics which the "East" and "South" consider defensible. Verbosity – over the top for a Finn – is an earnest Italian's way of being explicit. Shows of emotion in a business context – embarrassing for Germans or Brits – illustrate the basic humanity of Mediterranean peoples. Volatility – seen as whimsical or fickle by northerners – may be viewed as light-heartedness, buoyancy or sprightliness by Africans and South Americans. Japanese opaqueness – disconcerting for Americans – is intended to guard privacy, not to deceive, while Chinese invasion of Western privacy (are you married? how much money do you earn?) is meant to show interest in the life of one's interlocutor. French and Portuguese tendency to interrupt (detested by the British or Nordics) is also intended to show that one finds the other's conversation stimulating. The Brazilian's lateness in arriving at your party indicates his reluctance to embarrass you by showing up before you expect him. Russian and Latin "flexible truth" gives you the luxury of exercising your own interpretation of it. Brazilian and Korean "elastic" truth is used to introduce an element of optimism while Chinese ambiguous statements allow you (and them) to keep one's options open as long as possible. Nepotism – common in Spain and Arab societies – is frowned upon in the West but assures trust for those who practise it. Absenteeism – condemned by Western managers – is common in Thai and some Mediterranean cultures to cultivate business relations outside the office environment.

Some Latin and Middle Eastern cultures have a tendency to mix or interrelate your joint project with others they are dealing with. This irritates single-minded Germans or Americans, but nonlinear people do this to "get the whole picture" and may in fact facilitate your project through third party influences. Bypassing officialdom, pulling strings and seeking favours from key people horrifies Nordics and Swiss, but are seen as sensible shortcuts to get things done in Greece, Turkey or Italy. This is more serious when open or covert bribery is involved, but in some countries, such as Russia, Ukraine, Iran, Indonesia and many parts of Africa, nothing gets done if "facilitation payments" are refused.

Although the tripartite categorization of cultures (linear-active, multi-active and reactive) is reasonably distinct – it is a fact that the second and third categories understand each other's behaviour more than do linear-actives. The multi-active peoples of Africa, the Middle East, the Mediterranean and South America are quite unlike the reactive (Confucian and Buddhist) inhabitants of China, Japan, Korea, Vietnam, Thailand, etc., but there is nevertheless a common denomination of understanding between the two categories regarding relationship orientations, the primacy of family, the context of truth, the concept of hierarchy, the exercise of power distance, the influence of religion

(or philosophy), the value of networking, the mixing of the social and professional, the flexibility of planning, the importance of reputation and face protection, the observance of protocol, the exercise of formality, the willingness to bypass
officialdom, the elasticity of rules and regulations, the value of indirectness
and the prioritizing of market share and long-term profit over short-term gain.

In short, there are two business worlds – the West and the Rest. In fact the
Rest live in two separate worlds, but, interestingly, they seem to agree on what
makes the world go round! To cater to multi-active and reactive aspirations,
what must Western business people do? Is one change of approach necessary,
or two? Do they need to develop different business strategies and policies to
woo the Chinese on the one hand and the Italians and Latin Americans on the
other? The answer is certainly yes. Let us consider first the steps that need
to be taken to increase the West's acceptance by reactive – largely Eastern
– cultures.

Golden rules for dealing with reactive cultures

1. Speech is to promote harmony

In the West the primary purpose of speech is to exchange information. In
multi-active cultures, e.g. France, it is to express opinions. In Eastern cultures,
what is actually said is of less importance than how and when it is said and
who says it. Platitudes – ineffective in the West – are trotted out in profusion
in Japan; flattery is also included. Platitudinous conversation, when prolonged,
strikes Westerners as time wasting and pointless; in the Eastern view, the
longer this harmonious exchange is maintained, the more likely it is that successful business will ensue. Americans, particularly, have difficulty in understanding this. The "platitudinous imperative" is observed in all first meetings
between Chinese and Japanese and often results in participants leaving the
room with only a vague understanding of what has been decided, as meaning
is easily lost in a fog of impeccably polite behaviour. Subsequent meetings will
of course clarify objectives. This process slows down decision-making in the
East, and often tests Westerners' patience when they are confronted with it.

2. Good listening is important

Reactive and particularly East Asian people tend to speak less than Western
Europeans and Americans. They usually hear you out first, then reflect unhur-

riedly, then attempt to be concise in reply. As they are high context cultures, their message, though relatively brief, may be highly charged with secondary, implicit meaning. For instance, if a Japanese says "We shall make every effort to deliver these goods in the brief period you have allowed us", he is actually telling you that he can't do it. There are other reasons for listening carefully: many East Asians have a poor command of Western languages and it is advisable to query meaning if their statements are unclear – misunderstandings of a linguistic nature are common when doing business with the East. Finally, attentive listening is courteous, which brings us to Rule 3.

3. Never interrupt

Britons and Nordics do not like to be interrupted when making a point; Americans and Australians can take it. In East Asian cultures (apart from Hong Kong) it is taboo. One must remember that they are probably making an effort to speak in English, have reflected first on what they are going to say, so it is only fair to hear them out. Even minor interlocutors must be allowed to express their views; to interrupt a senior person would be sacrilege. We shall discuss the question of loss of face later.

4. Never confront

Linear-active cultures have a sneaking fondness for confrontation: it is direct, honest and saves time. There are different levels of confrontation: Germans, Americans and Australians are much blunter than, for instance, Britons, New Zealanders and Swedes (who are partly reactive). In the East, in the interests of harmony, it is generally avoided. Koreans and Chinese may use it tactically, but not in their general comportment. The Westerner has little to gain by being too directly critical of people he hopes will be customers. Japanese and Chinese often say that the foreigners they get on best with are British, Swedes and Danes – the subtler ones. Again we have to consider face protection.

5. Never disagree openly

There are times in life when we feel we have to disagree with an interlocutor – he or she may be a friend, colleague, superior or opposing negotiator. Expressing disagreement comes more easily to some cultures than to others. Germans disagree openly, considering it to be the most honest way. Americans and Finns are also admirably frank and direct. French people disagree openly, but politely. In the East Asian cultures open disagreement is taboo – indeed most Asians are nervous about it.

British people also dislike open conflict and use various instances of coded speech to soften their opposition in conversation. The examples below indicate how ways of expressing disagreement may be affected by Swedish love of consensus, Chinese fondness for ambiguity, Italian indirectness, Japanese concern about loss of face, American cynicism, Swiss correctness, Filipino deference to superiors, Brazilian cheerfulness and Finnish humorous reticence.

▪ I don't agree	German
▪ I'm afraid I don't share your opinion	French
▪ I agree, up to a point	British
▪ Let's agree to disagree	British
▪ We agree	Japanese
▪ We agree if all of us agree	Swedish
▪ We agree and disagree at the same time	Chinese
▪ Have another cup of coffee	Finnish
▪ I agree with you, but I don't think my board of directors will	Swiss
▪ You gotta be kidding	US
▪ You are the boss	Filipino
▪ I suppose anything's possible	Brazilian
▪ Let's go and have a Campari and talk about it tomorrow	Italian

6. Never cause anyone to lose face

No understanding of Asian mentality is complete without a grasp of the concept of face. Having face means having a high status in the eyes of one's peers, and it is a mark of personal dignity. Especially Chinese, Japanese and Koreans are acutely sensitive to having and maintaining face in all aspects of social and business life. Face can be likened to a prized commodity: it can be given, lost, taken away or earned. You should always be aware of the face factor in your dealings with Asians and never do or say anything that could cause someone to lose face. Doing so could ruin business prospects and even invite retaliation.

The easiest way to cause someone to lose face is to insult the individual or to criticize him or her harshly in front of others. Westerners can offend Asians unintentionally by making fun of them in the good-natured way that is common among friends in the West. Another way to cause someone to lose face is to treat him or her as an underling when his or her official status in an organization is high. People must always be treated with proper respect. Failure to do so makes them and the transgressor lose face among all others aware of the situation.

Just as face can be lost, it can also be given by praising someone for good work in front of peers or superiors or by thanking someone for doing a good job. Giving someone face earns respect and loyalty, and it should be done whenever the situation warrants. However, it is not a good idea to praise others too much, as it can make you appear to be insincere.

You can also save someone's face by helping him or her to avoid an embarrassing situation. For example, in playing a game you can allow your opponent to win even if you are a better player. The person whose face you save will not forget the favour, and will be in your debt. A person can lose face on her own by not living up to others' expectations, by failing to keep a promise or by behaving disreputably. Remember, in business interactions that a person's face is not only his own but that of the entire organization that he represents. Your relationship with the individual and the respect accorded him is probably the key to your business success in China and the rest of Asia.

7. *Suggestions, especially criticism, must be indirect*

Open criticism, especially of a personal nature, is taboo in reactive cultures. If one disapproves of a statement or course of action, alternatives may be suggested in a humble manner, as indirectly as possible ("we tried something like that in Sweden last year . . ." or "another thing we found useful . . .").

Asians are experts not only at introducing other ideas indirectly, but also using indirect questions to elicit information or opinions: "I don't suppose you would have Tanaka's figures . . ." or "in the event that . . . could we consider . . .?

Japanese, who are critical of your stated intent or your suggestion, will not say so openly. Silence avoids discord; what they are likely to do is refrain from engagement with your idea. They will quickly pursue another course of action without drawing too much attention to it. Westerners can also do this with impunity; Asians will understand.

8. *Be ambiguous, so as to leave options open*

This is a frequently-used tactic by Asians themselves. Where Westerners normally are looking for commitment, Asians see no advantage in premature engagement. During a negotiating period or preparation for action, circumstances may change. Delaying a commitment may carry with it risk, but alternatively new opportunities may surface. Asians like options. Concepts such as right and wrong, good and bad, true and untrue are not written in stone as they are in the West. A course of action, for instance, may be right or wrong according to conditions or context. It may be right and wrong at the same time. Decisions must be made at appropriate times in order to be right. For a Chinese, a decision (apart from being right or wrong) must be virtuous. It is often said that Japanese, for their part, often delay decisions so long that all options except one are eliminated, leaving them the correct course of action. Though Westerners, particularly Germans, Americans and Norwegians, may feel uncomfortable with ambiguity, they have little to lose by exercising it with Asians, who might respect them for it. Asians are uncomfortable with unalterable commitments.

9. Prioritize diplomacy over truth

Purely factual truth is viewed with suspicion by all Asians. Things are not always what they seem, as any scientist will tell you. Unless it is positive, truth can be a dangerous concept in China, Japan and Korea and if too bluntly expressed is risky anywhere east of Istanbul. The English, with their coded speech, are not wedded to the open expression of truth; diplomatic Swedes and Danes, though lovers of veracity, win medals by using diplomacy in the Far East; Finns at least know when to keep their mouths shut. Unless trained in diplomatic speech or manners, most Australians, Americans, Germans, Norwegians and Dutch are simply too blunt to avoid offence. Face protection is of course the issue.

10. Follow the rules but interpret them flexibly

Americans, Germans, Swiss, Dutch and to a lesser extent Britons and Nordics habitually respect officialdom. This is partly because their officials and institutions are generally efficient and deliver permits, judgements, mail, etc. within a reasonable time period. In many multi-active societies – Mediterranean, African, Middle Eastern and east Balkans – this promptitude is lacking. Consequently people in these areas have less respect for rules and seek shortcuts.

Reactive people in the Far East lie somewhere between these two worlds. Punctuality and rules are certainly respected and adhered to in Japan, China and Korea, but they are viewed more as wise arrangements rather than unalterable edicts or commandments. Asians, when confronted with an inconvenient statute or ordinance, do not break the law, but they look at the obstacle from a series of different perspectives and seek out the most lenient interpretation. This often involves Asian "common sense", a variety of its own, which attracts compliance from officials, advisers, interested parties, even erstwhile opponents.

11. Utilize networks

Asian societies make great use of networks. In China the basis is the family system which operates not only in the People's Republic, but also among its overseas Chinese members in Hong Kong, Singapore, Taiwan, Indonesia, Europe and North America. There are Wongs in London and Zhangs in Vancouver. The Korean family network, though not quite so ubiquitous, is similar in character. In Japan networking takes place also among families but more so among classmates and university colleagues. Westerners who have been able to secure one or two good friends in Japanese society are able to reach anyone in the business community through their friends' intermediary. For instance, let us say that you wish to obtain an appointment with the advertising manager of Mitsubishi Heavy Industries. Your friend Takeshi Sato does not work for Mitsubishi, but Okada, who was at Keio University with him, does. Sato contacts Okada, who works for Mitsubishi Electric and is therefore able to go across the Mitsubishi conglomerate to his opposite number in the Heavy Industries Division, Kawamura. Kawamura is not close to the advertising manager, but he plays tennis once a week with Kishi, who knows him well. The Japanese networking system obliges Kishi to help Kawamura who must help Okada who is obliged to help Sato his Keio colleague, who, because of your friendship, must help you. This type of networking takes place a thousand times a day in Japan and you are perfectly entitled to make use of it (provided of course that your friend Sato *owes* you). It is important therefore for Westerners to cultivate meaningful personal relationships in Asian societal structures.

12. Don't rush or pressure Asians. Do things at appropriate times

The comments we have made above concerning promotion of harmony, face protection, leaving options open and use of diplomacy indicate manifestly that Asians do not like to be hurried. Kipling mentions an epitaph that read "A fool lies here who tried to hustle the East". It is advisable to do business with Asians at their preferred tempo, which is likely to be at a slower pace than your own (Hong Kong is the exception). Even more important is to understand the Asian proclivity to recognize the *appropriateness of timing*. In his previous publication *When Cultures Collide* (Nicholas Brealey, 2000) Richard Lewis comments at length on this phenomenon, and quotes:

> "The Japanese have a keen sense of the *unfolding* or *unwrapping* of time – this is well described by Joy Hendry in her book 'Wrapping Culture'. People familiar with Japan are well aware of the contrast between the breakneck pace maintained by the Japanese factory worker on the one hand, and the unhurried contemplation to be observed in Japanese gardens or the agonizingly slow tempo of a Noh play on the other. What Hendry emphasizes, however, is the meticulous, resolute manner in which the Japanese **segment** time. This segmentation does not follow the American or German pattern, where tasks are assigned in a logical sequence aimed at maximum efficiency and speed in implementation. The Japanese are more concerned not with how long something takes to happen, but with how time is divided up in the interests of properness, courtesy and tradition.
>
> For instance, in most Japanese social gatherings, there are various phases and layers – marked beginnings and endings – for retirement parties, weddings, parent-teacher association meetings and so on.
>
> In Japan's conformist and carefully regulated society, people like to know at all times where they stand and where they are at: this applies both to social and business situations. The mandatory, two-minute exchange of business cards between executives meeting each other for the first time is one of the clearest examples of a time activity segment being used to mark the beginning of a relationship. Another example is the start and finish of all types of classes in Japan, where the lesson cannot begin without being preceded by a formal request on the part of the students for the teacher to start. Similarly, they must offer a ritualistic expression of appreciation at the end of the class.
>
> Other events that require not only clearly defined beginnings and endings but also unambiguous phase-switching signals are the tea ceremony, New Year routines, annual cleaning of the house, cherry blossom viewing, spring 'offensives' (strikes), midsummer festivities, gift-giving routines, company picnics, sake-drinking sessions, even the peripheral

rituals surrounding judo, karate and kendo sessions. A Japanese person cannot enter any of the above activities in the casual, direct manner a Westerner might adopt. The American or Northern European has a natural tendency to make a quick approach to the heart of things. The Japanese, in direct contrast, must experience an unfolding or unwrapping of the significant phases of the event. It has to do with Asian indirectness, but in Japan it also involves love of compartmentalization of procedure, of tradition, of the beauty of ritual."

To summarize, when dealing with the Japanese, you can assume that they will be generous in their allocation of time to you or your particular transaction. In return, you are advised to try to do the "right thing at the right time". In Japan form and symbols are more important than content.

13. Observe fixed power distances and hierarchy

Most Asian companies, large and small, have a fixed hierarchy among their employees and management. It is not an exaggeration to say that in a Japanese company of 50 people, each one would know his exact "number", i.e. on which rung of the ladder he stood. This is normally fixed in terms of rank; one ascends the ladder, of course, by getting older. New, younger employees start on the bottom rung. In the Confucian manner (China, Japan, Korea) each individual advises and instructs the person one rung down. This system does not take into account the relative intelligence or competence of the individuals. In a collective society, age and date of university degree count for more than merit. Asians are generally content with this system and bypass it at considerable risk. As far as the Westerner working in an Asian company is concerned, he should try to ascertain "which rung he is on" and behave accordingly. If he is number 5, he will obey and show great respect to numbers 1–4. He is entitled to instruct and show less respect (though he must be courteous) to numbers 6–100. Most Asians are uncomfortable talking to "equals" or to persons whose rank they have not ascertained. Talking up or talking down is no problem. That is why the meticulous exchange of business cards (which indicate rank) is mandatory in Asian countries. Westerners should never try to interfere with power distance or promote employees to a position above their "ranking" (it can be disastrous for the person concerned). Inequality is willingly acquiesced to among reactive Asians.

14. *Work hard at building trust*

Building trust with Asians is a slow process, though not necessarily difficult. Again, it is a question of timing. Americans and linear-active Europeans arrive in the Far East ready to do business. Americans, particularly, like to get down to brass tacks. In all Asian countries they will encounter a reluctance to discuss business in initial encounters. What has to take place is a procedure which could be described as a courtship dance. Westerners are invited by their hosts to sit down and drink tea. Conversation ranges over many subjects, but business is not mentioned. Americans grow impatient. They consider there are many nice people they can sit down and drink tea with, but they want to discuss *deals*, which are relatively scarce. Asians have the opposite view: deals and products are plentiful and ubiquitous; what is scarce are people you can trust.

The courtship dance may take hours, days, weeks or months. It may involve lunches, dinners, theatre outings, golf, excursions – in Thailand kick boxing. During these activities anything may be discussed *apart from* business, except in the most general terms. The "deal" itself must not be mentioned for some time. What Asians want is to see you, listen to you and evaluate you. They are in the process of deciding whether they want to do business with you or not. They may be considering entering into a relationship which could last 20 years or more. This is a serious undertaking on their part. Linear-actives, by entering into the spirit of sociable intercourse, friendly exchange of views and even details of their private lives, can best serve their cause (a solid business relationship) by postponing its realization until they feel their Asian partners are ready for it. Most linear-actives, particularly Americans, fall into the trap of discussing details of profit-sharing and obligations at too early a stage. Until trust has been established, Asians shun such minutiae like the plague. Among linear-actives, Swedes, Finns, Britons, Canadians and South Africans are the most likely to exercise the necessary patience in early meetings and preliminaries.

Golden rules for dealing with multi-active cultures

If the golden rules for dealing with reactive cultures have emphasized the key characteristics in which East Asians differ from Westerners (e.g. obsession with face protection, the search for harmony, tendency towards ambiguity, collective deportment) there are nevertheless certain traits which linear-actives have in common with reactives, in spite of the geographical and historical distance between the two categories. These include: punctuality, calm, patience, some introversion, sense of reserve, limited body language, non-tactility, disdain for verbosity, dislike of rhetoric or open emotion, good listening, reluctance to interrupt, general reliability, steadfastness, forward planning, willingness to compromise, hatred of debt and fondness for understatement (Americans excepted).

These commonalities enable Brits and Nordics to work in relative comfort in Japan, Malaysia, Singapore and Hong Kong as well as Americans in Thailand, the Philippines, Korea and Vietnam. The cultural categories are dissimilar, yet to some extent compatible. *This is less true if we compare linear-actives with multi-actives.* In this comparison we see that the salient characteristics of linear people are *diametrically opposed* to those of multi-actives (e.g. introversion v. extroversion, reticence v. verbosity, calm v. emotion, results orientation v. relationship orientation).

Linear-active behaviour is an Anglo-Germanic phenomenon originating in northwestern Europe and rolling out through colonization to North America, South Africa, Australia and New Zealand. Among non-Germanic peoples, only Finns have joined this category and even they are partly reactive. Two continents – North America (minus Mexico) and Australasia – are completely linear-active. The strikingly different destinies of North and South America (the latter colonized by multi-active Spaniards and Portuguese) are an indication of the yawning behavioural gap between the two categories. How history would have been different if Columbus had continued on a northwesterly course to Florida or if the Pilgrim Fathers had been blown off course (like Cabral) and settled northeastern Brazil!

It is important to note that, through a quirk of fate or historical accident, the Anglo-Germanic bloc from the 18th century onwards began to regard itself as *superior* in efficiency, both in commerce and ability to rule, than other cultural categories. This conviction of superiority, with its accompanying drive, may have had its roots in cold climate competence and energy, Protestant reforming zeal or German thoroughness. It certainly blossomed subsequent to the English industrial revolution, the rapid development of British and American manufacturing (fuelled by abundance of coal) and the continuous existence of democratic institutions in the Anglo and Nordic communities. However this may be, the linear-active "powers" leading up to and after the two world wars, emerged with *de facto* world leadership based on military might and, even more significantly, over 50% of global GDP.

This sense of pre-eminence, particularly in the English-speaking world, but also shared in no small measure by Germans, Dutch, Swiss and Nordics, *has not yet subsided*. The BRIC (Brazil, Russia, India and China) quartet are showing rapid gains in manufacturing, technology, financial muscle, access to commodities and market share (China the star performer), but Western complacency has not yet been eroded. There is still a lingering notion among the linear-active countries that our systems of governance, our concepts of justice, our attitude to human rights, our intellectually vibrant societies, our cocktail of work and leisure, our right to lead and instruct others, our business methods and our ability to maintain our levels of production and high living standards are viable in the future. We may be right about everything but the last two or three. We are content with our way of life and worldview. We feel we have got it right, the others not yet.

The danger of such thinking is believing that the others *want* to be like us. In fact most multi-actives do *not* and the French have often said so. Even more dangerous is our tendency to show little respect, even disdain, for characteristics of other cultures. Examples are American contempt for Mexican timekeeping, British amusement at French body language and Scandinavian derision at Latin verbosity. Linear-actives and multi-active cultures see each other in an entirely different and often unfavourable light. In *The Cultural Imperative* (Nicholas Brealey, 2003) Richard Lewis describes the cultural spectacles through which Germans and Italians see each other:

"Italians through German Eyes

Values and Core Beliefs. Italians seem to be among the most disorganized of Europeans, with a multitude of political parties and changing governments every few months. Prime ministers and other leaders are in and out of power as if they were in a revolving door. Even failed and tainted politicians are re-elected regularly and are often simultaneously in court on corruption charges. More than one ex-prime minister has been linked convincingly with the Mafia (often seen as the best-organized political force in the country). Northern Italians are so fed up with the chaotic and clan-ridden south, they have formed a party whose aim it is to split the country in two. Italians seem to have little respect for Parliament, government, law, or the Church, remaining loyal only to their own families and the clique to which every Italian male belongs. Their standards of probity and commitment fall far short of our own, and though they rank as the world's ninth industrial nation, we have no idea how they managed it.

Communication. We Germans are capable of conversing and analysing things at great length, but we are taciturn compared with the Italians. We argue in a fairly straight line, but they go around in circles – ever-widening ones. The problem is that at the end we are not all sure what they have said or in which direction they are heading. We usually make the agenda for meetings, but they avoid it conscientiously. When they make an agenda, it reads like a short story.

Social and Business Behaviour. Italians set great store by their charm and charisma and think they can pull the wool over German eyes with their tactics. They are pleasant enough characters and confide in us greatly, telling us all about their families, their professional and social lives, where they were educated, where they go for their holidays, and so on. They don't realize that we do not want to know all these personal details – their hopes, aspirations, disappointments, and so on. *It is none of our business.* They want to get too close to us too quickly – and not only spiritually, but physically, too; they have little hesitation about touching us, even hugging and sometimes *kissing* us after only a short acquaintance! Who do they think we are – pets? However, we must admit their general manners are better than ours, and they never seem to be insulted. Although we are often very dry and ironic with them, they don't seem to notice.

Italians don't appear to understand that business in Germany is done strictly according to the law and that we follow rules and procedures rather than getting things done 'through the back door' and using key acquaintances. We know that sometimes influence counts in our country, too, but we don't talk openly about it. During meetings Italians often talk two or three at a time and make a mockery of any agenda we attempt to start with. In general they agree to most of our proposals but only follow up on those that interest them. They are somewhat unreliable suppliers and late payers. When they negotiate a price, they start high and come down a lot, their final prices often being reasonable.

Other. With their relaxed nature and natural exuberance and optimism, they are in many respects the opposite of Germans, but they are pleasant companions (for a while).

How to Empathize and Motivate. We listen to their joys and woes and pretend we are interested. We go easy on the irony and play the 'flexible price' game with them. We make allowances for late deliveries and payments. We hug them occasionally and try to enjoy their humanity.

Germans through Italian Eyes

Values and Core Beliefs. The Germans are always telling us how honest and reliable they are; we suspect they are comparing themselves with us. They strive to lead good, orderly lives and respect the law so much they won't even cross an empty road at midnight if the light is red. They also pay their taxes regularly, keep only one set of books and are quite ungenerous in giving little presents to officials. They all seem to want to get into Heaven rather badly, but we aren't sure we want to get into a German Heaven!

Communication. German communication style is so frank and open that we know the whole story in five minutes and wonder how we can begin to negotiate or even make interesting conversation. If we start to show a little artistic creativity with their cold facts and figures, they attack our logic and criticize us mercilessly. If we pretend to be upset, they say they are only trying to help us. Humour doesn't help either – they don't think our jokes are funny, and *they* won't tell any while doing business. We must admit they are truthful, sensible people, but they come across as a bit heavy at times.

Social and Business Behaviour. Germans spend a lot of money on new clothes, but we would not go so far as to say they are well dressed. They go in for a boring charcoal grey rather a lot – it's like a uniform for executives. When we show up in tastefully designed sports jackets, they ask us if we have just arrived back from holiday. On introducing themselves, they shake hands snappily in military fashion. Mentally, they've got to be clicking their heels. They don't smile much initially (in Germany smiling is only for friends); we try to be their friends, but if we try too hard, they get suspicious.

They are very formal at business meetings and use titles a lot. Most of them are "Doktors." You can always tell who the delegation leader is because the others always glance at him before they say anything they think is important. Our bosses are autocratic, too, but in our case we pretend not to be. Germans expect us to arrive on time at their meetings and come fifteen minutes early to ours, before we are ready. Agendas, schedules, timetables, and contracts are all holy documents in their eyes. We like to ad-lib a lot at meetings, and they try to write down everything we say, but after a while, they give up.

Other. Germans seem to indulge in a lot of soul-searching and worry about whether they are leading good lives or not. We think they are, but they are not sure about us.

How to Empathize and Motivate. Although the Germans criticize us, we are not offended because we know that nobody is perfect. We usually agree to everything they say; we can always modify things in due course. We share the dream of a United Europe with them, and we don't challenge their leadership, as the French do."

Both sides have a right to see each other in their own way (the descriptions are only partly humorous). Each side sees its worldview as superior.

The problem for linear-actives is not only do we show too little respect for multi-actives, but that we shall have to get them to buy our products in order to maintain our living standards. We want them to be our customers: the other consideration is that there are five billion of them, including one billion Latins and another billion on the African continent. What must we do to woo them?

1. Speech is for opinions

Communication patterns differ sharply from culture to culture. We have commented above how a harmonious atmosphere can be created by the appropriate use of speech in the reactive category. East Asians use conversation as a give-and-receive-respect mechanism and are able to establish relative status and rank in a few sentences. Linear-actives use speech primarily to give and receive information. In multi-active cultures – France is a good example – words tend to convey opinions rather than facts. French, Italian and Portuguese people, for instance, believe that they can convince anyone of just about anything, provided they can gain sufficient personal access. They see speech as a powerful weapon in terms of eloquence, fluency and persuasion. Northern Europeans, particularly Finns and Norwegians, are suspicious of any kind of verbosity which they see as a tool for hiding facts rather than disclosing them. They tend to retreat into their shells when faced with a barrage of views. A better policy is to respond, by expressing one's own opinions in a similar manner. This brings us to rule number two.

2. Let them talk at length and then reply fully

Multi-actives in general and French and Spaniards in particular want to develop their ideas at length and wish to be heard out. They permit interruptions, but continue to reinforce their message by completing their argument. There is nothing to be gained by denying them this completion – they are grateful if you permit this and subsequently listen to your reply with equal attention. You should in fact reply fully; they will not find your loquacity out of order. It is normal for them. If you are too laconic or taciturn, they may well be disappointed, even miffed. Not to engage them sufficiently is like refusing to bargain with an Arab, who is disgruntled at your failure to haggle.

3. Be prepared to discuss several things at once

Linear-actives like straightforward utterances illustrating the salient point they wish to make. One sentence deals with one subject. In German, sentences have rigid word order in a tight grammatical straitjacket, with the conclusive verb at the end. Multi-actives, even when speaking English, tend to use longer, more convoluted sentences with one or more subordinate clauses and, even worse, occasional references to other points of interest. Multi-actives have busy minds; they tend to relate the subject under discussion to other concerns present in their thoughts. Where an American when envisaging raising salaries would concentrate on its economic viability, a Frenchman might draw into the discussion questions of the company's reputation in society, the mood of the trade union, the effect it would have on certain individuals, even his or her own position.

   For the same reason, multi-actives are reluctant to segment business issues and decide on piecemeal solutions. All has to be discussed to get the whole picture; decisions should be holistic, or problems will ensue. Such thinking leads to lack of respect for strict agendas.

4. Be prepared for several people talking at once

Meetings in linear-active countries generally follow an agenda and people speak in turn, one at a time. This is not the case in meetings held in multi-active societies. Apart from the agenda question, speakers tend to *talk over each other* (in meetings, informal conversations, television and radio interviews) in places as far apart as Italy, Brazil and Hungary as well as in all Arab and African countries. A German executive, sent out to manage his company's subsidiary in Brazil, experienced great difficulty in running orderly meetings in his firm. Little respect was shown to the chair and it was normal for three or four people to be speaking simultaneously at almost any time. The German, a disciplinarian, as many of his countrymen tend to be, was not only frustrated by these proceedings, but was personally unable to follow the gist of concurrent conversations. His Brazilian colleagues assured him that they were missing nothing that was said in the room. Finally the German pulled out yellow cards which he brandished to anyone who spoke out of his turn. If the transgression was repeated, he showed the miscreant a red card and sent him out of the meeting for half an hour. For football-minded Brazilians this measure was effective and the chairman had orderly meetings as a result. When he asked them the reason for holding four conversations at the same time, they told him they got four times as much work done that way.

5. Display feelings and emotion

Spaniards, Arabs and others give full vent to their emotions, leaving you in no doubt as to their disappointment, anger, joy or surprise according to the situation. British, Nordics and Canadians often find this difficult to do, as their national conditioning encourages them to present a calm exterior, composure and avoidance of open emotion. This works well with reactive Japanese and Chinese, but Latins, Arabs and Africans are gratified more by observing your honest reaction through at least facial expression. They want to know you are human! Don't be too gruff. For multi-actives, feelings are more important than facts.

6. Interrupt when you like

In multi-active cultures it is not rude to interrupt another's speech as long as this is done politely. In fact interruptions are viewed favourably, as they are interpreted as a sign that you are showing interest in your interlocutor's remarks. No interaction would give the other the impression that you are bored or simply not listening. Good interruptions are, for instance: "What exactly do you mean by . . ." or "I agree with most of what you say, however . . ." or "That's very perceptive". By the same token, you must be prepared to accept interruptions from multi-actives. Finnish officials in Brussels have to be strongly encouraged to interrupt French or Italians, otherwise they may never get a word in.

7. Truth is flexible and situational

Only linear-actives stick entirely to scientific truth, and even that is restricted to North Americans, Nordics, Germanics and Australians. British, with their coded speech, as well as understated New Zealanders and culture-conscious

South Africans are not averse to white lies or economy of truth when the occasion demands. Multi-actives in general see truth as a malleable concept dependent on situation and context. Italian truth has been described as flexible (even negotiable), Portuguese as tailored, conciliatory; Spanish use "double truth" (immediate or long-term?), preferred Arab truth is moralistic, Hungarian opportunist, African poetic. French truth is usually dressed up, Brazilian elastic and optimistic (don't bring bad news). Russian truth, in public at least, is a convenient lie.

As a linear-active you will be most comfortable using scientific (factual) truth but it is wise to accept that other versions exist; don't rush to condemn others' variations. Above all, don't face anyone down.

8. Be diplomatic rather than direct

Though multi-actives are less sensitive than reactives to direct assertions or criticism, it pays to exercise diplomacy in attempting to get them to do what you want. The French are the most direct of the multi-actives, though they pride themselves on their *savoir faire*.

9. Socialize enthusiastically, be gregarious

Multi-actives mix business with pleasure much more than linear communities. Office hours are more flexible, especially in the evening. Italian businesspeople usually go to a nearby bar after work and socialize with colleagues before going home. Madrid's bars and restaurants hum with activity until the early hours. Venezuelan cocktail parties can last till midnight – people go out and eat after that. Germans and Scandinavians work hard from 9 to 5, but head quickly home thereafter. Germans particularly like to compartmentalize their working and leisure hours. Hungarians and Eastern Europeans linger in their coffee houses, Portuguese ask business colleagues and customers to dinners which may commence at 9–10pm. Brazilian get-togethers often seem interminable to Northerners.

10. Think aloud

Latins, Greeks, Arabs and Africans habitually think aloud as they pace up and down reflecting on future courses of action. This is rare in linear societies (outside of the United States) and unthinkable in Nordic countries (or Japan, for that matter). If you can train yourself to indulge in this practice in the company of multi-actives, you have more to gain than to lose. Voluble speakers often have difficulty second-guessing the intentions or thought processes of opaque Finns or Swiss, and may be relieved by oral transparency.

11. Complete human transactions

Linear-actives are good at completing action trains; that is to say, when they have embarked on a course of action or project they will concentrate on its completion and are reluctant to allow human interference while they are thus engaged.

Multi-actives are less single-minded about action trains, but very much concerned with completing *human* transactions. That is to say, once they have embarked on a meaningful conversation or other significant engagement with a fellow human, they drop all other matters until the human errand has been brought to a satisfactory conclusion. To illustrate the point, if an American businessman is on the phone when a close friend of his suddenly enters his office, he will wave his friend into a corner to wait till he has finished his phone call. An Italian, by contrast, will quickly terminate the phone call in order to greet his friend in a cordial manner.

12. Seek and give favours with key people

Multi-actives, often hampered in their countries by inefficient officialdom, have no hesitation in seeking help from key connections they may have (cousins, uncles, schoolmates) to obtain shortcuts to gain advantage in business. They are not obsessed by the linear-active idea of a "level playing field" for all. If they can obtain favours, they will go for them. As good colleagues, they will generously offer the use of the key connection to linear-actives who normally do not indulge in such activities (they may even consider them nefarious). It is a mistake not to accept help and assistance from such sources. If the proffered favour is refused, there will be three unfortunate interpretations of the event: (1) you will be seen as "holier than thou" (or stupid); (2) your friend will feel rebuffed; (3) help from the key connection will not be available in the future, in time of need. A corollary of favour seeking is favour granting. An Italian or Arab who considers you to be a close friend will have no hesitation in demanding favours from you. You may not be in a position to provide the help requested, but you cannot refuse outright. In principle you have no option but to grant the favour. If it is not possible, you have to show you made your best endeavour.

13. *Overt body language and tactility are acceptable*

All multi-actives use considerable body language (facial expressions, gestures, postures) though they vary in style and degree. As a linear-active you need not imitate them, but you should not fall into the trap of assuming that extrovert body language indicates unreliability. All unreliable Italians gesticulate and use many facial expressions. But all reliable Italians use them too. Tactility is another matter. Each culture has its "distance of comfort". Linear Northerners (like many Asians) function comfortably at a distance of 1.2 metres from their interlocutor. Latins, Arabs and Africans prefer about 50–80 cm. Most multi-actives are tactile, especially Mexicans and Arabs. In many multi-active societies, males may kiss each other on the cheeks. Use your own judgement, but do not retreat too quickly or too far or you will offend your partner.

14. *Reputation is as important as profit*

Most cultures are profit minded, but both multi-actives and reactives consider the reputation of a company more important than profit. This is particularly noticeable in France where managers are expected to be well educated and caring towards subordinates. In France, as in Sweden, state-owned firms are national symbols. In Russia firms or individuals who are openly (too) profitable or asset-rich are disliked by the people as a whole.

15. *Accept unpunctuality*

In most multi-active countries, poor time-keeping is endemic. It has little to do with laziness; people in cold climates show up more readily for work than in hot ones. In temperate climates, Italian, Spanish and East Europeans simply attach more importance to the mood and atmosphere in which business is transacted than to the actual time it is supposed to take place.

16. *Remain relationship oriented*

In linear-active cultures and especially those with a history of manufacturing, people are product oriented, that is to say they believe in the primacy of products – that if of good quality, they will make their own way in the world – they will sell readily and be accepted by the majority. Having won over the customer, linear individuals will then develop a comfortable relationship with him in order to perpetuate custom.

In multi-active and reactive cultures, things do not work that way. That might have been the situation in the 19th and the first half of the 20th century, when most manufacturing was carried out in linear-active Britain, Germany, Sweden and the United States, and the modern products emanating from these cultures dominated consumption. Now, the situation is different. China is the factory of the world; in addition goods are provided in abundance in nonlinear countries such as Japan, Brazil, India, Korea, France and Italy, while Middle Eastern countries and Russia provide the world with oil and gas. Customers in Asia, Africa, South America and Europe have a wide choice as to what and where they buy. Spaniards, Indians, Arabs, Turks and Africans buy from people who are nice to them. Instead of the product paving the way for business relationships, the cultivation of relationships paves the way for the sale of products. Probably 80% of purchases are made on the basis of viable, close relationships between buyer and seller, not on consideration of the quality-and-price ratio of the item concerned. Primacies of relationships exist at the personal level, also between corporations and governments. China and India are currently competing for African acceptance and affections in order to tap the vast African consumption of the 21st century.

If one could only give linear-active businesspeople one piece of advice – one principle to follow – in order to succeed in business in the other cultural categories, it would be this:

PUT RELATIONSHIP BEFORE PRODUCT

when dealing with your customer.

This cannot be done in a day, a month or a year. It is a process that involves cultural dynamics over a protracted period – in all likelihood a fundamental reorientation of well-worn commercial principles in order to cater for a new, changing world which offers a plenitude of possibilities on a scale we could only dream of.

In the next chapter, we will discuss the nature of the crisis, which can hit a company at any time, but often will coincide with it navigating a transformation point.

9

In this chapter we will examine the nature of the corporate crisis. We will study eight of the most typical sources of an existential corporate crisis and use examples from our cases to better understand the root cause and highlight the influence of the national culture.

A crisis is a defining moment in any organization's life. Will it prevail or falter? Overcoming a crisis often embeds deep values in the psyche of the corporation. A company facing financial disaster where, in its view, it was mistreated by the banks, may decide never again to be reliant on external funding – if it survives the experience. However, not all organizations will or should survive such a disaster. Sometimes, the forces of creative destruction as suggested by Schumpeter will simply play out; the organization will disappear unceremoniously and other, more efficient, organizations will take its place.

However, some organizations like P&G, Siemens, Shell, GE and Exxon have prevailed over many decades, and continue to add value to society. We are not arguing that all companies should or could prevail for centuries. In our global society with its higher level of transparency and accountability, there is less room for inefficient companies, or companies that don't comply with basic legislation and human rights. By enhancing insight into their own cultural strengths and history, we believe more companies could prosper for longer, which is one of the main reasons for writing this book. If we can inspire just a few companies to add value to society for longer, we have indeed achieved one of our objectives.

These seven sources of a crisis, which we will discuss in turn, include:

- Poor strategy facing competition
- Poor execution

- Disruption:
  - Technology
  - Process
- Success
- Time
- Change of leadership
- Navigating a transformation point

It is a philosophical discussion as to whether corporate decline is inevitable or not. The reality is that the oldest business organizations are only a few hundred years old at most, so in the timescale of eternity or humanity, business organizations have a limited lifespan. However, this is not the same as arguing that a business can't expand its useful life. In Diagram 9.1 we show the original lifecycle model by Dr Adizes.

By understanding the dynamics of the crisis, you, the company management and the board will be able to navigate its perils more effectively. In Diagram 9.2 we link the crisis and the resurgence of an organization to our lifecycle model, though it is important to note that a life-threatening crisis can hit at any point in time, as indicated in Adizes' lifecycle model, and not only in the maturity period.

Let's look at each of the causes of a crisis in turn and examine how different organizations responded to them and the role the national culture played.

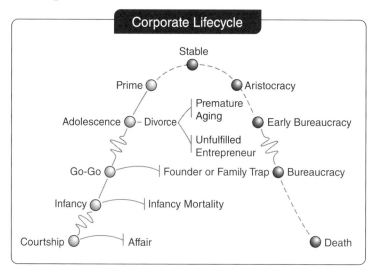

Diagram 9.1: Dr Adizes' original lifecycle model
Source: Adizes, Ichak (1999) *Managing Corporate Lifecycles*. Santa Barbara, CA: Adizes Institute, reproduced by permission.

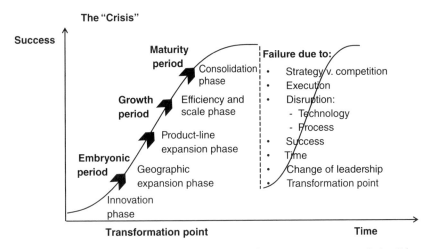

Diagram 9.2: Link between crisis and resurgence of an organization and the lifecycle model

These seven types could be described as being archetypical, and thus transgress borders and cultural differences. Where national culture plays a distinct role, we will highlight it. But in most situations, the influence of national culture will be through enabling or derailing cultural dynamics. In the last section of the chapter, we will review the national influence for each type of crisis.

Strategy v. competition: being "outplayed"

This is a classic business situation, where the competition simply had a better strategy and "outplayed" the organization. Let's go over 200 years back in time and look at what happened when the disciplined Prussian Army met Napoleon's motivated army and was "outplayed", and how it responded in both a very Germanic and a very un-Germanic way.

The Prussian Army and Field Marshall Von Moltke

On a foggy October day in 1806, the Prussian Army suffered a simultaneous and devastating defeat when two of Napoleon's forces acting almost as one destroyed it in the twin battle at Jena and Auerstedt.[1] The Prussian Army was until then seen as the ultimately well-oiled war machine, run with iron discipline

[1]Bungay S. (2011) *The Art of Action*. Nicholas Brealey, p. 27.

and clear top-down control and command, by experienced generals often recruited from the Prussian upper classes. The defeat led to a fundamental review of the lessons learned, and resulted in a fundamental change in the people, the leaders, the culture and the skills and leadership capabilities of the top officers. This transformation also required a new set of behaviours that would challenge deeply rooted German national traits and the traditional military work practices.

It fell to the philosophical thinker Clausewitz to examine the root cause of the defeat. In his book *Vom Kriege* (On War), he reflected on the reality of battle based on his own experiences during a 40-year career in the Prussian Army, including being on the field during the defeat in 1806. He led a disciplined and intellectually objective review, as one would expect of a German thinker, of the lessons learned from 1806. He coined the expression "Friction" as a summation of the uncertainties, errors, accidents, technical difficulties, the unforeseen and their effect on decisions, morale and actions in battle.[2]

His central insight was that during war you need to match the unavoidable chaos in a battle with operational agility and empowerment while maintaining the strategic direction. Chaos should not be matched with the rigidity of a command-and-control organization, with limited or no empowerment to act at the operational levels, which until then had been the trademark of the Prussian army. In the chaos of battle, if you have to wait for orders, precious time and thus the battle may be lost – thus it was concluded that the only way to remedy this was through a professional officer corps with the ability, authority and willingness to make decisions in real time.

In 1808 general conscription was introduced, and the officer ranks were officially opened to all, regardless of social position. Promotion was driven by performance rather than years of service; however, the transformation slowed during the long peace after Napoleon's final defeat in 1815. In 1857, Field Marshal von Moltke was promoted to Chief of the Prussian General Staff. His leadership philosophy was heavily influenced by Clausewitz, as to how an organization should reconcile the dichotomy of strategy and tactical execution in the foggy chaos of battle, where the best laid out plans meet the independent mind of an opponent and the reality of random circumstances.

Over the next 30 years Von Moltke would personally transform the work practices and thus culture of the Prussian Officer Corps. He set about creating

---

[2] Bungay (2011), p. 29.

a culture of intelligent and independent thinking, to create an effective system of command that ensured cohesion in execution. In 1869 he laid down his principles in *Guidance for Large Unit Commanders*,[3] which laid out the principles for higher command and remained unchanged for 70 years. After analyzing the effectiveness of these principles, they were embraced by both the US Army and the British Army following the first decades after WWII.

Von Moltke's principles were simple. He expected the operational commanders to understand the strategy and the tactical intentions well enough so that they could make tactical decisions during battle, without referring to a more senior officer. He would sensibly encourage risk taking, and, as long as it was aligned with the strategic intent, failure would not be criticized. He would praise individual initiative within these boundaries and actually required junior people to depart from the letter of their instructions if the situation demanded it. In modern language we would call this strategic transparency – principles far remote from the old thinking in the Prussian Army where lower levels were only expected to execute and not to understand.

He also emphasized the need to plan only for what can be planned, trusting that the operational levels were capable of making judgements and timely decisions in the situation, without compromising the overall intent and the operational cohesion.

In today's parlance he thus believed in setting a clear strategic objective for the organization and giving directives that were broad enough for the operational units to understand the ultimate goal – on a day-to-day basis – while empowering them to act according to the situation. For Von Moltke, strategy development and strategy execution was one and the same thing.

To expedite the cultural change, he created the General War School as the primary development vehicle. Every year from 1858 to 1881, he would personally lead two staff rides with 20–40 officers for up to two weeks and supervise the conduct of war games that could last for months. The result was, as Von Moltke himself said, that in a given situation, 99 out of 100 officers would think like him. He thus created a unified operating model by working on the minds of his generals, allowing them to absorb a common doctrine based on principles rather than rule. He would only admit officers among the high potentials to the General Staff who had proven they were willing to disobey

[3]Bungay (2011), pp. 57–59.

orders – at least in exercise. Creating a common culture around new work practices and habits is a long and difficult process, which requires constant, personal, hands-on leadership from the top.

An essay from 1860 tells a story of a staff officer dutifully carrying out an order without question, only to be pulled up short by a high-ranking general with the words: "The King made you a staff officer because you should know when *not* to obey." Not exactly the perspective you would expect of a law-and-rule-abiding German with a liking for *Ordnung*.

As a curiosity, Von Moltke first used these new principles when the Austrian–Prussian Army defeated the Danish Army at Dannevirke in 1864. This led to the loss of one-third of Denmark's territory (Saxe-Lauenburg, Schleswig and Holstein) and started a period of introverted mourning. However, it also inspired the industrial revolution in Denmark, where entrepreneurial companies like FLSmidth helped rebuild the Danish economy, as we saw earlier in the book, proving that a "crisis" can be the source of rejuvenation.

The effect of national traits

The dogmatic nature of the Prussian Army, which displayed many of the typical characteristics of a mature organization, reinforced the work practices of being hierarchical, disciplined and control–command oriented. The crisis came when that strategy and its work practices proved ineffective against Napoleon's enthusiastic troops inspired by the French Revolution. However, normative (truth finding) German characteristics also helped the organization recover and find a way to transform its work practices – yet to enact the transformation it required a great intellectual mind and a determined leader dedicating over 30 years of personal leadership to embed these new values in every single officer and in the organization.

Any organization, whether in the embryonic period or in the maturity period, can suffer from choosing an unsuccessful strategy. The mid-size Danish toy company LEGO floundered when an unsuccessful strategy of brand and product diversification in the late 1990s led to financial disaster. A new CEO refocused the company on its roots and today the company is more successful than ever – and the crisis may well have revitalized the company beyond what would have been possible without it. Similarly, a start-up company often has to change its business model and strategy several times before hitting a successful one. But even if you have the right strategy, you also have to execute it well to succeed.

Problems in execution

Examples – Sony and GM

In the case of Sony versus Samsung, the difference in performance was rooted in their different abilities to execute. Sony had the right strategy, having predicted the event of the converged and connected digital world, and had the financial might to execute this strategy. However, it got caught between the execution-oriented Samsung on the one hand and innovative Apple on the other. Both had superior technical skill and capabilities, though fewer financial resources at the time. To navigate this dual challenge successfully would have required Sony to execute to perfection. However, instead the urge for consensus, the shortage of relevant software skills in the organization and in Japan, combined with a leadership vacuum after the founder generation passed away, prevented Sony from taking the necessary assertive actions.

Similarly, at GM the leadership never got to grips with the significant cost disadvantage it had slowly been building. Over several decades, when GM was highly profitable, powerful unions secured not only attractive salaries for their members, but also perpetual retirement and health benefits. As GM's market share declined and its scale advantage with it, GM could no longer command the same levels of profits. No matter how well it executed its commercial strategy – which it didn't – the structural rigidity and cost it carried ultimately became insurmountable. In contrast, Ford managed to navigate this more effectively, and was not bailed out by the US government, despite also having generous employee benefits by US standards.

The effect of national traits on poor execution

Many industries evolve to maturity with only few global winners of similar size. Consequently, executing well is the key to staying competitive. There can be multiple reasons for poor execution, some of which are rooted in the national culture. It could be the culturally based misjudgements of Asian companies acquiring declining European brands, not fully realizing the impact and rigidity of local employee laws. Or it could be a European or American company entering a new market assuming that the work practices that were successful in the home market will make them successful in the new market too, like Walmart in Germany. Or it could be a derailing cultural dynamic that prevents the company from executing the strategy.

If the organization needs to execute a strategy that requires capabilities that are at odds with its national profile, it may find that challenging. A Danish company executing a strategy requiring disciplined process execution could struggle against companies from countries with a stronger process orientation. Likewise a Korean company that needs to execute a strategy of being creative and diverse may find this challenging. However, in both cases you may be able to identify leaders from that country with the appropriate personal competencies who can guide the effort with success. People fortunately come with a broad range of personal capabilities, whatever their national upbringing.

Failure of execution may also simply be caused by the fact that a competitor was more urgent and sharper at the game. Two young men walk leisurely in the jungle. Suddenly, a hungry tiger appears in front of them, growling, ready to attack. One of the young men bends down and starts putting on his running shoes. The other one looks at him in amazement and asks: "Why are you doing that – you can't outrun a tiger." He responds as he finishes tying the final lace: "Well, I don't have to outrun the tiger!"

Disruption

One of the most common causes for a crisis is a disruption. Few have written more convincingly about this than the Harvard professor Clayton Christensen in his book *The Innovator's Dilemma*.[4] The two most common forms of disruption are the technology disruption and the process disruption.

Technology disruption

A technology disruption is essentially when a new technology replaces an old one. Steam power replaced animal and hydropower. Then, electrical power and the combustion engine largely replaced the steam technologies. Among the computer mainframe companies, only IBM survived. The rest of what was then called the "bunch" (Burroughs, UNIVAC, NCR, Control Data and Honeywell) disappeared. The mainframe companies were then replaced by the mini-computer companies where only HP survived as an independent organization – the other main players Digital and Tandem were acquired by HP, and Sun by the software company Oracle. The mini-computer was then replaced

---

[4]Christensen C. (1997) *The Innovator's Dilemma*. HBS Press.

by the personal computer, which in turn may be replaced by the mobile phone and the tablet. At every technological transition point, old players were left behind and new emerged, though sometimes it can take decades for such a transition to take place.

Sony and Nokia both grew to global dominance in the first technology cycle, then were challenged by a technological disruption as their industries entered a new period. In Sony's case it was the transition from mechanical technologies to digital technologies and in Nokia's case it was the transition from customized embedded software and highly specialized components to operating systems and content-based ecosystems, more akin to what was used in the PC industry.

In both cases, the companies understood the potential for disruption, but either dismissed it or didn't react forcefully in time. In his book, Clayton Christensen outlines five principles of the company facing disruption:

1. **Companies depend on customers and investors for resources.** The implication of this principle is that it is difficult for existing companies to allocate resources to a new idea, which has a different resource profile in terms of business model, skills and capabilities and work practices, i.e. a company competing in the high-end may struggle to be profitable with the low-cost model of a new technology. The best option is often to create an independent organization with the appropriate cost structure and culture.
2. **Small markets don't solve the growth needs of large companies.** Many large companies adopt a strategy of waiting until the new market is large enough. This creates a difficult dilemma for them. They are not organized to nurture multiple new business ideas that have the potential to disrupt, but may or may not be successful. However, once the disruptive technology is identified, it often requires different skills and capabilities and a new business model, making it difficult to successfully merge it into the larger company.
3. **Markets that don't exist can't be analyzed.** As we discussed in Chapter 7, the mature company tends to be more analytical and facts based, and thus well placed for sustaining evolutionary technological innovation – but maybe not for more creative "out-of-the-box" disruption. If a disruption challenges the "mental model" of the organization, it usually is very difficult for the incumbent to recognize the threat and act on it – a bit like fish-can't-see-water. Large companies are inflexible, dogmatic and set in their ways of looking at the world. Thus a new disruptive trend that poses a challenge will easily be dismissed.

4. **An organization's capabilities define its disabilities.** As we have seen repeatedly, a company carries with it the capabilities and skills set of the earlier phases. In the case of Sony, mastering semiconductor and components manufacturing was seen as the task for sub-suppliers, and not central innovation in the mechanical era. However, when those skills became the source of innovation and standardization in the industry, Sony found it difficult to compete with Samsung. Had Sony, however, succeeded in establishing an overarching technical architecture for its home entertainment products, it might have turned out differently – but the skills for this were in short supply at Sony and in Japan. In such situations, the forces of creative disruption will dictate that the company either changes or decays.

5. **Technology supply may not equal market demand.** The simple observation is that disruptive technologies, though they initially can only be used in small markets remote from the mainstream, are disruptive because they subsequently can become fully performance competitive within the mainstream against established products. When the first 20-pound heavy mobile NMT phones were introduced, it came with limited coverage and was used mostly for travelling salesmen and executives. Few, if any, fixed-wire operators would see them as a threat to their core business.

The effect of national traits on technology disruption

The forces of disruption are omnipresent across borders. One could argue that being agile, open and flexible may prepare a company better for dealing with a disruption. However, business books are full of examples from every nation of the effects of disruption. What you, the management and the board should watch out for is the emergence of a derailing cultural dynamic that may make the company less open and agile to recognize a threat of disruption.

Given that P&G only had one new successful product category launch in 15 years, this should have alerted the board and the management to the fact that something was amiss. American short-termism and corporate power play may have played a role in this; however, national culture can only explain some dynamics, definitely not all of them.

Process disruption

Another key source of disruption is through a transformation of the work processes and work practices. Online retailing is a good example of the impact of the supply-chain revolution that has changed the face of retailing globally. At one level it is of course based on a technology disruption; however, to embrace this, new technology companies had to redefine their workflow completely. New players like American Amazon and eBay are radically different from the traditional retailer. They employ different people – who are often young, analytically minded and brilliant at mining Big Data. As a consequence they have developed distinctly different corporate cultures from the established competitors in book publishing and traditional retailing.

The effect of national traits on process disruption

In the Toyota example we showed how unique work practices deeply rooted in the Japanese culture helped Toyota gain a sustained competitive advantage over a 20-year period or more. It proves the point that an established player can innovate in a mature industry when bringing a different perspective to the "game" that is being played. Toyota, for instance, established a supply-chain of primarily Japanese companies that they would work closely with, sharing technologies and giving financial support at times. This structure was consistent with Toyota viewing itself as a typical Japanese vertical *keiretsu*, seeking harmonious relationships with its partners. The structure contrasted the more adversarial relationship Western automakers had established with their suppliers. It enabled Toyota to remain nimble and agile for a long period, while in particular American car manufacturers pursued a strategy of vertical integration. That strategy in turn laid the foundation for establishing bloated and inefficient bureaucracies, as most visibly seen in the case of GM, which over time made them less competitive.

Success – the success crisis

That success can lead to disaster has been known for centuries and is often referred to as corporate hubris. Hubris indicates an overconfident pride and arrogance that is associated with a lack of humility, though not always with the lack of knowledge.[5] Hubris often becomes visible through a cultural dynamic that is fuelled by national influences. Jim Collins' excellent book *How*

---

[5]http://en.wikipedia.org/wiki/Hubris.

the Mighty Fall[6] is a *tour de force* of describing the nature of the downfall of the American corporation and its potential resurgence. In essence once a company believes in its own infallibility, it risks closing its eyes to external threats and thereby opens the gate for disaster – and that can happen in any culture or country. Let's look at some of the key aspects of "the success crisis" for a business corporation.

Success makes blind – the success trap

Success makes an organization blind, and hubris easily sets in with the top team becoming internally focused rather than externally focused, competitive and agile. This happened at GM, it happened at IBM in the 1990s and it happened at Nokia. Organizations that successfully navigate the success trap often have a humble and normative perspective on the world, combined with strong values that are aligned with achieving their core mission. The philosophy of Gerstner at IBM was that the right leaders have a sense of urgency in good times and bad times and whether they are faced with a crisis or not – that urgency is not cultural, it is simply good leadership. During a period of success, the leadership and the owners of a corporation should watch out for any indication of a derailing cultural dynamic.

Success has no memory

Success or the perception of success is the mechanism that reinforces behaviour. However, success is indiscriminate in the sense that it will reinforce enabling behaviours present, as well as any derailing ones at the time of success, and disregard whether they had anything to do with the success or not.

We have talked about the time lag of up to five years between a culture change and the strategy change. The current success of the large organization is often based on actions taken a while ago. However, *success has limited memory*, in particular if there has been a change of leadership or strategy. The current team will take credit for the current results and will link the results with their own immediate contribution and implicitly to the strategy present at the time of success. This way success can sow the seeds for later failure by reinforcing derailing behaviours that had little to do with the success at the

[6]Collins J. (2009) *How the Mighty Fall.* Random House.

time, as we saw in the cases of Nokia, GM and Sony. This effect may be a contributing factor to companies hailed by management gurus as being outstanding in one period only to fail in the next period.

The share price trap

A company's share price is the ultimate measure of success, in particular in linear-active countries. A high share price will in itself focus the organization on maintaining that share price at all costs in the short term, and can make the company short-term oriented and strategically less agile, in particular if the company is publically listed and share price-based bonuses are a key part of the executive compensation philosophy. This, in itself, can then sow the seed for failure by reinforcing derailing behaviour.

Dell invented the direct model in the late 1980s; however, the market changed in the early 2000s, when competitors became able to replicate its efficiency. It has since proved difficult for Dell to balance its desire for keeping the share price up, while investing in finding a new business model in retail, consumer products or services to replace the direct model. A company whose basic business model is threatened often faces the dual challenge of having to maintain a high share price in a market that has already peaked, while funding the new business that could save them. Kodak unsuccessfully struggled with moving from its legacy film business to the digital era. It ultimately went bankrupt, despite realizing the threat over 15 years in advance, and inventing the digital camera.

This is one of the reasons for the success of private equity in the linear-active Anglo-Saxon part of the world, and the resurgence of family-owned companies. A company that needs to go through a period of transition and investment may find it difficult to do this when publically quoted. You rarely hear a chairman say: "The company needs to go through a tough transition period and therefore the shareholders will need to be patient and brace themselves for four to five years of poor financial results and lower share price as we manage this transition." He or she would rarely last through the next AGM, even if it would be in the best long-term interest of the company.

Private equity companies can take a company out of the limelight for a period – typically up to five years – to invest in the necessary transformation. Likewise, family-owned companies do not have the short-term pressures of the stock market. It can often take an even longer-term view of the business and be willing to accept riskier investments for the long term.

Failure may be the best preamble for change in a publically quoted company – as it creates a burning platform, which the company can use to transform its work practices and culture. The key challenge for the management, the board and the shareholders is to seize this opportunity for change!

The burning platform

Times of failure are often the best point to introduce new work practices and to change behaviours. It normally takes a recession or a dramatic drop in financial performance to motivate an organization to fundamentally change. GM wasn't able change its ways and had to be bailed out by the US government, despite top management and the board knowing for many years that the company was not in a sustainable situation. There are numerous examples of companies that changed too late. The same happened with Polaroid and Bethlehem Steel in the USA, the same with ICL Computers in the UK, Bull in France, the East Asiatic Company in Denmark, and so on. They saw it coming for a long time but couldn't or wouldn't change.

Yet, an exclusive group of companies have managed to recover from the depths of failure: Apple was failing when Steve Jobs returned as CEO in the late 1990s and went on to become the highest valued company by 2011. P&G has reinvented itself several times during its 175-year history. So have Caterpillar, IBM and GE in the USA, ABB and Siemens in Europe and Samsung in Korea. What characterizes these companies is a combination of strongly held long-term focused business values, combined with determined leadership at the time of crisis and an ability to use a burning platform to revolutionize their way of thinking and work practices. As we mentioned before, having a strong normative inclination at the heart of the culture and being willing to face the truth when it matters greatly facilitates this ability to change with the times.

The subject of cultural change management is beyond the remit of our book. Many excellent books have been written on the subject including Dan Denison's recent book *Leading Culture Change in Global Organizations: Aligning Culture and Strategy*.[7] The discussion in the final chapter of how a company needs to identify and inculcate new habits and replace old habits is excellent and very much in line with our experience with enabling and derailing behaviour as discussed in Chapter 4.

[7] Denison D., Hooijberg R., Lane N., Lief C. (2012) *Leading Culture Change in Global Organizations*. Jossey-Bass.

However, a burning platform ultimately is just as it says, a platform for change – but not a guarantee that it will happen.

Time – if you don't move forwards you move backwards

Economic theory dictates that over time returns will revert to normal. A new product may start out commanding a higher return, maybe through patent protection, but ultimately competition or the end of the patent will ensure that returns revert to normal. The art of business is to create market situations where the company can command a higher return to the shareholders on their investments. However, the gravity of competition and innovation also means that if you don't move forwards – invariably you move backwards. This goes for all of us as individuals and for corporations.

Fifty years ago, owning a small car dealership for a young entrepreneur was as attractive as starting a PC dealership in the 1980s or a specialized social website in 2012. Today, car and PC distribution are mature industries, dominated by large players, with little room for the entrepreneurial owner. The independent retailers find it more and more difficult to compete with the larger and more efficient chains. When radio and TV were a novelty, they were sold by specialist shops and educated sales people. Today they are just two of many product lines sold by electronic goods retailers and increasingly sold online.

In 1912, the list of the top 25 most valued companies included 20 rail and infrastructure companies, one steel company, one telecommunications company, two oil companies and one clothing manufacturer.[8] In 2012,[9] the top 10 list was dominated by four technology companies, four oil companies, a bank and an industrial conglomerate, showing the inevitable results of the lifecycles of industries. However, three companies – GE, Shell and Exxon (Standard Oil) – were in the top 25 in both centuries, proving that large companies can thrive for decades if not centuries.

[8]http://www2.e.u-tokyo.ac.jp/~sousei/WARDLEY3.pdf.
[9]http://qvmgroup.com/invest/2012/03/31/worlds-30-largest-public-companies-by-market-cap/.

Change of leadership

The founders and their family-related successors have a deep and often permanent influence on the success and embedded values of an organization. Some companies like P&G and Samsung have been blessed with talents within the family that could lead the company for up to three generations or, in rare cases, even longer. However, if a company is to exist beyond the founders, ultimately it will need to transition from a founder to a managerial regime. This transformation is always a testing point in time for the organization. If it coincides with a "crisis" as we saw in the case of Austin and Sony, it can exacerbate that crisis.

In the technology sector, three out of five of the highest market cap companies are still founder led. IBM successfully moved to a managerial regime in 1971, while Apple only did it in 2012. Microsoft, Google and Oracle are still founder led. If Apple is hit with a disruptive trend or crisis in coming quarters, this may well turn into an existential crisis, as the company seeks to establish a new managerial regime. In the 1990s, Apple failed partly because it moved to a managerial regime too early in its lifecycle. If the consumer electronics industry continues to innovate at the current rate, the success of Apple this time will depend on its success with truly inculcating continued innovation in the organization, both from a cultural and organizational perspective. Managing the transition to a managerial regime is a key responsibility for the board of any family or founder-led business that transgresses national borders – and it can never be taken lightly.

Navigating a transformation point

In Chapters 5, 6 and 7 we discussed how a few companies navigated the transformation from one phase to the next and the critical role national traits played in this. As a company rushes through the lifecycle phases, ultimately it will face a transition point that will require it to fundamentally change. This is where the perils of failure will be most prominent. Predicting the severity of the next transition point is a key responsibility for the management and the board, which until now has been taken quite lightly – "we will handle it when we get there" seems to have been the instinctive response.

Whether increased pace in international business is an indication of a shorter corporate lifecycle – only the future will tell. In the digital era, Web 2.0

companies need to go global in a few short years to be successful and some even speak about companies needing to be "born global". In social media-based segments, the company that gets there first often becomes the winner in its segment; just look at companies like Google, Amazon, eBay, Yahoo, LinkedIn, Facebook and Twitter.

However, even for these digital giants, transformation points have to be navigated. They have expanded at a mind-boggling pace, creating enormous shareholder value in the process which, however, may mask underlying issues. In some countries such as China, India and Russia, local competition with a better understanding of the consumers and local politics has blocked the dominance of the digital giants and some have not yet expanded beyond their initial single-line-of-business and one-size-fits-all models.

The challenge for the board is not simply analyzing the present situation and identifying potential derailing cultural dynamics, it is also a question of understanding "where the ball will bounce" in the next period. A central question for the leadership and the board in any corporation should be: What will the effect on our corporate culture and values be, once we have implemented the new work practices dictated by our strategic imperatives? This is a very sensible exercise when considering profound changes in work practices, and can help significantly to reduce the execution risk.

Finally, let's now explore how the national character may influence the response to each of these "crises" in a bit more detail.

Differing cultural performances in times of crisis

Poor strategy facing competition

There is little doubt that the British, notwithstanding their long experience in international business, have often been slow in coining new strategies, compared with arch rivals in manufacturing such as Germany, Japan and the United States. Their 19th century successes, largely due to the Industrial Revolution – born in Northern England – gave them manufacturing pre-eminence for the best part of the century. This enabled them to supply the inhabitants of their 15 million-square-mile empire – stretching from England to the Americas, Australasia, the furthest reaches of Africa and Asia itself – including the vast subcontinent of India – with iron and steel goods of all kinds, including engines, tools, arms, boats, cargo vessels, liners and a variety of manufactured items the whole world needed or wanted. British coal fuelled the building of the Empire, the ships that patrolled it, the railways that distributed its products and the guns that defended it.

Such industrial (along with political) dominance inculcated in the minds of the English elite a sense of superiority over other people – especially non-whites – that lingered for decades after the Empire had disappeared. Such complacency, persisting between the World Wars and even post-1945, left the British unprepared for challenges such as the German Miracle, the rapid burgeoning of American post-war industry, and, most surprising of all, the runaway success of the (non-white) Japanese. We discussed earlier the decline of Austin and the lack of strategy in the automobile industry. In other areas, the British were equally lethargic, persisting in retaining and investing in industries that they had no chance of sustaining, e.g. coal, steel, textiles and shipbuilding. Insularity and love of tradition are continuing factors impeding British alacrity. Only in the sphere of financial services have British strategies led the field; for the most part they have a reputation for "muddling through".

The French, also conservative and traditional, are nevertheless more quick-witted than the British. They often make changes on impulse. They cannot be regarded as slow-coaches. However, their reluctance to learn English is poor strategy for pursuing business in China, Japan, the United States and most of the world. In this regard, the British can certainly outperform them.

The Italians, invariably adaptable, are quick to change strategies – especially pricing – when facing competition. They have been particularly adept in marketing cars and white goods.

The Americans, change oriented by nature, generally are skilful in adopting the right strategy to meet competition – their ubiquitous presence in the world's market means they often set benchmarks.

The Chinese and Indians face competition with confidence in many areas of manufacturing. Their overarching strategy – that of rock bottom wages in their factories – is normally triumphant.

Poor execution

The Germans, with their renowned efficiency and sound planning, outplay most rivals in terms of good execution. They excel in quality, timeliness and exactitude. This is largely due to structure based on experience and *Ordnung*, perhaps lacking to some degree in, for example, companies in the Hispanic world or Eastern Europe.

Koreans pride themselves on good execution, exemplified by industry leaders such as Samsung, Hyundai, LG and Kia. The Koreans' incentive to maintain high standards emanates from their burning desire to "beat the Japanese". Switzerland and the four Nordic countries excel in execution. As far as the Americans are concerned, they have few problems with quality or timeliness but are slow to analyze differences in local cultures. They may not always be giving foreign customers what they want.

Disruption

This is often caused by the rapid emergence of new technologies which cause previous ones to suddenly become outdated or obsolete. The Americans are best placed to deal with such phenomena. Most, though not all, new technologies emerge in the United States. Computers and mobile or smartphones have evolved at a bewildering pace and, as we have pointed out, certain US firms have suffered acute crises as a result. Adaptable companies such as Sony and Nokia encountered serious disruption, though in general one would expect technologically strong countries such as Japan, Korea, China, India, Sweden, Finland, Germany and the UK to cope. However, considerable financial losses can be incurred when popular technologies become obsolete.

Success

If we scrutinize the names of the companies currently in the top 100 Fortune firms, we shall see that only just over a dozen survive from the comparative list compiled a hundred years ago. Success can breed hubris, decline, bankruptcy and disappearance. How can one avoid this happening? It is partly a question of national culture. We have discussed British "colonial-style" complacency, which was one of the reasons why Britain slipped from number one economic power to sixth (and soon to be eighth, ninth or tenth). France-centred France suffers from equal smugness. Large French firms, especially in the automobile industry, have slipped badly (though enterprising Michelin is a shining exception). Hubris was one of the causes of Daimler's disastrous merger with Chrysler. Again, American blind overconfidence resulted in Walmart's repeated failures in trying to "do it the American way" in both Europe and Asia. In general, the USA is the chief culprit in pushing American "success" methods in cultures that disdain them; Japanese, Canadians and Australians are more modest in their approach to foreign markets. Koreans, eager to win but realistic in their expectations, strike the right balance. Korean chaebol owners do not fall into the share price trap, so lethal in the USA, where shareholders' demands can prejudice a marginally profitable operation. Even though the chaebols are now run by professional managers rather than by the owners or their relatives, there is little pressure on them to provide profits that might endanger the fate of the enterprise. Finns, too, in spite of Nokia's setbacks, try hard to remedy problems caused by the firm's temporary (though uncharacteristic) hubris.

Time

In the last 20 years, China has outplayed everyone in moving forwards, though Korea has been a good second. Concentrating on technology, the United States, India, China, Korea and small Finland are likely to be leading innovators and maintain momentum, while Brazil is finally "beginning to move". Japan, however, has stagnated for two decades, due to her postwar alacrity encumbered by fearsome bureaucracy and lethargic political parties. Mature conglomerates like Shell and Unilever are content to move forward at their own pace. Norway's giant Statoil has deliberately slowed its development in the interests of conservation and long-term solvency!

Change of leadership

Change of leadership occurs more easily in some cultures than others. In meritocratic, change-oriented USA, it is a natural event although firms justly hang on to intelligent, charismatic leaders until they begin to fail. In Germany, change of leadership is not a huge problem, as successors are expected (and inclined) to follow strict procedures and established processes that created the successful enterprise in the first place. Changing a manager is more complicated in France. While mistakes by German leaders are not easily forgiven and American managers are summarily fired if they lose money, there is a high tolerance in France for management blunders. The humanistic leanings of French and other Latin-based cultures encourage the view that human error must be anticipated and allowed for. Managers assume responsibility for their decisions, but it is unlikely that they will be expected to resign if these backfire.

If they are of the right age and experience and possess impeccable professional qualifications, replacing them would not only be futile, it would point a dagger at the heart of the system. For the French, attainment of immediate objectives is secondary to the ascribed reputation of the organization and its socio-political goals. The exalted position of French chief executives (one cannot fire a mediocre one) is often seen as a drawback for the enterprise and the national economy.

Leadership change in Japan often produces *no change*, both in companies and at government level. Vigorous leaders such as Morita, Matsushita, Nakasone and Koizumi are few and far between. Leadership change has been successful in Brazil and Korea inasmuch as in both countries there took place a fortunate transition from centralized management to one exercised by a staff of professional managers. In Brazil, rule was originally vested in rich families who were hand in glove with the army. In fact, for decades, business was run primarily by the military. Given the size and eventual growth of the country, conduct of commerce just became too complex for a small number of key people to control and thousands of managers were educated and trained to run the economy. The same happened in Korea, where the families owning the chaebols had to found a large managerial class to achieve efficiency and growth.

Navigating transformation

Navigating transformation and predicting its effects is the responsibility of the management and the board, but such decisions often have to be taken considering the background of the national economy. The most traumatic change is due to take place in China, where declining speed of growth dictates an urgent transition from a decades-long export-led economy to a domestic-led one. Tens of millions of rural Chinese people are moving to the big cities. By 2020, there will be numerous metropoles with more than 20 million inhabitants. These cities, with their incalculable capacity for consumption, will transform the imperatives and goals of Chinese enterprises, both state and in the private sector. Resolving the thousands of crises that will arise during this transition will define the eventual commercial face of China for the rest of the century.

Russia, too, faces an inevitable transitional crisis of enormous proportions. Currently 80% of Russian GDP is resources based (oil, gas, minerals). Commodities are presently abundant and highly priced. Russian state and private enterprises are acutely aware of the problem and are already active in international organizations such as G20 and the WTO, exploring long-term solutions and agreements with governments and conglomerates.

India faces more transformation problems than any other country, given her widespread poverty levels and fragile infrastructure. Some cultures are more adept at handling chaos than others – India, Russia and Italy are among them. The BRICS group (Brazil, Russia, India, China and South Africa), if successful, can solve a lot of problems for each other. China not only can buy Brazilian crops, but also already sends peasants to farm (neighbouring) Russian land. India will need to find a meaningful role in this quartet. Land-and-resource-rich Canada and Australia could undergo favourable transformations. Asset-poor Japan faces demographic problems and may have to transform her immigration policy.

American, British and other Western companies with their numerous subsidiaries in Europe, Asia, Africa and South America will need to predict and handle crises with sufficient agility as they arise. This will have to be done with respect to and in conformity with local cultural tradition and in sync with the current politico-economic climate of the countries they operate in.

Meeting crises

Below you will find an overview of the instinctive reaction to a crisis in different countries:

Fast moving	Slow moving
China	UK (conservative traditional)
Hong Kong	Germany (process dominated)
Korea ("beat the Japanese")	Sweden (obsession with consensus)
USA (innovative)	Japan (stagnating)
Finland (innovative)	Vietnam (communist)
Denmark (innovative)	Argentina (myopic politics)
India (*jugaad*)	Switzerland (comfortable with status quo)
Italy (adaptable)	Norway (comfortable with status quo)
Netherlands (international experience)	Canada (comfortable with status quo)
Chile (agile)	
Russia (must find economic and cultural identity)	

Chapter closing

This completes our exploration of the nature of a "crisis" and how an organization's national character influences the corporate response to it. It also marks the end of the final main chapter, before the concluding chapter that will summarize our observations and discuss its implications.

National culture and corporate culture are simply one lens through which one should analyze a company and their performance. It doesn't replace other perspectives, but adds a complementary view to the currently more popular business strategy and execution orientation. This rational perspective has become prevalent in particular in companies in linear-active countries and among their business advisers and bankers. Regrettably, we argue, in recent years the softer cultural perspective has become rather unfashionable with many simply dismissing its importance over other, easier-to-measure, factors.

Our modest hope is that we have presented a convincing case that, in our increasingly global world, national heritage still matters and for leaders and students of management it is worthwhile and rewarding to revisit this perspective.

10

Changes in global commerce, political or socio-demographic spheres may cause the same traits that facilitated a company's success in one evolutionary period to derail it in the next. This may necessitate rapid adaptation of its business strategy and corporate culture. Boards and management play a vital role in ensuring the company has adequate cultural alignment with the chosen strategy. Herein lies the risk. Companies are often blind to their own national culture. And because corporate culture is so soft and complex, dysfunctional behaviour is easily swept aside with subjective arguments and dismissed as not being important. Who can argue with numbers that are audited by a reputable global and government certified auditor? But it seems that anyone is free to argue with the interpretation of culture to support whatever agenda they have. Therefore, we suggest that companies elevate the cultural discussion so it is more data driven, without losing the important nuances and the soft nature of the subject – to ensure it is taken seriously!

To achieve this, the board and the management must create a governance framework that allows for a more objective discussion of culture – even when it is difficult – and create a culture that allows management to look in their own cultural mirror in a non-threatening manner. *Diversity of thinking and respect for other people's perspectives* are two critical virtues that should govern this for the leadership of most global corporations.

In this chapter we outline the eight actions companies must take to create a culture of openness and respect based on factual analysis. We will also briefly discuss some of the ramifications for countries as they compete to enhance their competitiveness in a global world.

Seeing the water that surrounds you

The framework presented in this book will help companies and their leadership navigate the challenges of strategy and cultural alignment. It has five simple steps:

1. Determine the main dimensions of the company's strategy and cultural alignment using the Cultural Dynamic Model®
2. Classify the national type that reflects the embedded national values using the Lewis model
3. Identify where the company is in its lifecycle
4. Establish how national culture may have enabled and/or derailed success at the most recent transformation point and could impact the organization at the next
5. Diagnose signs of a potential crisis accentuated by a cultural dynamic with the potential to create a life-threatening situation for the company.

In the Appendix, we have listed some of the most common current national enablers and derailers for some of the main economies. These characteristics are often blind spots for the management, as they are part and parcel of their belief system and therefore critical for boards and management to be aware of. Ignore them at your peril! Yet they also present an often unexplored opportunity to enhance performance by embracing deeply rooted national traits and behaviours that can help the organization gain a sustainable competitive advantage, as we saw in the Toyota case.

The national lifecycle fingerprint

In addition to these common national traits, every country has a unique cultural profile or fingerprint that underpins its companies as they develop over the corporate lifecycle. Below we have briefly outlined the national profiles of three countries: Denmark (Diagram 10.1), Japan (Diagram 10.2) and the USA (Diagram 10.3) as examples.

The national profile of Denmark reflects the respect for the individual, the collectivism, the pragmatism and openness, but also the independence that makes Danes react negatively to rules and regulations they have not themselves defined. These characteristics support Danish companies in particular in the embryonic period, as evidenced by the high number of small and

Denmark

Short term	✖	Long term
Bias-for-action	✖	Analysis
Flexibility	✖	Rules
Pragmatism	✖	Normative
Openness	✖	Dogmatism
Agility	✖	Process

Diagram 10.1: Outline of national profile of Denmark

Japan

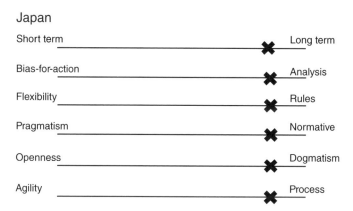

Short term	✖	Long term
Bias-for-action	✖	Analysis
Flexibility	✖	Rules
Pragmatism	✖	Normative
Openness	✖	Dogmatism
Agility	✖	Process

Diagram 10.2: Outline of national profile of Japan

▲ The embryonic company

✖ The mature company

USA

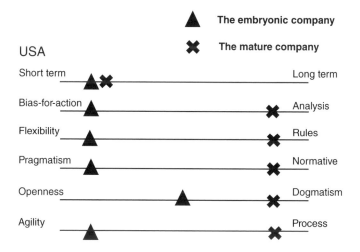

Short term	▲✖	Long term
Bias-for-action	▲ ✖	Analysis
Flexibility	▲ ✖	Rules
Pragmatism	▲ ✖	Normative
Openness	▲ ✖	Dogmatism
Agility	▲ ✖	Process

Diagram 10.3: Outline of national profile of the USA

medium sized companies (SMBs) with a global presence. The largest and most successful Danish companies typically dominate a global niche industry such as William Demant in hearing aids, Novo Nordisk for diabetes medicine and Lego in educational toys. However, there are far fewer truly large global Danish corporations, compared to neighbouring Sweden with its national profile more aligned with that of the mature company and large-scale industrial pursuit.

A key challenge for Denmark is that a globalized world requires bigger scale, which will challenge SMBs with global growth ambitions. This may help explain why the Danish economy has become less competitive internationally in the past decade.

Japanese companies are supported by a national profile well suited for the mature global company requiring adherence to processes and the disciplined application of technical competences. Compared to neighbouring Korea, Japan is less urgent and more collectivist. This leads to different execution capabilities as evidenced in the case of Sony and Samsung. A complex written language and poor English skills accentuate Japan's lack of openness, and can make it appear detached. The recent cases of Toyota's hesitant public response to the accelerator crisis in the USA, and the debacle surrounding the apparent fraudulent behaviour at camera-maker Olympus, are evidence that Japanese companies and their boards may not always fully appreciate the perspective of the global community and include it in their decision-making when facing a crisis.

The USA is unique with a national profile that supports both the innovative start-up company and the mature organization, though through different aspects of its national culture. The start-up company is underpinned by American ambition, the frontier spirit of always moving on and trying new things, the perseverance to continue until the job is done, the American Dream, the desire for success and the opportunity to be successful by influencing your own destiny.

In contrast, it is the more masculine aspects of the American psyche that support the large mature corporation; the results orientation, the acceptance of power and the use of it, the dogmatism that the American way of doing business will prevail, the acceptance of hierarchy and the rules and processes that go with it. However, the American short-term orientation may at times work against the large corporation as it reacts to a crisis in a knee-jerk rather than strategic manner. Together with Britain, the USA may have a blessing in disguise by naturally speaking the global lingua franca, English, leading to less openness to other cultures.

A local company in any country that manages to break out of the pack and onto the global scene is often blessed with founders whose personal values helped neutralize potentially derailing national traits. At Sony, Ibuka and Morita embedded the traits of being creative, ambitious and open. At Nokia it was the ambition and agility of Jorma Ollila and the early leadership team that helped it break out. At Apple it was Steve Jobs' relentless pursuit of design perfection in a country with a short-term utilitarian mentality of value-for-money and bigger-is-better. At P&G it was the founders' conservative and normative traits that enabled the company to take the long-term perspective.

Examples of 17 national traits that both enable and derail

Table 10.1 outlines how a strong national trait can take a different form – being an enabler or a derailer dependent on the situation. For each country there will obviously be additional traits that can have the same effect, as suggested in the Appendix.

Two recommendations to investors

1. Watch out for the tell-tale signs of a derailing cultural dynamic and promote diversity in the board

Many outstanding books have been written on the subject of corporate hubris, each with its own unique perspective and cultural bias. In his excellent book *Why Good Companies Go Bad and How Great Managers Remake Them*,[1] Don Sull lists the tell-tale signs of Active Inertia. This list includes:

- Your company boasts superior performance
- Your CEO appears on the cover of a major magazine
- Management gurus pronounce your company as outstanding
- You build monuments to your success
- You name monuments after your success
- Your CEO writes a book
- Your top executives look alike
- Your competitors all have the same zip code you do.

[1]Sull D. (2005) *Why Good Companies Go Bad and How Great Managers Remake Them*. Harvard Business School Press.

Table 10.1 Examples of cultures where a single national trait originally enabled success then morphed into a derailer

Culture	Trait	Enabling	Derailing
Finland	Rural values, go-it-alone streak	Simplicity, agility, speed	Loses nimbleness after rapid expansion
UK	Individualism	Inventiveness	Lacks scale and process
France	French-centred self-esteem	Confidence	Complacency
Germany	Devotion to process	Optimal procedures and structure	Slow (reluctant) to switch
Sweden	Consensus	Welfare State	Too costly to maintain
Brazil	Euphoria	Many ventures	Poor follow-up
Russia	Aggressive	Exploited vast resources	Non-renewable
China	Single-minded growth	Record exports	Domestic neglect
Denmark	Individualism	Nimbleness	No big companies
Canada	Laid back	Popularity	Slow development
Norway	Conservative	Conserves resources	Ties up wealth
Japan	Company is sacred	Excellent collective work ethic	Lacks invention, stagnates
Italy	Adaptability	Gets business	Changeable execution
Switzerland	Banking secrecy	Prosperity	Vulnerable to challenge
Belgium	Compromise	Avoids dogma	Split nation
USA	American Dream	Super-confidence	Fails to learn others' cultural values and strengths
India	Great improvisers (Jugaad)	Opportunistic growth in IT & some industries	Lack of process, structure & discipline leads to endemic corruption

Jim Collins, in his equally inspirational book *How the Mighty Fall*,[2] lists the five stages of the typical American company's success and decline with some of the tell-tale indicators for each stage in brackets:

- Stage 1: Hubris born of success (the rhetoric of success, decline in learning orientation)
- Stage 2. Undisciplined pursuit of more (success breeds ambition, bureaucracy subverts discipline, personal interests placed above organizational interests)

[2]Collins, J. (2009) *How the Mighty Fall*. Random House.

- Stage 3. Denial of risk and peril (amplify positive/discount negative information, increasingly big bets with limited validation, obsessive reorganizations)
- Stage 4. Grasping for salvation (seeking the silver bullet, grasping for a leaders-as-saviour, initial upswing followed by disappointment)
- Stage 5. Capitulating to irrelevance or death.

We would add a few additional tell-tale signs to look out for across countries:

- A lack of diversity of thinking at the board level and in the management group
- Limited evidence of strategic and cultural change capabilities when approaching a transformation point
- Limited evidence of a normative mind set
- Cultural references in the annual report suggesting a myopic national cultural mind set
- Promotion from within and a lack of success of outsiders coming into senior roles
- A crisis coinciding with a business cycle transformation point
- An upcoming transition from founder to managerial regime.

The simple point being that if a company displays some of the characteristics listed above, the investment may be riskier than the numbers on their own would indicate.

Investors should actively promote diversity on the board. It may not always be in the best interest of shareholders to diversify the executive suite from a nationality or mind set perspective, as evidenced in the Samsung case. However, the board has the ultimate governance responsibility for ensuring that cultural blind spots are recognized by the management in particular when facing a strategy change, a transformation point or a crisis.

2. Analyze the cultural implications carefully when merging two organizations

Companies are usually merged or acquired for sound strategic reasons: underperformance that the buyer believes can be changed; the restructuring of an industry; strategic and operational synergies; achieving a higher market share and a more dominant market position: efficiency of scale, stronger financial muscle, more diversity, and so on. However, in many M&A situations, the expected financial benefits did not materialize – and that is often because the issue of culture was not considered properly – Daimler-Chrysler was a glowing example.

Culture is difficult to analyze in advance of a M&A transaction. In the data room, the acquiring company has access to relevant financial, operational and market data information. Through this they will acquire a good feel for the numbers side of the business. However, all too often the question of culture is dismissed or ignored, not because it is not recognized, but simply because it requires complex and soft data, which it is difficult to get in an intense M&A situation – where you have access to financial data for a few weeks, but only limited access to the people.

Our advice is that money invested ahead of time in this area can create significant shareholder value and avoid disappointment. The rational perspective easily prevails in these situations: "If you can't measure it – it doesn't exist." This can be very costly when evaluating a potential M&A situation. An expert on corporate culture once said: "In a M&A situation, I am often the most unpopular person. The advisers, the banks and the leadership usually will stand to make quite a bit of money or getting a bigger and better job." Here is the lone voice of an individual who doesn't look like them – the investment banker, the senior management consulting partner or the senior executive – who with limited hard data to support his perspective is saying "be careful, this could go horribly wrong!"

Two recommendations to boards

1. Conduct a full strategy and cultural dynamics audit at least every five years

It is rare that boards consider the corporate culture of a company in detail. They audit the finances, they audit the green and social responsibility credentials, they audit the overall strategy, they have even recently started auditing themselves, but rarely the culture. We recommend that boards should request a review of this on a regular basis. This review should include:

- An analysis of the company's current strategic and cultural alignment specifically discussing potentially enabling and derailing cultural dynamics at play

- A future alignment analysis, based on scenario forecasting such as: approaching a transformation point, a strategy change, an upcoming M&A situation, or a crisis situation that could challenge status quo
- A specific discussion of what the water may be that we the board and the management cannot see.

2. Promote diversity at the board and in the executive team

There is increasingly strong evidence that diversity and diversity of thinking positively impact the bottom line. We believe in the value of national, gender, age and line of thinking diversity. However, it is important to note that individuals who are thought of as being diverse and have worked in the organization successfully for many years may not always provide the diversity of thinking expected.

One can argue that in a stable environment, with a clear strategy, a lack of national diversity may not hamper performance but on the contrary could enhance it. If everyone speaks the same language, grew up in the same country, went to the same university and lives in the same neighbourhood then the communication in the group will be easier and decision-making smoother. However, we believe that in our rapidly changing world, the ability of management to view an issue through different lenses and have an open and respectful debate about it will prove a winning strategy for most companies.

Four recommendations to management

1. Carefully balance diversity with day-to-day performance and make the organization culturally aware

Management face the challenge of balancing short- and medium-term performance with the ability to prosper long term. In our quarterly focused, execution-oriented world with stock analysts commenting on every action, that is a tall order.

From a shareholder perspective, it is much preferred if the company change before there is a burning platform and before the board orders them to do so. The responsibility of the management is to ensure that the effects of potentially derailing dynamics are minimized and enabling dynamics are supported. Diversity of thinking is one way of identifying if something is amiss – as is monitoring the culture with hard and soft data.

As a head-hunter, Kai Hammerich has often experienced companies requesting candidates that can help create or stimulate a cultural change. "Find us someone who will challenge us", the clients say. It is often based on a real desire, but in effect is an abdication of responsibility for actually changing the culture. All too often, when the candidate is hired, he or she finds that when they challenge the existing rules and norms it leads to unavoidable conflicts over habits and values with the "old organization". The management will initially and enthusiastically support it, but more often than not, over time the leadership support wanes and the "challenger" ends up leaving the company. Cultural change and leadership must come from the top. Change agents need unrelenting support from the leadership to be able to change deeply rooted patterns of behaviour. Old habits die hard and expecting an outsider to do that job is not realistic, unless that person is the new CEO, with unwavering support from a committed board.

If the outside perspective is too easily dismissed by the organization, it may be the clearest signal that the management has a big task ahead of them to make the organization culturally aware and open.

2. Establish a recurrent methodology for making culture discussion more data driven and establish a cross-functional task force to systematically monitor culture

Because culture is such a soft area, having hard data to support the arguments will simply help to enhance the acceptance and facilitate the discussion in both linear-active cultures and professional cultures that are analytically inclined. The company should choose one or more diagnostic tools to monitor the key aspects of the culture on a regular basis. A number of methodologies exist such as McKinsey's Organizational Health Index, Denison's culture survey, as well as widely used psychometrics, behavioural preference and cultural and employee engagement survey methodologies. The hard data should be supported by observation-based analysis and structured interviews to ensure that the hard data is interpreted correctly and complemented by the essential soft data as not all of these methodologies allow for analysis of the impact of national culture.

The objective is obviously not to just analyze, but to act if there is a derailing cultural dynamic and to promote good habits and cultural dynamics that will enhance performance.

Normally the human resources function is responsible for monitoring corporate culture. However, we believe many companies would benefit from establishing a cross-functional group including the head of human resources, head of strategy and the heads of a couple of business units and main subsidiaries/regions. The remit of the group would be to direct the strategy and cultural alignment discussion, supervise the regular audits and pass recommendations to the firm leadership.

3. Ensure there is a clear strategy for embedding key elements of the corporate culture globally

In Chapter 7, we discussed the three generic cultural subsidiary strategies companies pursue as they expand internationally. It is more often than not a strategy that has evolved over time and implicitly becomes the accepted modus operandi, rather than being a designed strategy. The three strategies are:

1. National culture domination
2. The hybrid global/local culture
3. Local culture domination.

Each will have advantages and disadvantages, in terms of speed of expansion, cost and resources required. Which one is the best choice will depend on the company's particular circumstances and the country it originated from.

A company from a large country with an ambition to dominate a global industry may be well advised to pursue a strategy of national cultural domination. This means that the key work processes are shared across all subsidiaries, with limited opportunity to localize, as we saw in the Toyota and P&G cases. The strategy requires a significant investment in aligning the behaviour and habits of the employee base with the core values.

At the other end of the scale is the small company from a small pragmatic country that needs to expand rapidly. It may be well advised to pursue a local culture domination strategy, where it deliberately compromises cultural alignment over pace of expansion. The downside obviously being that it will have fewer levers by which to influence the work practices of the subsidiary system. This strategy will require establishing a few control processes, typically financial reporting, but may also include key processes such as "Lean", to ensure a minimum level of oversight and alignment.

If we accept that culture is the glue that keeps an organization together, then most organizations will benefit from being explicitly aware of what those values are. However, when articulating corporate values the company needs to be cognisant that those come in four different flavours as discussed in Chapter 4, each with a very different objective, namely:

1. Aspirational values
2. Fashionable values
3. Actual values
4. Corrective values.

4. Align the talent and leadership agenda with the cultural imperatives

The board and management should analyze their need for diversity and act on it. In many organizations there are glass ceilings preventing diversity talent from moving forward. History shows that these glass ceilings are complex to break and often based on deeply rooted assumptions, values and habits. If the board and management believe in diversity, it is imperative for them to establish processes and cultural change programmes that will break the diversity glass ceilings. In Europe and America many companies have a gender diversity policy to increase a low level of female executives. They may ask headhunters to specifically recruit more women, but that often ends up being a musical chair exercise – one company's gain is another company's loss – which will make the price go up and not increase supply. Companies, in particular large corporations that set the tone for best practice, need to recognize their responsibility for working on the supply side of the diversity equation.

A few years ago Kai Hammerich was instrumental in establishing a Danish CEO network representing most of the largest companies in Denmark. Recently, they discussed gender diversity at the executive level, where Denmark scored surprisingly low, just above Japan but well below most other Western and emerging market countries. The group had invited Barbara Annis, a world leader in gender diversity, to come and speak to the group sharing her experience, data and anecdotes. After lengthy discussions, the group of CEOs concluded that ultimately it was their individual duty and responsibility to increase the flow of female talent in their companies – though each firm would have to design its particular programme, based on its history, market position and culture.

Some argue that you can only change deeply rooted cultural behaviours through a change of leadership and key people. Struggling companies often feel they need to clear the deck to fundamentally change the culture. However, some companies such as P&G, Shell and GE have thrived for decades if not centuries, and have inculcated an ability to adapt, while still primarily promoting from within. Paradigm shifts with an entirely new leadership team from the outside are normally risky for the investors and expensive, though sometimes unavoidable.

Implications for countries

Most countries make a deliberate effort to enhance their global competitiveness. Using the results of our framework and analysis, they should consider the following:

1. **Identify potential accelerators**, i.e. where in the lifecycle the national culture best supports companies, and consider action to further enhance this in the educational system and in the business support structure:
   a. Identify industries/technologies that lend themselves to areas of national strength
   b. Enhance systemic efforts to support the development of companies in those areas
   c. Nurture the application of enabling traits and establishing best practices
2. **Identify potential national derailers** and consider actions to neutralize those:
   a. Focus the business and professional educational system on enhancing the understanding of areas of weakness
   b. Establish a national support structure to promote best practice of how to neutralize potential derailers through post-graduate education and adoption of better work practices
3. **Entrepreneurism**
   a. Recognize that the traits of entrepreneurs that can help a national company break onto the global scene often will be that of the "cultural challenger".

The primary educational system in all countries plays a critical role in embedding national values. Likewise, the post-graduate and professional education system can play a pivotal role in enhancing the appreciation of nationally rooted cultural dynamics and the effect of national enablers and derailers.

Countries may be well advised to invest more in understanding how to compensate for apparent cultural weaknesses and promote areas of strength. A country like Denmark, being culturally inclined to developing smaller companies, may put more emphasis on the art and science of growing larger companies. Part of this could include asking the business education institutions and industry associations to more systematically explore and develop best practices for a global company culture that is distinctively Danish.

Finland may benefit from exploring how it can use the thousands of engineers that have left Nokia and given it a unique technical platform with skills and capabilities rarely found in Europe. The Finns are creative and tenacious and through Nokia have gained valuable experience in rapidly globalizing a company while keeping a Finnish identity and overcoming national derailers. Maybe Nokia could be complemented by a plethora of smaller companies like Rovio Entertainment, a games company that created the global success Angry Birds which has already exceeded one billion downloads to mobile devices.

Similarly, reactive countries such as Korea, Japan and China may benefit from gaining a deeper understanding of entrepreneurism and how to nurture entrepreneurial "cultural challengers" that otherwise may feel excluded from the "group". As they say, "you can't make an omelette without breaking some eggs", and thus entrepreneurs in countries that value conformity and seek harmony may find that the environment is hostile to their seemingly diverging talents. If those countries truly desire nurturing more innovative entrepreneurs who can compete on the global stage, they may have to challenge some of their deeply rooted values and habits.

Chapter and book conclusion

We hope we have convinced you that national culture matters more than ever in a globalized world; companies need to take note of their cultural heritage, use it to their advantage and not be blinded by it. We have shown you the power of the enabling and derailing cultural dynamics over the corporate lifecycle. These cultural dynamics are often fuelled by national values and severely impact performance.

The management, the board and the investors have a critical role in helping companies navigate our rapidly changing global world – but they can only do so if they are prepared to take off their cultural sunglasses, so to speak, and observe the water around them.

One key question remains: Will corporations be affected more or less by their national culture in the future? For the next 20 to 30 years our answer would be definitely "more". Beyond that – who knows, it could go either way. The energy of young emerging market corporations is forceful. Many of their leaders were trained in a nation-state-centric tradition, with limited international exposure. They will not be restricted by a linear-active way of thinking about business, and will find new ways of doing business, establish new innovative work practices and ways of getting things done. These emerging market businesses will challenge the corporations from linear-active cultures and through this redefine the business world as we know it. Over the past 60 years we have lived in a world where America dominated the landscape militarily, economically and philosophically. This era may be coming to an end. However, the American domination has resulted in a far more open accessible world, with greater social and economic mobility. This openness has created the platform from which emerging market countries will grow their economic wealth, hopefully adhering to the principles that made it possible in the first place. While the 20th century was all about the Americas, the 21st may well belong to the emerging markets and their middle classes.

As these emerging markets' companies meet the rest of the world on its home turf, they too will need to recognize their own cultural profiles with its strengths and weaknesses, and learn to adapt in new ways. Their success will most likely encourage them to cherish and nurture many of the national values that made them successful in the first place. Why aspire to be like America – or Europe – when they themselves are equally, if not more, successful?

Learning languages – and in particular English being the lingua franca for business – is becoming a requirement in a globalizing world. Richard D. Lewis knows this first-hand having been a tutor of English to people from over 40 countries for over 50 years. English will create a foundation for thickening the global veneer of cooperation, but it will *not* in itself create a uniform global culture. In his book *The World is Flat*,[3] Thomas Friedman explained how uniform supply chain processes have enabled companies across the world to work together in one seemingly seamless process. However, that didn't make the Chinese PC assembler an American company, it simply created an interface, which made the differences less visible, to the benefit of everyone.

What is certain to happen is that the average person's exposure to other cultures, anywhere in the world, will increase in the coming years. People travel more and at a younger age. More students will study at a university

[3]Friedman T. (2005) *The World is Flat*. Farrar, Straus & Giroux.

abroad early in their career. Children from linear-active cultures are far more likely to end up working for a company with reactive or multi-active cultural roots, unlike their parents, who would most likely work for a foreign company with linear-active roots, if not one from their own country.

Over a billion people in the world today can read the daily "international electronics newspaper" – being connected to and getting daily news from the Internet. This invariably will increase their curiosity and awareness of other people's way of thinking. However, we also live in a world competing for limited natural resources. The success of the emerging BRIC countries (Brazil, Russia, India and China) may lead to a desire to redefine the "game" played internationally if they feel it is unfair to them. This could lead to more nationalism and insular national thinking – as we experienced during the Cold War.

However, we remain optimistic that the world will become a multicultural one. After all, we have come a long way in the last hundred years. Our hope is that we will live in a world where diversity is appreciated and where the perspectives of other cultures with benign ambitions will be respected and valued. Organizational culture is the result of all the decisions made and actions taken in an organization over time. Culture is behaviour and behaviour defines culture. Culture is man-made and therefore can be directed by man. Thus, whichever direction the world takes, we can only point the finger in one direction – towards ourselves. And herein lies our biggest opportunity!

APPENDIX

The enablers and derailers listed here are obviously a stereotypical subset of the complex web of key national characteristics. However, these are traits we see as having a particularly strong impact on the culture of companies from each of these countries. It is important to remember that national characteristics often are performance neutral, meaning the same trait can be an enabler in one period and a derailer in the next, or be irrelevant. The responsibility of the board and the management is to ensure that they understand the effect of characteristics that may create a performance enhancing Cultural Dynamic and recognize the ones that may lead to a dysfunctional Cultural Dynamic – and then deal with them.

Country	Enablers	Derailers	Comments
Argentina	Vast resources Excellent population ratio to land area	Corrupt governments	Should be in top 20 economies in the world
Australia	Culturally well placed between UK and USA Proximity to Asia (esp. China) Laid back pragmatic Vast mineral resources	Insular Find it difficult to adapt to Asian cultures Emptiness of desert centre	"Tyranny of distance" now becoming geographic luck (near China)
Brazil	Optimists Future oriented Favourable demographics Vast natural resources	Lack follow-up Always looking for next "El Dorado" Difficult rainforest terrain Don't bring "bad news"	Favourable transition from military dictatorship to democracy Huge home market

(Continued)

Country	Enablers	Derailers	Comments
Canada	Great diversity Proximity to US market Internationally popular Laid back Vast land area and mineral wealth	Lack aggression in business Failed to integrate French Canadians	Favourable future, based on resources and popularity Access to Atlantic, Pacific and Arctic
China	Work ethic Huge labour force Low wages Their turn to develop One party decides Pragmatism Emerging middle class	Rural people move to cities Wages are rising Public will demand more comforts (e.g. car) Lack of entrepreneurship Insular language problems Military spending	Overheating economy Rural poverty Poor infrastructure will give future social problems Communism unlikely to survive next 20 years Exports-led economy needs changing to domestic-led
Hong Kong	Can morph rapidly when required Eliminate red tape Work ethic	Uneasy situation within PRC	Best example of culture adapting to change in business strategy
India	Big labour force Great improvisers (*Jugaad*) IT strength	Future overpopulation Lack process Disorganized	Endemic corruption Poor infrastructure
Japan	Face protection, honour Ultra-courtesy The company is sacred Long-termism	Poor linguists Age-based hierarchy Risk averse in personal matters Long-term perspective hampers quick action when needed "Salaryman" – lacks spontaneity Slow reaction to global changes	Fukushima disaster revealed collusion between government and big industry Toyota arguably world's best car producer but would not admit mistakes in time (face) Reflexive obedience, unable to solve systemic crisis over 20 years

Country	Enablers	Derailers	Comments
Korea	Nationalism Pull together Work ethic Confucian hierarchy	Excessive patriotism Insular Lack diversity Too rigid	Aim to "beat the Japanese" has been largely achieved Rising wages threaten competitiveness
Mexico	Favourable demographics Proximity to US market Tourist receipts	Drug problems Often exploited by USA Unemployment	Violence common Frequent culture clashes with USA
Russia	Patriotism Collective spirit Vast natural resources Physical toughness Well educated esp. engineering	Overcollective under communism Great distances hamper unity Uneven work tempo Inclination to apathy	State is too bureaucratic and corrupt Populace dissatisfied politically Adverse demographics (declining)
Singapore	Work ethic Controlled economy Discipline Favourable geographic location Good relations with Beijing	Overregulation Creeping red tape	Second only to Hong Kong in terms of adaptability
Turkey	Work ethic Low wages Good demographics Stable political arrangement between army and Islamists	Failed to solve Kurdish question Uncertainty about relations with EU	Currently enjoying impressive growth (c. 7% – 2012)
USA	Confidence (the American Dream) Bias for action (speed) Bottom-line focus Masculinity	Ignoring other cultures Waste – extravagance Lack patience (unlike Asians) Weak at building relationships	Success has bred arrogance Global dominance now being challenged Never underestimate US resilience
EUROPE			
Belgium	Sound economy based on diligence and ability to compromise	Often bitter rivalry between Flemish and Walloons	Future of unified state uncertain

(Continued)

Country	Enablers	Derailers	Comments
Denmark	Intelligent planning of small-but-good economy Belief in the strength of the communal Danish Model Creative Agile	Belief in the Danish Model Lack of scale in a rapidly globalizing world Pragmatic, yet sometimes not open	Many SMEs Few big companies
Finland	Agility Innovation Rural values	Decline of agility post 2005 (Nokia) Lack of emotional engagement Go-it-alone inclination	Nokia's prolonged success engendered arrogance Go-it-alone dangers
France	France-centred, self-esteem Strong on theory, ideas, process Sense of intellectual superiority	Ideas often trump pragmatism France-centred focus on French language Difficult to fire failures	Poor English language skills Loss of English-speaking markets
Germany	Factual planning and process *Ordnung* Work ethic Focus on exports Precision engineering	Hierarchical bureaucracy Holidays getting longer Exports-lead challenged by Korea, China, Japan	Financially sound Resilient, like USA Location at heart of EU
Italy	Humanitarianism Flexibility Idealism	Southern inefficiency Mafia Weak government	Indebtedness Split state
Netherlands	Individualism Pragmatism Good linguists Global outlook	Stubbornness Overdirectness	Historically international Solid economy and finance
Norway	Thrift Prudent exploitation of oil, etc.	Too cautious in global conditions Content with status quo Too reliant on its natural resources	Even Norwegians impatient with "oil reserve fund"

Country	Enablers	Derailers	Comments
Poland	Hard workers Unified nationally Obsession with survival	Ultra-defensive Frequent scepticism Delicate relations with two neighbours (Russia and Germany)	Often underestimated
Spain	Drive Originality Pride in past	Poor language skills Neglect other cultures	Strong links to S. America High indebtedness (2013)
Sweden	Ideal welfare state Obsession with human rights Femininity Once consensus is reached, most will align	Some exploit benefits, but neglect duties of system Complacency Consensus system causes slow decision-making	Technology lead being eroded by Korea, Japan, etc. Attempt to rebalance the economy (less state, more private enterprise)
Switzerland	Diversity Discipline Language skills Quality	Strong currency	Seasonal labour force Temporary immigrants – some friction
UK	Individualism and inventiveness Engineering strengths Creativity in design and the arts Stable institutions	Weak on process Overtraditional Slow to change Educational standards declining Class system Insularity	Manufacturing base mostly lost (cars, textiles, coalmining, shipbuilding) Overemphasis on financial services

REFERENCES AND WEBSITES

Adizes, I. (1999) *Managing Corporate Lifecycles*. Adizes Institute.

Bungay, S. (2011) *The Art of Action*, Nicholas Brealey.

BusinessWeek, March 2010, quote from IBS Center for Management Research. Case on Toyota, BSTR/385.

Chang, S.-J. (2010) *Samsung vs Sony*, Wiley.

Christensen, C. (1997) *The Innovator's Dilemma*, HBS Press.

Church, R. (1994) *The Rise and Decline of the British Motor Industry*, Economic History Society.

Collins, J. (1995) *Built to Last: Successful Habits of Visionary Companies*, Harper Business Essentials.

Collins, J. (2009) *How the Mighty Fall*, Random House.

De Mente, B.L. (2004) *Korean Business Etiquette*, Tuttle.

Denison, D., Hooijberg, R., Lane, N. and Lief, C. (2012) *Leading Culture Change in Global Organizations*, Jossey-Bass.

Drachmann, P. (1932) *FLSmidth & Co., 1922–1932* Egmont H. Petersens Hof-Bogtrykkeri.

Friedman, T. (2005) *The World is Flat*, Farrar, Straus & Giroux.

Hakkarainen, A. (2011) *Behind the Screen*, eBook, Amazon.

Hino, S. (2006) *Inside the Mind of Toyota*, Productivity Press.

Hofstede, G. (1980) *Culture's Consequences*, Sage.

Hofstede, G., Hofstede, J. and Minkov, M. (2010) *Cultures and Organizations*, 3rd Edition, McGraw-Hill.

Hoover, B. and Hammerich, K. (2009) Building the "A" Team in America, White paper, Russell Reynolds Associates.

Jones, G. (2005) *Renewing Unilever; Transformation and Tradition*, Oxford University Press.

Kosonen, M. and Doz, Y. (2008) *Fast Strategy*, Wharton School Publishing.

Kotter, J. and Heskett, J. (1992) *Corporate Culture and Performance*, Free Press.

Lewis, R.D. (2003/2007) *The Cultural Imperative*, Nicholas Brealey.

Lewis, R.D. (2005) *Finland, Cultural Lone Wolf*, Intercultural Press, Nicholas Brealey.

Lewis, R.D. (2006) *When Cultures Collide*, 3rd Edition, Nicholas Brealey.

Liker, J.K. and Hoseus, M. (2008) *Toyota Culture, the Heart and Soul of the Toyota Way*, McGraw Hill.

Michel, T. (2010) *Samsung Electronics*, Wiley.

Morita, A. (1984) *Made in Japan*, Dutton.

Pagel, M. (2012) *Wired for Culture*, Allan Lane.

Peters, T. and Waterman, R.H. (1982) *In Search of Excellence*, HarperCollins.

Porter, M. (1980) *Competitive Strategy*, Free Press.

Riisager, K. (1922) *FLSmidth & Co., 1882–1922 (40 years)*, Trykt i Langkjaers Bogtrykkeri Ad.

Schein, E.H. (2004) *Organizational Culture and Leadership*, Jossey Bass.

Schisgall, O. (1981) *Eyes on Tomorrow*, Doubleday Fergusson.

Sharratt, B. (2000) *Men and Motors of 'The Austin'*, Haynes.

Sull, D. (2005) *Why Good Companies Go Bad and How Great Managers Remake Them*, Harvard Business School Press.

Which?, October 2010.

Websites

http://denning.law.ox.ac.uk/news/events_files/USCEOsPaidMore_2012_05_21_(2).pdf

http://en.wikipedia.org/wiki/British_Motor_Corporation

http://en.wikipedia.org/wiki/History_of_Ford_Motor_Company

http://en.wikipedia.org/wiki/Hubris

http://en.wikipedia.org/wiki/Lee_Kun-hee

http://en.wikipedia.org/wiki/Leyland_Motors

http://en.wikipedia.org/wiki/List_of_corporations_by_market_capitalization

http://en.wikipedia.org/wiki/Myers-Briggs_Type_Indicator

http://qvmgroup.com/invest/2012/03/31/worlds-30-largest-public-companies-by-market-cap/

http://seekingalpha.com/article/259736-china-surpasses-japan-in-percentage-of-world-market-cap/

http://www.bbc.co.uk/news/business-17865117

http://www.bbc.co.uk/news/technology-16832990

http://www.businessweek.com/stories/2003-07-06/p-and-g-new-and-improved

http://www.helium.com/items/1086171-how-do-key-success-indicators-or-kpi-work

http://www.mobilenewscwp.co.uk/2011/05/nokia-market-share-slips-to-lowest-in-14-years/

http://www.prweb.com/releases/2006/02/prweb342169.htm

http://www.samsung.com/uk/aboutsamsung/management/boardofdirectors.html; http://www.samsung.com/us/aboutsamsung/management/usexecutiveteam.html

http://www.sony.net/SonyInfo/CorporateInfo/History/history.html

http://www.telegraph.co.uk/expat/4190728/Frances-educational-elite.html.

http://www.toyota-global.com/company/vision_philosophy/toyota_production_system/origin_of_the_toyota_production_system.html

http://www.vanityfair.com/online/daily/2012/07/microsoft-downfall-emails-steve-ballmer

http://www2.e.u-tokyo.ac.jp/~sousei/WARDLEY3.pdf

INDEX

Index compiled by Annette Musker

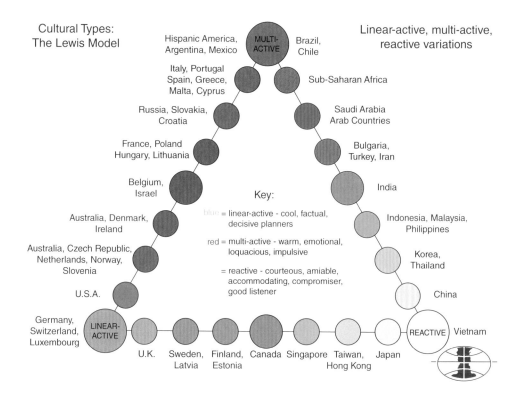

Cultural Types:
The Lewis Model

Linear-active, multi-active,
reactive variations

Hispanic America,
Argentina, Mexico

MULTI-
ACTIVE

Brazil,
Chile

Italy, Portugal
Spain, Greece,
Malta, Cyprus

Sub-Saharan Africa

Russia, Slovakia,
Croatia

Saudi Arabia
Arab Countries

France, Poland
Hungary, Lithuania

Bulgaria,
Turkey, Iran

Belgium,
Israel

Key:

India

Australia, Denmark,
Ireland

blue = linear-active - cool, factual,
decisive planners

Indonesia, Malaysia,
Philippines

Australia, Czech Republic,
Netherlands, Norway,
Slovenia

red = multi-active - warm, emotional,
loquacious, impulsive

Korea,
Thailand

U.S.A.

= reactive - courteous, amiable,
accommodating, compromiser,
good listener

China

Germany,
Switzerland,
Luxembourg

LINEAR-
ACTIVE

REACTIVE

Vietnam

U.K.

Sweden,
Latvia

Finland,
Estonia

Canada

Singapore

Taiwan,
Hong Kong

Japan

Diagram 2.1: The Lewis model